Eisenhower Center Studies on War and Peace
Stephen E. Ambrose and Günter J. Bischof, Editors

Eisenhower and the German POWs

☆ ☆ ☆ ☆ ☆

Eisenhower and the German POWs

Facts Against Falsehood

☆ ☆ ☆ ☆ ☆

Edited by

Günter Bischof and Stephen E. Ambrose

Louisiana State University Press • *Baton Rouge and London*

Designer: *Amanda McDonald Key*
Typeface: *Times*
Typesetter: *G & S Typesetters, Inc.*
Printer and binder: *Thomson–Shore, Inc.*

Library of Congress Cataloging-in-Publication Data

Eisenhower and the German POWs : facts against falsehood / edited by
Günter Bischof and Stephen E. Ambrose.
    p.   cm. — (Publications of the Eisenhower Center)
  Papers presented at a symposium held Nov. 1990 at the Eisenhower
Center, University of New Orleans.
  Includes bibliographical references and index.
  ISBN 0-8071-1758-7 (cloth : alk. paper)
  1. World War, 1939–1945—Prisoners and prisons, American—
Congresses. 2. Prisoners of war—Germany—History—20th century—
Congresses. 3. Eisenhower, Dwight D. (Dwight David), 1890–1969—
Congresses.   I. Bischof, Günter, 1953– . II. Ambrose, Stephen
E. III. Eisenhower Center (University of New Orleans) IV. Series.
D805.U5E35   1992
940.54'7244—dc20   92-3908
                                                         CIP

Portions of the arguments and data presented in Albert E. Cowdrey's essay first appeared
in briefer form in the *Canadian Bulletin of Medical History,* VII (1990), 187–91, and are
reprinted with the kind permission of the editor. A quotation of Nikolai Tolstoy in
Thomas M. Barker's essay is from *Contemporary Authors,* Volumes 81–84, edited by
Frances Carol Locher (copyright © 1979 by Gale Research, Inc.), and is reprinted by
permission of the publisher.

To the historians of the Maschke Commission
and to Josef Bischof, who was a prisoner of war
in American captivity

Contents

Preface • xiii

Introduction
Günter Bischof and Stephen E. Ambrose • 1

I   The United States and the German POWs

Eisenhower and the Germans
Stephen E. Ambrose • 29

The Diplomatic and Political Context of the POW Camps Tragedy
Brian Loring Villa • 52

A Question of Numbers
Albert E. Cowdrey • 78

II   Germany in 1945 and German POW Historiography

Food Shortages in Germany and Europe, 1945–1948
James F. Tent • 95

German Historiography, the War Losses, and the Prisoners of War
Rüdiger Overmans • 127

Some Reflections on the Maschke Commission
Rolf Steininger • 170

III   Conspiratorial History

A British Variety of Pseudohistory
Thomas M. Barker • 183

Contents

Bacque and Historical Evidence
Günter Bischof • 199

Appendix A
Report on the Food Situation in Western Germany, 1945 • 235
Appendix B
Volumes of the Maschke Commission • 241
Selected Bibliography • 245
Contributors • 251
Index • 253

Illustrations

Map

American POW Camps in Germany • 14–15

Photographs

(following page 38)

Surrendering German conscripts

Three German soldiers give up

Captive Wehrmacht troops fourteen and fifteen years old

Americans moving east, captured Germans west at the Rhine

Column of German POWs, Remagen

Germans fleeing the Russians surrender to the 82d Airborne

German civilian refugees fleeing west

Captured German battalion in town square in Bavaria

Wehrmacht officer, "300,000th prisoner," entering enclosure

Some of 82,000 POWs in open field, Gummersbach

Prisoners in temporary "cage" outside Kaiserslautern

Mass of prisoners in town square, Worms

Remagen, one of the most overcrowded "Rhine meadow camps"

Dachau survivors greet American liberators

Some of the dead of Dachau

Eisenhower, Patton, and Bradley at concentration camp, Gotha

American generals see demonstration of Nazi torture methods

Some of the dead of Ebensee concentration camp

Survivors of Ebensee

Half-starved American prisoners liberated from the Germans

Hermann Göring surrenders to General Dalquist

Illustrations

Captain Edward Levy interviews captive Hans Goebbels
SS troops apparently beaten, perhaps by Americans
Fifteen-year-old Hitler Youth being processed for discharge
Two members of the Volkssturm just before release
German "soldiers" from the Volkssturm

(following page 112)

German women give food and water to POWs
Army K rations distributed to POWs
Earth holes for shelter, Rheinberg
POWs dig well for water
Sinzig on the Rhine
Officers' compound, Ludwigsburg
Büderich on the Rhine
POWs line up for water, Büderich
German priest holds Catholic services for POWs
K ration distribution, Gummersbach
POWs unload train filled with K rations for Rheinberg camp
Bread allotment at POW enclosure
German women POWs, Remagen
POW field kitchen in temporary enclosure
POW barracks mess hall, early 1946
Some of 35,000 POWs at Bad Aibling airport before V-E Day
Bad Aibling enclosure some eight months later
German civilian with "tracing service" album after war
Woman finds picture of her grandson in tracing service album
Woman writes down data on missing grandson
Tracing service employee questions returned POWs
Malnourished infants, Berlin, 1947
Berliners harvest potatoes in the Tiergarten
German children looking for scraps of food
Eight-year-old with tin of potato soup, Berlin
Children with cartload of bread, Bamberg
Food donated by U.S. civilians arrives by ship, Bremen, 1948

Preface

THE EISENHOWER CENTER at the University of New Orleans is very pleased to see its first conference volume published. The Eisenhower Center is a small research center studying the life and times of General and President Dwight D. Eisenhower, a man who shaped two crucial decades (1940–1960) as few men did in the twentieth century. In the spirit of broad and fair historical inquiry, the Center felt called upon to investigate the serious charges against Eisenhower and the United States Army—as well as the smear campaign against the entire historical profession—that the Canadian novelist James Bacque launched in his sensationalist best seller, *Other Losses*. In 1990, the centenary year of Eisenhower's birth, Bacque's trumped-up allegations tainted the celebrations of a genuine American hero.

The editors thank many people for their help in putting this volume together. Above all, we would like to express our deeply felt gratitude and appreciation to the contributing scholars from two continents. With enthusiasm and scholarly integrity, they responded to our invitation to meet for a two-day symposium at the Eisenhower Center in December, 1990. A long day of critical discussions helped us to sharpen our theses. Neil Cameron, a documentary producer of the BBC, London; Axel Frohn of the German Historical Institute in Washington, D.C.; and Sol Litman, a Canadian journalist and researcher, also participated in these discussions to share their knowledge of the Bacque affair. We particularly thank the contributors for putting their regular work aside and concentrating on researching and preparing these papers with dispatch. Trans-Atlantic communications were not always easy, but in the age of fax machines, problems with manuscripts were worked out.

The contributors to this volume encountered many helpful and kind archivists: at the Bundesarchiv in Koblenz, Germany; the Militärgeschichtliches Forschungsamt in Freiburg, Germany; the Hoover Library in West Branch, Iowa; the resourceful William Mahoney and Edward Reese at the Military Branch, as well as the archivists at the Still Picture Branch of the National Archives in Washington; Richard Boylen and David Pfeiffer at the Washington National Records Center in Suitland, Maryland; Daniel Holt, David Haight, Jim Leyerzapf, and Hazel Stroda at the Eisenhower Library in Abilene, Kansas; and Jane Yates at the Citadel Library and Museum in Charleston, South Carolina. The librarians at the University of New Orleans and Tulane University went out of their way to be helpful. The BBC's Cameron and Andrew Mitrovica of the Canadian Broadcasting Corporation investigated Bacque's allegations in superb television documentaries. Both the BBC and the CBC documentaries deserve praise for their level-headed approaches to a controversial subject. It was a privilege to share research results with these able producers.

We are particularly grateful to the following institutions for giving us permission to reprint photographs from their holdings: the National Archives in Washington, D.C., the Dwight D. Eisenhower Library in Abilene, Kansas, the American Friends Service Committee Archives in Philadelphia, and the German Red Cross *Suchdienst* (Tracing Service) in Munich. The Gieseking Verlag in Bielefeld was kind enough to give us permission to reprint an adapted version of its map showing American POW camps in Germany.

We also express our appreciation to Charles Maier, Brian Villa, and Albert Cowdrey for reading parts of the manuscript and improving it through their wise counsel. Brian Villa, who is at work on his own book on the Bacque affair, prospectively entitled *Writing History, Writing Fiction: The James Bacque Charges and Controversy,* has been the most helpful of colleagues in sharing some of his research with us. Rüdiger Overmans was most helpful in locating some "Maschke Commission" volumes for us. Major Overmans and Professor Tent performed special service in locating rare photographs.

Above all, we thank the many individuals who shared their solicited and unsolicited personal experiences with us. We managed to accumulate a small archive on the German POW experience in World War II by collecting oral-history interviews, personal reports, diaries, and letters. *Die Furche,* a Vienna weekly, printed Günter Bischof's review of Bacque's German edition and collected many personal reponses to this article. We thank editor Hannes Schopf and his team, as well as the men who responded to the article by summarizing their personal experiences as POWs. Among them, Dr. Otto Stur of Vienna was particularly hospitable in granting a long interview and providing his POW diary. Dr. Shea Halle, Nicholas Gordon, and Dr. Albert Hammon—all three involved in building and supervising the Remagen-Sinzig POW enclosure—eagerly shared their memories and furnished copies of citations.

At the University of New Orleans we thank Chancellor Gregory O'Brien, Provost John Mangieri, Vice-Chancellor Gordon Mueller, and Dean Robert Dupont of Metropolitan College for their enthusiastic support of all Eisenhower Center activities. In the History Department, chairmen Gerald Bodet and Arnold Hirsch and our mentor Joseph Logsdon have been accommodating and supportive at every step of the way. Our team at the Eisenhower Center has done first-class work in making local arrangements for the December symposium and in helping with the preparation of the manuscript: our thanks to Kathi Jones, Carolyn Smith, Maria Romain, Scott Peebles, Jerri Bland, and Peggy Iheme, as well as to Tracy Hernandez and Marissa Ahmed, for their cheerful work. In Metropolitan College, Gloria Alvarez and Carol Walker helped in preparing conference brochures for the Eisenhower Center.

The Eisenhower Center is fortunate in having an exceedingly supportive board of directors. Ollie Brown and Arthur Davis made the symposium a memorable event with their gracious southern hospitality toward the participants. Jack Dunlap, Richard Holtz, Samuel Krauss, Mary Mohs, and Richard Stephens, as well as a generous grant from the Peter Kalikow Foundation of New York, made the conference possible. We sincerely appreciate their generosity.

At Louisiana State University Press, Margaret Dalrymple's enthusiasm for this project was infectious, and Catherine Landry's helpful advice and the superb copy editing of Gerry Anders made this a much better manuscript. We also thank the anonymous reviewer for his or her suggestions toward improving the manuscript.

We dedicate this book to one Austrian POW in American hands as well as all historians who do research on World War II POWs. Josef Bischof, Günter Bischof's father, was a POW at Camp Carson, Colorado, during and after World War II. He would have liked to stay in the United States after his captivity but was forced to return home. His memories are not bitter.

This is a book on historiography and is, therefore, duly presented as a tribute to all historians who quietly work on the vast topic of World War II POWs. Among them stand out the historians of the official German Maschke Commission, who labored for sixteen years to tell, in impressive detail, the tragic story of 11 million German POWs during and after

World War II. Their professional standards should be an inspiration to all historians.

Last but not least we thank our wives, Melanie Boulet and Moira Ambrose, who have carried us through the completion of this project with their usual—which is to say extraordinary—love and support.

A few words concerning the various editions of James Bacque's book and this volume's references to them may spare the reader some confusion.

Both the Canadian *Other Losses* and the German edition (*Der geplante Tod*) were published in 1989. The authors met at the Eisenhower Center in December, 1990, to discuss their papers, citing from these two editions. The American edition appeared in the summer of 1991, when these essays were going through copy editing. For simplicity's sake, we decided to stick mainly with references to the original Canadian edition. The citations in the Overmans essay are from the German edition, with the Canadian edition cited in parentheses. Only the Introduction and the Steininger and Bischof essays contain references to the American edition, always identified as (Los Angeles, 1991). The American edition differs very little from the Canadian in the main text, except that Bacque added two new paragraphs on pp. 116–17 (characteristically suggesting non sequiturs of the sort that there could not have been a food shortage in France since French wheat production in 1944 was higher than French wheat consumption and French meat production in 1946 was much higher than in 1941!). These two paragraphs throw the pagination in the American edition forward by one page for the rest of the main text; also, eight new endnotes are added to this chapter. More important, the American edition features a new Epilogue and two new appendixes (10 and 11) with accompanying endnotes. Otherwise, the Canadian and American editions are largely identical.

In the American edition, Bacque corrected some obvious mistakes that appeared in the Canadian edition—for instance (p. 41), a citation of a wrong volume from the Maschke Commission. His corrections, however, are not always so cleanly accomplished. In the case of a supposed "Adenauer" citation, Bacque plainly misstates the matter. According to the Canadian edition (pp. 153–54), the German Chancellor spoke out in the German Bundestag on the fate of 1,407,000 missing German soldiers (with the original citation from the book *One Great Prison*, by Helmut M. Fehling [Boston, 1951], rendered incorrectly). Bacque corrects the mistake in the American edition, noting that it was in fact the West German Ministry of Refugees that announced these numbers of missing POWs, not Adenauer (Los Angeles, pp. 154–55). Yet in both editions Bacque neglects to give the subtitle of Fehling's book, *One Great Prison: The Story Behind Russia's Unreleased POWs,* which clearly demonstrates that Fehling is talking about German prisoners missing in the Soviet Union—not POWs missing in the West as Bacque suggests to his readers (see also the Overmans essay, esp. pp. 168–69).

There are also incongruencies between the Canadian and the German editions of the sort that ought to inspire caution. For example, in the German edition Bacque acknowledges the help of a researcher (Jessica Daniel) with German interviews, which is not mentioned in the acknowledgments of the book or in the respective endnotes of the Canadian and American editions. Thus, oddly enough, whereas "Mavis Gallant and the author" did the interview with the German witness Heinz T. [*sic*], and "the author" interviewed Werner Steckelings in the Canadian (225*nn*17–18) and the American editions (266*nn*25–26), in the German edition Jessica Daniel is acknowledged as an interviewer and "translator" (*Der geplante Tod,* 223*nn*16–17). What does this mean? Did Bacque use a researcher for his German interviews and translations whom he does not want to acknowledge as such in his English writings? Does he pretend he knows German when he does not?

As the reader will see, oddities of this kind are far from the only things to be wary of in reading Mr. Bacque.

Eisenhower and the
German POWs

Introduction

Günter Bischof and Stephen E. Ambrose

I feel that the Germans should suffer from hunger and from cold as I believe such suffering is necessary to make them realize the consequences of a war which they caused.

—Lucius D. Clay to John J. McCloy, June 29, 1945

IN THE FALL of 1989 the Canadian novelist James Bacque rocked the scholarly community with the publication of his book *Other Losses,* charging that General Dwight D. Eisenhower personally, and the United States and French armies institutionally, were responsible for the deaths of up to a million German prisoners of war at the end of World War II. According to Bacque, the U.S. Army circumvented the 1929 Geneva Convention by inventing the category "disarmed enemy forces" (DEFs) for German POWs. This change allowed Eisenhower and the American army to withhold adequate food rations and shelter from the DEFs. The result, according to Bacque, was starvation and disease in the American POW/DEF enclosures in Germany and France, causing the deaths of from 800,000 to 1 million Germans held as prisoners of war. These alleged mass deaths in Eisenhower's "death camps" were, according to Bacque, hidden in army records by way of a category listed as "other losses." [1]

Bacque went a step farther: he charged that ever since these heinous crimes were committed, professional historians had participated in a vast American conspiracy by failing to uncover the mass deaths. Only Bacque,

---

1. See James Bacque, *Other Losses: An Investigation into the Mass Deaths of German Prisoners at the Hands of the French and Americans After World War II* (Toronto, 1989). Except as otherwise noted, all references are to this Canadian edition. (See our Preface for a brief discussion of differences among the Canadian, German, and American editions of *Other Losses.*)

through his single-minded pursuit of the available archival evidence, set the record straight after a "long night of lies."[2] Did he? The following essays look into Bacque's charges concerning the American treatment of German POWs/DEFs at the end of World War II.

World War II, unleashed by Hitler's Germany, has been characterized as the "total war."[3] It stands as the *Massenkrieg* par excellence. Masses of civilians dislocated and masses of prisoners taken characterized the war as much as did mass armies. An estimated 55 million people died as a direct result of World War II, among them 4 million Germans. Some 35 million prisoners of war were taken worldwide, among them some 11 million Germans. The fate of the German POWs of World War II has to be seen as "part of the mass destiny which people experienced in the course of the war."[4]

Beginning in early April, 1945, and swelling to a climax in the first weeks of May, an unprecedented mass migration of civilians and soldiers took place in Central Europe. Supreme Headquarters, Allied Expeditionary Force (SHAEF), under the command of General Dwight D. Eisenhower, was forced to cope with a population upheaval the scope of which had hardly been seen before in history. By May 8, when the war ended in the European theater, the Allied armies were swamped with some 7 million displaced persons (DPs) in Germany and 1.6 million in Austria—among them slave laborers from all over Europe and the barely surviving inmates, including some 100,000 Jews, of the liberated and ghastly German concentration camps.[5] Adhering to the agreements made at Yalta, the Allies

2. *Ibid.*, 4.

3. For solid general surveys of World War II, see John Keegan, *The Second World War* (New York, 1989); Peter Calvocoressi and Guy Wint, *Total War: Causes and Courses of the Second World War* (London, 1972); and M. K. Dziewanowski, *War at Any Price: World War II in Europe, 1939–1945* (2d ed., Englewood Cliffs, N.J., 1991).

4. Hergard Robel, "Vergleichender Überblick," in Erich Maschke et al., eds., *Die deutschen Kriegsgefangenen des Zweiten Weltkrieges: Eine Zusammenfassung* (Munich, 1974), 233, Vol. XV of the Maschke Commission. See also Erich Maschke, "Das Schicksal der deutschen Kriegsgefangenen des Zweiten Weltkrieges als Aufgabe zeitgeschichtlicher Forschung," Introduction to Kurt W. Böhme, *Die deutschen Kriegsgefangenen in Jugoslawien, 1941–1949* (Munich, 1962), vii–xx, Vol. I, Pt. 1 of the Maschke Commission. Given the chaos that prevailed at the end of World War II and the numbers that were involved, all figures cited here have to be seen as rough estimates.

5. Michael R. Marrus, *The Unwanted: European Refugees in the Twentieth Century* (New York, 1985), 296–313; Leonard Dinnerstein, *America and the Survivors of the Holocaust* (New York, 1982), 9 ff.; Mark Wyman, *DP: Europe's Displaced Persons, 1945–1951* (Philadelphia, 1989). On the liberation of the concentration camps and the number of 100,000

repatriated 2 million displaced "Soviet citizens"—the United States alone repatriated 1 million—most against their will. Approximately 5.25 million Western European DPs were also repatriated before the end of 1945.[6]

General George Patton's Third Army, in Bavaria, kept the Jewish DPs—most of whom were barely alive after their liberation from the German concentration camps—behind barbed wire, sometimes still dressed in their old "KZ-pyjamas."[7] In some instances they were penned together with their former Nazi guards. Conditions in the Jewish DP camps improved only after the highly critical Harrison Report, appearing in August, 1945, described the reprehensible treatment of Jews in those camps. Among other things, the report charged: "Generally speaking, three months after V-E Day and even longer after the liberation of individual groups, many Jewish displaced persons and other possibly non-repatriables are living under guard behind barbed-wire fences, in camps of several descriptions (built by the Germans for slave-laborers and Jews), including some of the most notorious of the concentration camps, amidst crowded, frequently unsanitary and generally grim conditions, in complete idleness, with no opportunity, except surreptitiously, to communicate with the outside world, waiting, hoping, for some word of encouragement and action on their behalf. . . . They are in concentration camps in large numbers under our military guard instead of S.S. troops. One is led to wonder whether the German people, seeing this, are not supposing that we are

---

liberated Jews, see Jon Bridgman, *The End of the Holocaust: The Liberation of the Camps* (Portland, Ore., 1990), 13 and *passim*. On the Jewish DPs in the American zone, see also Juliane Wetzel, " 'Mir szeinen doh': München und Umgebung als Zuflucht von Überlebenden des Holocaust, 1945–1948," in *Von Stalingrad zur Währungsreform: Zur Sozialgeschichte des Umbruchs in Deutschland,* ed. Martin Broszat, Klaus-Dieter Henke, and Hans Woller (Munich, 1989), 327–64. On DPs in Austria, see Thomas Albrich, *Exodus durch Österreich: Die jüdischen Flüchtlinge, 1945–1949,* Innsbrucker Forschungen zur Zeitgeschichte, I (Innsbruck, 1987), and Klaus Eisterer, "Französische Besatzungspolitik in Tirol und Vorarlberg: Aspekte der sozialen, politischen, und ökonomischen Entwicklung, 1945/46" (Doctoral dissertation, University of Innsbruck, 1990), 79–212.

6. SHAEF gave the repatriation of Soviet citizens high priority in allocation of transport, and in the summer of 1945 up to 30,000 were delivered per day. See Cathal J. Nolan, "Americans in the Gulag: Detention of U.S. Citizens by Russia and the Onset of the Cold War, 1944–1949," *Journal of Contemporary History,* XXV (1990), 531; Nicholas Bethell, *The Last Secret: The Delivery to Stalin of Over Two Million Russians by Britain and the United States* (New York, 1974); Eisterer, "Französische Besatzungspolitik," 150–55. On the Western European DPs, see Marrus, *The Unwanted,* pp. 310f.

7. Out of 60,000 Jews liberated from concentration camps, 20,000 died within a week. See Dinnerstein, *America and the Survivors of the Holocaust,* 28.

following or at least condoning Nazi policy." By way of contrast, the very George S. Patton who is Bacque's shining hero noted in his diary that others "believe that the Displaced Person is a human being, which he is not, and this applies particularly to the Jews who are lower than animals." [8]

With most German towns lying in ruins, the Bavarian villages in the American zone faced 15 to 25 percent population increases from the influx of DPs and refugees, and Munich alone had to cope with 75,000 DPs. The local population considered the foraging DPs a plague.[9] In addition, the German civilian population was swollen by 12 to 14.5 million ethnic German refugees expelled from Eastern Europe. The Allied armies had not anticipated such masses of people, most of them striving to survive in what one historian has called "a rubble-strewn wasteland in which the living often envied the dead." [10]

8. Harrison Report quoted from Alfred D. Chandler, Jr., and Louis Galambos, eds., *The Papers of Dwight David Eisenhower: Occupation, 1945* (Baltimore, 1978), VI, 267 n 1, 417 n 4. This volume (VI) and the five volumes of Eisenhower's wartime papers edited by Chandler, Stephen E. Ambrose, *et al., The Papers of Dwight David Eisenhower: The War Years* (Baltimore, 1970) are hereinafter cited by volume as *Eisenhower Papers*. Earl Grant Harrison was the American representative on the Inter-Governmental Committee on Refugees, a nonmilitary agency whose primary function was the resettlement of nonrepatriable and stateless persons. Eisenhower protested that charges like those quoted here were "misleading," since all the U.S. Army was trying to do was to protect the DPs against "depredation and banditry by displaced persons themselves." Dwight D. Eisenhower to Henry L. Stimson, August 10, 1945, Eisenhower to Harry S. Truman, October 8, 1945, *ibid.,* 266–69, 414–18. On conditions in the camps and their improvement after the Harrison Report, see Wetzel, " 'Mir szeinen doh,' " 342–45, and Dinnerstein, *America and the Survivors of the Holocaust,* 39–71. Patton is quoted in the latter, 16–17. This is the very same Patton whom Bacque portrays as representing "to a high degree the honor of the army and the basic generosity of the American people." Bacque, *Other Losses,* 149.

9. Paul Ecker, "Revolution des Dorfes?," in *Von Stalingrad zur Währungsreform,* ed. Broszat, Henke, and Woller, 368–425. See also Otto Burianek, "The Politics of Rectification: The U.S. Army and Displaced Persons in Munich, 1945–1951" (Ph.D. dissertation in progress, Emory University). Almost half the population of the Tyrolese town of Landeck were DPs in May, 1945. See Eisterer, "Französische Besatzungspolitik," 189.

10. Marrus, *The Unwanted,* 324–31; Heinz Radke, "Das Schicksal der Ost- und Osteuropadeutschen von 1945 bis heute," in *Geflohen und vertrieben: Augenzeugen berichten,* ed. Rudolf Mühlfenzl (Königstein, 1981), 241–59; Jean Edward Smith, ed., *The Papers of General Lucius D. Clay: Germany, 1945–1949* (2 vols.; Bloomington, 1974), I, xxix. The latter, hereinafter cited as *Clay Papers,* is an excellent primary source for the general economic chaos that prevailed in Germany in the early occupation period. Jean Edward Smith's *Lucius D. Clay: An American Life* (New York, 1990) and Wolfgang Krieger's *General Lucius D. Clay und die amerikanische Deutschlandpolitik, 1945–1949* (Stuttgart, 1987) are crucial secondary sources. With the exceptions of two of the twenty-two volumes produced by the

Introduction

On top of what amounted to as many as 20 million dislocated civilians from all over Europe, and in addition to the badly demoralized German civilian population, the U.S. Army also had to cope with most of the surrendered German army. Eisenhower had anticipated capturing 3 million German soldiers on the Continent. The actual total was as many as *ca.* 5 million in American hands in June (7.6 million in Allied hands in northwestern Europe alone, not counting the 1.4 million in Allied hands in Italy); probably 1 million were German soldiers who had fled west to avoid surrendering to the Red Army. One must keep in mind that given the vast numbers of POWs/DEFs taken at the end of the war, the American counting was initially slipshod and not very reliable, which probably explains the conflicting figures in the literature.[11]

The British left the Americans to deal with the vast majority of the surrendered German personnel. The British and the Americans had agreed in 1945 that they would share the captured Germans on a fifty-fifty basis, but at the end of the war the British refused to take their half, "arguing," as one historian has noted, "that they did not have places to keep them or

Maschke Commission, the wartime *Eisenhower Papers* (but not the instructive two volumes on the German occupation!), and Arthur L. Smith's *Heimkehr aus dem Zweiten Weltkrieg: Die Entlassung der deutschen Kriegsgefangenen* (Stuttgart, 1985), James Bacque has utilized none of the basic sources cited in this Introduction, even though they are readily available in every basic research library.

11. There is no authoritative figure for German POWs and DEFs in Allied hands at the end of the war. Because of the impossibility of exact counts (see also Cowdrey essay), estimates differ widely, depending also on the exact moment in time between May and August of 1945 to which an author refers. Earl F. Ziemke writes of 5 million in SHAEF custody, 3 million of them being held by U.S. forces; see Ziemke, *The U.S. Army in the Occupation of Germany, 1944–1946* (Washington, D.C., 1975), 291. The Maschke Commission mentions 3.4 million in U.S. custody on the continent and 2.1 million in British hands there in the summer of 1945 (6.73 million including those in the United States and the British Isles); see Werner Ratza, "Anzahl und Arbeitsleistungen der deutschen Kriegsgefangenen," in Maschke *et al., Zusammenfassung,* 194–95, 206–207. Arthur L. Smith relies on the Maschke Commission figures and cites 7.74 million kept in the West including France, Belgium, etc. Arthur Smith, *Heimkehr,* 11. Bacque notes that U.S. Army reports about the numbers of DEFs captured differ between 4.36 million and 5.42 million; he operates with 5.22 million in U.S. hands in northwestern Europe, and 1.73 million in British/Canadian captivity; he also reprints a SHAEF facsimile that has a total of 7.61 million held in northwestern Europe (excluding Italy and the Mediterranean) on June 11, 1945. Bacque, *Other Losses,* 54, 177, 180. On the conflicting numbers in the historical literature, see also Axel Frohn, "Das Schicksal deutscher Kriegsgefangener in amerikanischen Lagern nach dem Zweiten Weltkrieg: Eine Auseinandersetzung mit den Thesen von James Bacque," *Historisches Jahrbuch,* CXI (1991), 468–72, 482–85.

men to guard them on the Continent and that moving them to England would arouse public resentment and adversely affect British morale." By June 1, Eisenhower had to report to the War Office that the British refusal to accept more German prisoners had produced shortages in U.S. food stocks amounting to "25 million prisoner-days' rations," which furthermore were "growing at the rate of 900,000 rations every day." [12]

Feeding all these unanticipated millions became a logistical nightmare of major proportions for SHAEF, which frequently had to resort to improvisation. The historian of the U.S. Army's occupation of Germany put it simply: "Food was the problem." [13] In mid-May, Eisenhower had outlined the food situation to the Combined Chiefs of Staff as follows: "In view of the critical food situation in Germany, it is necessary for me to take timely action to meet emergency conditions. It is therefore requested that I be authorized without prior reference to distribute in Germany imported foodstuffs if in my opinion the situation so requires. I have no intention of authorizing the use of imported foods in Germany except in areas where, after full utilization of indigenous resources, deficits would result in conditions prejudicial to military occupation." There is no conspiracy involved in Eisenhower's prioritizing of food distribution, given the "serious food situation" in his theater. [14] Eisenhower and SHAEF would initially use German food sources to feed the Germans; American supplies would then be added to prevent "disease and unrest" according to the provision of the basic American occupation directive for Germany, JCS (Joint Chiefs of Staff) 1067.

Eisenhower begged his government for additional shiploads of food from the United States, but there was a shipping shortage in the spring and summer of 1945. Ships were needed to bring to the Pacific the assault

12. Ziemke, *U.S. Army in the Occupation of Germany,* 291. In his prodigious praise for British treatment of German POWs (*Other Losses,* 132–41), Bacque ignores not only the fact that the British did not live up to their fifty-fifty wartime agreement on POWs with the Americans, but also that the British had their own category of "surrendered enemy personnel" to circumvent the Geneva Convention on the treatment of POWs.

13. Ziemke, *U.S. Army in the Occupation of Germany,* 292–96; Kurt W. Böhme, *Die deutschen Kriegsgefangenen in amerikanischer Hand: In Europa* (Munich, 1973), 9–59, 137–211, Vol. X, Pt. 2 of Maschke Commission. In August, 1945, General Béthouart, the French high commissioner in Austria, begged the Americans in their adjacent Bavarian zone of occupation to ship potatoes to the French zone in Austria. Eisenhower responded that export of any food was impossible, since he faced a critical shortage of food in Germany. See Eisterer, "Französische Besatzungspolitik," 29.

14. Dwight D. Eisenhower to Combined Chiefs of Staff, May 16, 1945, Eisenhower to Harold Alexander, May 18, 1945, in *Eisenhower Papers,* VI, 53–55, 63n1.

forces for the expected invasion of the Japanese home islands. The army's plans called for taking about half of the men who had just won the war in Europe and carrying them to the Pacific theater to make another amphibious assault against a dug-in enemy. This redeployment was not popular with the men, and it hurt the civilians, DPs, and POWs in Europe, as the Pacific had first call on shipping, where food had to be stockpiled for millions of American soldiers.[15]

The destroyed German transportation network left by the fierce Allied bombing campaigns was another logistical nightmare for SHAEF. The railroad lines had been torn up, the bridges destroyed, the terminals left in ruins. Two-fifths of the German transportation facilities had been wiped out by the end of the war. Of the 15,700 German steam locomotives, 38.6 percent were no longer operating; 31 percent of the remaining rolling stock was damaged. The "turnround" time for railroad wagons was five times the prewar average. Of 13,000 kilometers of prewar railroad tracks in the British zone, only 1,000 were operable. The Ruhr, Germany's industrial heartland, had been cut off by the Allied bombing raid of March 24, 1945. The transportation system in Germany had come to a virtual standstill in May, 1945, and it became the most critical bottleneck factor in the early reconstruction of the German economy.[16]

Moreover, SHAEF's entire logistical net had been set up to rush material to the front lines; suddenly, in early May, the flow had to be reversed. German troops were wandering around, still armed, trying to surrender. SHAEF had no way to move them in large numbers, given that it first

---

15. On Eisenhower's continuous problems with redeployment of SHAEF troops for the Pacific theater, see *ibid.*, VI, 77, 78, 91–92, 128, 140, 154, and *passim*. On the fears of the 101st Airborne Division about redeployment, see Leonard Rapport and Arthur Northwood, Jr., *Rendezvous with Destiny: A History of the 101st Airborne Division* (Fort Campbell, Ky., 1948), 757–58, and Lawrence M. Kuenzi oral history, in Eisenhower Center, University of New Orleans, hereinafter cited as EC.

16. Edward N. Peterson, *The American Occupation of Germany: Retreat to Victory* (Detroit, 1977), 114; Gustav Stolper, *German Realities* (New York, 1948), 66–67; Robert A. Pollard, *Economic Security and the Origins of the Cold War, 1945–1950* (New York, 1985), 90; Werner Abelshauser, *Wirtschaft in Westdeutschland, 1945–1948: Rekonstruktion und Wachstumsbedingungen in der amerikanischen und britischen Zone* (Stuttgart, 1975), 151–53. On "turnround" time, see John E. Farquharson, *The Western Allies and the Politics of Food: Agrarian Management in Postwar Germany* (Leamington Spa, Eng., 1985), 25. Contrary to this well-known evidence of tremendous destruction of German transportation networks due to the fierce Allied bombing campaigns, Bacque maintains that the rail transportation system was "in great shape" when the Allies entered Germany; see the Epilogue to Bacque's American edition (Los Angeles, 1991), 193.

transported home the Western European DPs, using every boxcar, army truck, and barge that was available.[17]

The army was ill-prepared for the staggering number of prisoners that surrendered in the final days of the war. In May, 1943, exactly two years earlier, Eisenhower had faced a similar situation when a quarter of a million Axis troops surrendered in Tunisia. In a postscript to a letter to Chief of Staff George C. Marshall at that time, Eisenhower complained that he had never been trained at West Point on what to do with such masses of prisoners. After writing up a long list of problems they caused, he concluded: "We should have killed more of them." This remark, which Stephen E. Ambrose regards as jocular, was taken seriously by the Department of Defense in 1969, when its reviewers ordered the sentence removed from Eisenhower's published papers, presumably for fear of offending NATO allies.[18] Nearly half a century after it was written, James Bacque charges that Eisenhower meant it—and did it at the end of the war in Germany.

The Germans captured in Tunisia fared relatively well. Transferred from camp to camp in the North African desert, many certainly experienced hunger and lack of shelter.[19] Once shipped to the United States, however, they were accorded every privilege of the Geneva Convention. They were housed in U.S. Army camps, and were fed well (during wartime, often exceedingly well). Most of them worked as agricultural laborers. Following the Normandy invasion, SHAEF continued to ship large contingents of POWs to the United States until the beginning of April, 1945.[20] Günter Bischof's father was captured in March, 1945, outside Kai-

17. On the repatriation of Western European DPs, see Marrus, *The Unwanted*, 310.

18. Dwight D. Eisenhower to George C. Marshall, May 25, 1943, in *Eisenhower Papers*, II, 1154–56. On the "suppression" of this sentence, see Bacque, *Other Losses*, 21, 206n23, 203n35.

19. See, for example, the illustrative report of a German POW reprinted in Kurt W. Böhme and Helmut Wolff, eds., *Aufzeichnungen über die Kriegsgefangenenschaft im Westen* (Munich, 1973), 73–186, Beiheft [supplementary volume] II of the Maschke Commission. For the POWs in French hands in North Africa, see Kurt W. Böhme, *Die deutschen Kriegsgefangenen in französischer Hand* (Munich, 1971), Vol. XIII of the Maschke Commission.

20. Arnold P. Krammer, *Nazi Prisoners of War in America* (New York, 1979); Judith M. Gansberg, *Stalag USA: The Remarkable Story of POWs in America* (New York, 1977); Hermann Jung, *Die Deutschen Kriegsgefangenen in amerikanischer Hand: USA* (Munich, 1972), Vol. X, Pt. 1 of the Maschke Commission; Böhme, *In amerikanischer Hand: Europa*, 10 (for the numbers involved), 16–31. In fact, the European theater of operations ceased to send prisoners to the United States in October, 1944, in anticipation of the end of the war; when

serslautern after fighting at the Colmar bridgehead. He was brought to the United States late in March, 1945, on one of the last convoys. Imprisoned in Camp Carson, near Colorado Springs, Colorado, he harvested beans and sugar beets and washed dishes in a hospital. He was treated well enough that he wanted to stay in America, but it was not allowed.[21]

In the final weeks of war in Europe, the numbers of German troops surrendering en masse simply became unmanageable. Resistance within the Ruhr encirclement (*Ruhrkessel*) ended on April 18; when Field Marshal Walter Model's Army Group B surrendered, 317,000 POWs were taken on one day—the largest mass surrender of German troops during the war. After such mass surrenders, the improvised and makeshift POW/DEF "temporary enclosures" quickly became overcrowded.[22] The transports were no longer available to ship back to the United States millions of German POWs.

The numbers of German prisoners taken by U.S. forces shot up from 313,000 to 2.6 million in early April, 1945, then to more than 5 million a month later.[23] These masses created vast problems for the Allies. By the terms of the Geneva Convention, which the United States had signed and which had the force of a treaty, SHAEF was required to feed German prisoners a ration equal to that of its own base soldiers. SHAEF had insufficient resources to meet those requirements. Anticipating huge food deficits in central Europe, Eisenhower's superiors on the Joint Chiefs of Staff had ordered him to change the designation of German POWs to "disarmed enemy forces" (DEFs), just as the British chiefs had changed the status of German POWs to "surrendered enemy personnel" (SEPs) for the same reason. This would allow the Allied commanders in Germany to feed German POWs at a lower level. No German government existed that could have spoken in favor of its soldiers in foreign captivity. While in the American and British zones the German Red Cross was allowed to con-

---

the winter offensives proved this decision overoptimistic, shipments were resumed in February, 1945. We are grateful to Albert Cowdrey for this clarification.

21. Josef Bischof to Günter Bischof, June 23, 1988, in EC.

22. Dwight D. Eisenhower to George C. Marshall, April 16, 1945, *Eisenhower Papers*, IV, 2588*n*1. For American unpreparedness and improvising, see Böhme, *In amerikanischer Hand: Europa*, 137–211.

23. Ratza, "Anzahl," in Maschke *et al.*, *Zusammenfassung*, 194–95; Bacque, *Other Losses*, 54, 175–86. All these numbers are estimates; for the wide range of other estimates of the number of captives, see note 11 to this Introduction.

tinue its work, the French and the Russians did not even permit the German Red Cross to operate in their zones. One observer summed up the fate of the German POWs: "Once hostilities ceased, the Germans were on their own—subject to the unconditional will of the occupier with no rights whatever." [24]

Due to the chaos prevailing in Germany at the end of the war, as well as the punitive American mindset (see the opening Clay quotation and JSC 1067), the German prisoners hardly ate at all in the first days of their captivity and very little during the first weeks of May and June, 1945. [25] German civilians and DPs fared little better. According to the SHAEF "Guide to the Care of Displaced Persons," DPs were supposed to be fed standard rations of 2,000 calories per day, first from German supplies, then from military government supplies and U.S. Army stocks. In Munich, German food stocks were used up by mid-May, and the U.S. military government was faced not only with feeding some 80,000 DPs—some of them marauding and foraging—but also with maintaining the basic ration for German civilians. The logistical problems were immense: 350 of Munich's 800 bakeries had been destroyed; there was no yeast or salt for baking and no coal for the ovens; flour production had been crippled by the bombing, and there was no transportation available to bring in flour from the outside; of 600 tons of stocks of dairy products and food, 540 tons had been looted before the U.S. military government took over. As one historian concluded, "Finding enough food to stay alive was the major problem faced

24. The Red Cross realized right away that the Allies had created these new categories to circumvent the protection of the Geneva Convention for the German troops captured en masse at the end of the war. On the Americans, see Böhme, *In amerikanischer Hand: Europa*, 69–72. On the British, their "surrendered enemy personnel" order, and their inability to fulfill the requirements of the Geneva Convention, see Matthew Barry Sullivan, *Thresholds of Peace: Four Hundred Thousand German Prisoners and the People of Britain, 1944–1948* (London, 1979), 21, 32. See also Arthur Smith, *Heimkehr*, 11–32 (quotation 14n17).

25. For a vivid description of the chaotic circumstances of the end of the war in Germany, see Heribert Schwan and Rolf Steininger, *Als der Krieg zu Ende ging* (Frankfurt am Main 1981). On the early days of the POWs, Charles P. Kindleberger, the well-known economist, who toured Germany in April, 1945, to check out the damage on and the dislocation American bombs had wrought in German industry, reports of a prisoner that a friend of his had rescued from a POW cage "where he had been with 10,000 others for four days without food and without a chance to wash in the literal sense." See Charles P. Kindleberger, *The German Economy, 1945–1947: Charles P. Kindleberger's Letters from the Field* (Westport, Conn., 1989), 207. These letters, with a historical introduction by Günter Bischof, are an excellent firsthand source for the general economic chaos that prevailed in Germany in 1945–1946.

by Germans under American rule for the first three years of the occupation." [26] The great scarcity of food supplies was a consequence of the chaotic conditions in Germany. The streets were clogged with foraging refugees of all types and nationalities; all needed to be fed. Most of the German infrastructure had been smashed; 4 million houses had been destroyed in Germany. In the American zone only 60 percent of the houses were usable (of which 4.5 percent were requisitioned for occupation troops and DPs).[27]

In 1945 the entire German population subsisted on starvation diets.[28] German agriculture had experienced serious decreases in production and productivity in 1944 and 1945. Since the available nitrogen and phosphates were channeled into ammunition production, a shortage of synthetic fertilizer had developed as early as 1943.[29] Without sufficient fertilizer, general crop levels had fallen by 20 to 30 percent by the end of the war. Production and distribution in the German Reich were already badly strained before the war was over. The Allied bombing raids destroyed thousands of farm buildings and made many food-processing plants such as dairies inoperative. Urban centers often had to be supplied with horse-drawn vehicles and handcarts. Lack of farm machinery, spare parts, and fertilizer caused an almost total disruption of agriculture when the war was over. After the release of Russian POWs and Eastern European slave laborers, German agriculture also experienced a serious labor shortage, which could only be alleviated by the quick release of German DEFs and SEPs. Roving bands of DPs and returning soldiers and civilians decimated the hog herds and chicken flocks of the German farmers.[30]

The most egregious dislocation of German agriculture, however, was caused by the zonal partition of Germany. The Western zones were cut off from Germany's "breadbasket," the Oder-Neisse areas, which had accounted for 35 percent of Germany's prewar basic ration scale, and which

26. For a very informative case study on the Munich area, see Burianek, "Politics of Rectification." See also Wetzel, " 'Mir szeinen doh.' " Quotation is from Peterson, *American Occupation of Germany,* 117.

27. Sullivan, *Thresholds of Peace,* 86; Peterson, *American Occupation of Germany,* 114–19.

28. A recently published German study depicts the widespread German starvation in the postwar period in impressive detail. See Günter J. Trittel, *Hunger und Politik: Die Ernährungskrise in der Bizone, 1945–1949* (Frankurt am Main, 1990).

29. Farquharson, *Western Allies and the Politics of Food,* 16, 28–29, 252ff. (Appendix 1, Table 2; Appendix 3, Tables 10, 11, on fertilizer production).

30. *Ibid.,* 1–29, 44–60, 252ff. (Appendices). See also Burianek, "Politics of Rectification," *passim.*

at the Potsdam conference in August were given to Poland. The Soviet Union, with millions of hungry people at home, was unwilling to share the foodstuffs of its zone; indeed, Soviet intransigence in the food sector was an important contributing factor to the outbreak of the Cold War in Germany. In January, 1945, the basic ration for normal consumers in Germany had been brought down to 1,625 daily calories; at the end of the war it was 1,100 calories in the British zone and remained so into the summer of 1945, varying from 840 in the Ruhr to 1,300 in Hamburg to complete breakdown in some areas. The situation was no better in the American zones in Germany and Austria. "By the high summer of 1945 hunger oedema was already visible in the Ruhr," concluded the historian of postwar Allied food policy toward Germany.[31]

On top of all else, the Allies had a strict policy of denazification and demilitarization of the entire German nation, not to mention the initial nonfraternization policy, which treated all Germans as lepers.[32] All POWs had to be screened. This purging of the German population of war criminals and petty Nazis required a huge bureaucracy administering the infamous questionnaires; in numerous cases this kept POWs/DEFs in the cages

31. For a detailed day-to-day documentation on the Western struggle at Potsdam to secure food from the Soviet zone, which turned into a crucial contributing factor for the outbreak of the Cold War, see Rohan Butler and M. E. Pelly, assisted by H. J. Yasamee, eds., *Documents of British Policy Overseas*, Ser. I, Vol. I: *The Conference at Potsdam, July–August, 1945* (London, 1984). On the serious dislocations in German agriculture and the resulting low ration scales, see Farquharson, *Western Allies and the Politics of Food*, 13–60 (quotation p. 45), 254 (Table 6), and John E. Farquharson, "Landwirtschaft und Ernährung in der Politik der Alliierten, 1945–1948," in *Kalter Krieg und Deutsche Frage: Deutschland im Widerstreit der Mächte, 1945–1952*, ed. Josef Foschepoth (Göttingen, 1985), 147–74. In May civilian rations in Munich were 1,007 daily calories; see Burianek, "Politics of Rectification." In June, 1945, the official daily rations for the American zone in Austria were set at 906 calories; on the critical food shortages in Austria, see Eisterer, "Französische Besatzungspolitik," 9–78, esp. 36–37. On the politics of food, see also Günter Bischof, "Between Responsibility and Rehabilitation: Austria in International Politics, 1940–1950" (Ph.D. dissertation, Harvard University, 1989), Chaps. 2 and 3. According to Bacque, however, 1,800-plus daily calories are considered the bare minimum subsistence level; giving the DEFs 1,150 calories per day (in June, 1945, 840 daily calories, and even less later) "was sentencing them to death in a fairly short time"; Bacque, *Other Losses*, 63, 213 n 1, 213 n 4.

32. Every basic postwar German history deals at length with the Allied policy of "de- and dis-," namely, the demilitarization, denazification, deindustrialization, decartelization, democratization, etc. mandated by the Potsdam agreements. See Krieger, *Clay;* Rolf Steininger, *Deutsche Geschichte, 1945–1961: Darstellung und Dokumente in Zwei Bänden* (Frankfurt am Main, 1983); Bischof in Kindleberger, *German Economy,* x–xxi.

longer than needed. By the end of 1945, the U.S. Army was detaining 100,000 "Nazis" in Bavarian internment camps—all of them very hungry, too. In this critical situation refugees and civilians were higher on the priority list of SHAEF's concerns—the prisoners came last.[33] No one went out of his way to make sure food got to the overflowing prisoner cages in May, 1945.

The historians of the German Maschke Commission pointed out with characteristic German scientific thoroughness long before Bacque that little else besides men got inside those cages.[34] The enclosures were makeshift affairs, little more than barbed wire and guardposts. Most POW camps provided inadequate shelter. In the ghastly Prisoner of War Transient Enclosures—popularly known as the "Rhine meadow camps" (*Rheinwiesenlager*; see map of American POW camps in Germany)—prisoners were not provided even with tents in the first few weeks. The weather made a bad situation worse; it was a rainy and at times cold spring, especially in the first weeks of May. The prisoners had to dig into the saturated ground to find some protection. Receiving no food, they boiled grass in water, paying the price of dysentery for quieting their hunger pangs. Many died. Conditions were severe enough that ever since 1945 there have been persistent rumors—based on the imprecise language of many survivors, such as that POWs "died like flies"—of mass deaths. The available evidence, however, clearly does not support such a conclusion.[35]

That there was American vindictiveness is indisputable. The guards, overwhelmed by the numbers of POWs/DEFs, did not treat them with kid gloves. The guards tended to be young, recently arrived recruits, men who had not been in combat against the German army. Many veterans have remarked that the new men who came in at the end, in March and April of 1945, were the ones most likely to find some way to show how tough they were. It also happened that when the generals picked officers to run the

33. Christa Schick, "Die Internierungslager," in *Von Stalingrad zur Währungsreform,* ed. Broszat, Henke, and Woller, 301–25; Lutz Niethammer, *Die Mitläuferfabrik: Die Entnazifizierung am Beispiel Bayerns* (2d rev. ed.; Berlin, 1982); James F. Tent, *Mission on Rhine: Reeducation and Denazification in American-Occupied Germany* (Chicago, 1982); Ziemke, *U.S. Army in the Occupation of Germany;* Peterson, *American Occupation of Germany,* 138–73; Arthur Smith, *Heimkehr,* 12.

34. For more detail on the Maschke Commission, see the essays by Steininger, Overmans, and Bischof in this volume.

35. Böhme, *In amerikanischer Hand: Europa,* 137–211. See also the diary from which Bacque has quoted very selectively, *ibid.,* 309–30. See also Frohn, "Schicksal deutscher Kriegsgefangener."

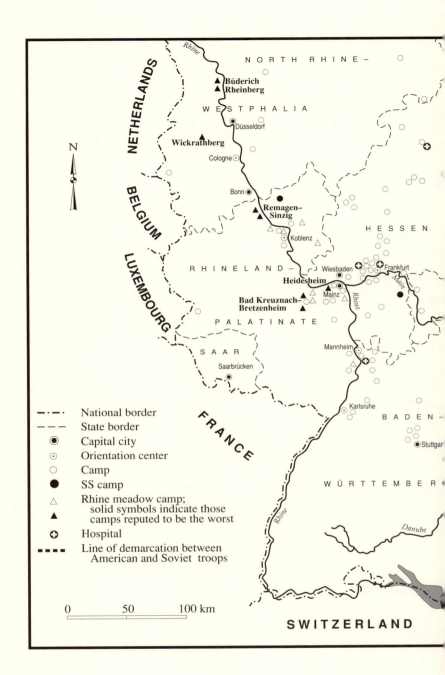

NETHERLANDS

BELGIUM

LUXEMBOURG

FRANCE

SWITZERLAND

NORTH RHINE–

WESTPHALIA

▲ Büderich
▲ Rheinberg

Düsseldorf

Wickrathberg

Cologne

Bonn

Remagen–
Sinzig

Koblenz

HESSEN

RHINELAND–

Wiesbaden   Frankfurt

Heidesheim

Mainz

Bad Kreuznach–
Bretzenheim

PALATINATE

Mannheim

SAAR

Saarbrücken

Karlsruhe

BADEN–

Stuttgart

WÜRTTEMBERG

Rhine

Main

Rhine

Danube

N

–··–··– National border
– – –   State border
◉   Capital city
⊙   Orientation center
○   Camp
●   SS camp
△   Rhine meadow camp;
▲   solid symbols indicate those
          camps reputed to be the worst
✛   Hospital
▬▬▬▬   Line of demarcation between
          American and Soviet troops

0   50   100 km

American POW Camps in Germany

Leipzig

S O V I E T   Z O N E   O F
O C C U P A T I O N

Erfurt

Zwickau

Chemnitz

Karlsbad

Main

Würzburg

CZECHOSLOVAKIA

Pilsen

Nuremburg

Klattau

Pisek

Regensburg

Budweis

Danube

BAVARIA

Munich

Linz

AUSTRIA

Source: Adapted from Kurt W. Böhme, *Die deutschen Kriegsgefangenen in amerikascher Hand: Europa* (2d ed.; Munich, 1973), Map 6 at end of book. With permission.

camps, at times they picked Jewish officers. One of those officers was quoted as saying the job gave him a chance to get a little revenge.[36]

By no means was a desire for revenge limited to Jewish soldiers. It was not uncommon among American and British troops in general. By May 8—V-E Day—most GIs had visited a concentration camp.[37] What kind of people were the Germans to be capable of such horrendous crimes? many asked.[38] They were already very angry at the unnecessary loss of men since January, 1945, when the Germans kept fighting after there was no question about the outcome, and what they saw in the concentration camps strengthened their hatred of the beaten enemy. After his visit to Buchenwald, Eisenhower wrote to Marshall:

> The things I saw beggar description. While touring the camp I encountered three men who had been inmates and by some ruse or another had made their escapes. I interviewed them through an interpreter. The visual evidence and verbal testimony of starvation, cruelty and bestiality were so overpowering as to leave me a bit sick. In one room, where they [there] were piled up twenty or thirty naked men killed by starvation, General Patton would not even enter. He said he would get sick if he did so. I made the visit deliberately, in order to be in position to give *first-hand* evidence of these things if ever, in the future, there develops a tendency to charge these allegations merely to "propaganda."[39]

In a follow-up letter to Marshall, Eisenhower added: "We continue to uncover German concentration camps for political prisoners in which conditions of indescribable horror prevail. I have visited one myself and I assure you that whatever has been written on them to date has been understatement."[40]

Clearly, Eisenhower was appalled by what he saw. So were the British. When they liberated Bergen-Belsen, a newspaper editor wrote: "This terrible degradation of humanity is the worst crime civilization can record

---

36. There were many Poles and Czechs and German Jews in American uniform at this time; see Sullivan, *Thresholds of Peace,* 22. For the testimony of some American camp guards, see the Bischof essay in this volume. Some of the treatment of German POWs is covered in Böhme, *In amerikanischer Hand: Europa,* 16–31, 176–80. See also Sullivan, *Thresholds of Peace.*

37. On the Holocaust, see Leni Yahil, *The Holocaust: The Fate of European Jewry* (New York, 1990), and Michael R. Marrus, *The Holocaust in History* (New York, 1989). On the opening of the camps, with pictures of some of the survivors, see Dinnerstein, *America and the Survivors of the Holocaust,* 24–34, and Wetzel, " 'Mir szeinen doh,' " 336–40.

38. Schwan and Steininger, *Als der Krieg zu Ende ging,* 68.

39. Dwight D. Eisenhower to George C. Marshall, April 15, 1945; in *Eisenhower Papers,* IV, 2615–16 (Eisenhower's emphasis).

40. Dwight D. Eisenhower to George C. Marshall, April 19, 1945, *ibid.,* 2623.

throughout the ages and no punishment devised can offer sufficient retri-
bution of these infamies."[41]

Not only American and British soldiers wept when they saw the skeletal
inmates of the liberated concentration camps for the first time. Many Germans themselves were no less shocked when forced to see the barbarism
of these camps. Some, like the mayor of Ohrdruf when he was forced to
see the concentration camp in the vicinity of his town, went home and
committed suicide. One German officer, upon seeing pictures of Camp
Ohrdruf, said sadly that "he had known that the Germans had lost the war,
but . . . he now realized for the first time that they had lost their honor."[42]

American soldiers entering Germany on the German-Dutch border
passed warning signs: Here Ends the Civilized World. Who could blame
the Americans for sometimes roughing up German POWs—or fault British
soldiers for sometimes "letting the Germans stew in their own juice for a
while"?[43] For by no means were the Americans alone in showing their
disgust with the German POWs. A German captured by the British in
September, 1944, received a daily ration of a tin can full of water and three
cookies, and every five or six days—together with six other POWs—a can
of corned beef. When some very thirsty POWs tried to fetch some water
before they were put on ships in Dieppe harbor, they were beaten back
from water fountains with rifle butts. Their diet started to improve in British POW camps.[44]

In spite of this widespread disgust with (Nazi) Germans and Germany,
the Allies did not have a policy of wholesale starvation of Germans. The
basic American directive for the German occupation, JCS 1067, provided
for rations that would prevent "disease and unrest" in Germany. According
to this order, Eisenhower argued SHAEF was not permitted to authorize a
"blanket release" of disarmed German forces "because their discharge
had to be 'strictly controlled in order to prevent widespread disorder.'"[45]
General Lucius D. Clay, Eisenhower's deputy, summed up the basic Allied
approach as follows: "As I see it, conditions are going to be extremely
difficult in Germany this winter and there will be much cold and hunger.
*Some cold and hunger will be necessary to make the German people re-
alize the consequences of a war which they caused.* However, between the
cold and hunger which is necessary for this purpose and the cold and hun-

41. Quoted in Bridgman, *End of the Holocaust*, 34.
42. Kindleberger, *German Economy*, 205.
43. Sullivan, *Thresholds of Peace*, 88, 32.
44. Rolf Steininger interview with Hermann Gladigau, transcript in EC.
45. Cited in Ziemke, *U.S. Army in the Occupation of Germany*, 293.

ger which brings about human distress is a wide range. We may not be able to avoid the latter, but certainly it is our duty to attempt to do so.[46]

There was, then, a volatile mix in Germany in May, 1945: angry GIs, frustrated recruits, and revenge-seeking Jewish officers, and former slave laborers and German soldiers packed into open camps. The result was unbearable conditions on a massive scale in a few of the large and grossly overpopulated holding camps on the Rhine River. But there is simply no evidence that it was part of an organized, systematic Allied effort.[47] Kurt Böhme, probably the best-informed expert on the treatment of German POWs in American hands, concludes that Eisenhower and the U.S. Army had to improvise for months in taking care of the masses of prisoners to prevent a catastrophe: "In spite of all the misery that occurred behind the barbed wire, the catastrophe was prevented; the anticipated mass deaths did not happen."[48] An authoritative study has concluded, regarding military control of DPs and refugees in Germany, that "seen in retrospect, one of the great achievements of the military period was the control of many infectious diseases, especially typhus, that in earlier periods regularly decimated large groups of refugees."[49] By and large, a similar conclusion can be applied to Allied treatment of German POWs and DEFs.

There are examples of mass deaths among POWs in World War II, particularly on the eastern front and in the Pacific theater. In 1941 alone, 2 million of 3.3 million Soviet POWs—about 60 percent—died in the hands of the German army or were executed by the special SS killer commandos (*Einsatzgruppen*) in collusion with the army.[50] By 1944, only 1.05

---

46. Lucius D. Clay to John J. McCloy, June 16, 1945, in *Clay Papers*, I, 24 (emphasis added; note that Clay reiterated these sentiments two weeks later in the letter to McCloy from which the epigraph for this Introduction is taken). Although there were punitive features in JCS 1067, it was not a derivative of the Morgenthau Plan, as Bacque maintains. Moreover, Clay never allowed himself to be hampered by JCS 1067 in any way and quickly formulated his own policy toward Germany in 1945; see Krieger, *Clay*, 28–94.

47. See the Villa essay in this collection.

48. Böhme, *In amerikanischer Hand: Europa*, 139. It was no better in some British camps; see Sullivan, *Thresholds of Peace*, 30–32.

49. Marrus, *The Unwanted*, 311.

50. Christian Streit, "The German Army and the Policies of Genocide," in *Genocide: Jews and Soviet Prisoners of War in Nazi Germany*, ed. Gerhard Hirschfeld (London, 1986), 12. For a more detailed study see Christian Streit, *Keine Kameraden: Die deutsche Wehrmacht und sowjetische Kriegsgefangene, 1941–1945* (Stuttgart, 1978). Omer Bartov's recent study *Hitler's Army: Soldiers, Nazis, and War in the Third Reich* (New York, 1991), gives overwhelming evidence of the complicity of the Wehrmacht in the ideological and genocidal warfare of the Nazis on the Eastern Front. See also Günter Bischof, "War Crimes Trials," in *The Harry S. Truman Encyclopedia*, ed. Richard S. Kirkendal (Boston, 1989), 386.

million of 5 million Russian POWs in German hands had survived, which amounts to a shocking mortality rate of 80 percent.[51] Of some 2 to 3 million German POWs in Russian hands, more than 1 million died—a mortality rate that may be as high as 50 percent. Moreover, whereas all German POWs had been returned by the Western powers by the end of 1948, the last Germans returned from Russia in 1956.[52] One historian has concluded from such staggering figures: "Human life was cheaper the farther one went east."[53]

Of the 132,000 British and American POWs taken by the Japanese army, 27 percent died in captivity—the Bataan death march being only the most notorious incident; it produced a death rate among POWs of between 40 and 60 percent.[54] By comparison, prisoners taken on the western fronts had an excellent chance for survival. In fact, 99 percent of the American POWs in German captivity were returned at the end of the war.[55] The editors of this volume think that as many as 56,000 German POWs—out

51. Wyman, *DP*, 23; Dziewanowski, *War at Any Price*, 254, cites 1.5 million of 5 million surviving.

52. The exact number of German POWs in Russian captivity is as uncertain as how many died. The Maschke Commission estimated about 2 million German POWs in Soviet hands at the end of the war, and roughly 1.1 million deaths from 1941 to 1955. See Ratza, "Anzahl," in Maschke *et al., Zusammenfassung*, 194, 224. Peterson, *American Occupation of Germany*, 116, 131–32n7, claims that of 3 million captured by the Russians, 300,000 returned. Steininger gives a mortality rate of 60 percent; see his essay in this volume. For a summary of Soviet treatment of German POWs based on the three pertinent volumes of the Maschke Commission, see Paul Carell and Günter Böddeker, *Die Gefangenen: Leben und Überleben deutscher Soldaten hinter Stacheldraft* (Berlin, 1980), 271–364.

53. Dziewanowski, *War at Any Price*, 268.

54. The rate of 27 percent appears in Philip R. Piccigallo, *The Japanese on Trial: Allied War Crimes Operations in the Far East, 1945–1951* (Austin, 1979), 27. Gregory J. W. Urwin argues in his careful study that 37.2 percent of American prisoners died in Japanese captivity, including 40 percent of the servicemen captured in the Philippines; he also cites a source that puts the mortality rate among Bataan POWs as high as 60 percent. Among the American servicemen captured on Wake Island, only 16.6 percent died in Japanese captivity because of their strong unit cohesion in the Japanese camps. Gregory J. W. Urwin, "The Defenders of Wake Island: Their Two Wars, 1941–1945" (Ph.D. dissertation, University of Notre Dame, 1984), 440, 446, 482n9.

55. David A. Foy, *For You the War Is Over: American Prisoners of War in Nazi Germany* (New York, 1984), 156. Piccigallo, *Japanese on Trial*, 27, says that 4 percent of the American and British POWs taken by German and Italian armies died during World War II. There was a great variety of treatment of American POWs in German hands. Captured fliers were treated well, but conditions generally deteriorated in 1944 and 1945 for the common soldiers. For slightly different death rates of American POWs in Japanese hands, see the Cowdrey essay in this volume.

of the 5 million captured at the end of the war—may have died in American captivity in the European theater in 1945. This rough estimate of a mortality rate of slightly more than 1 percent would roughly match the mortality of American POWs in German hands.[56]

The accounts in this volume of what happened to German prisoners in 1945 contrast sharply with that given by James Bacque in *Other Losses*. Bacque charges not only that prisoners were mistreated, but that General Eisenhower systematically denied food and medical care to them, his purpose being to starve them to death as an act of revenge and as an expression of his hatred of all Germans. Bacque writes: "The victims undoubtedly number over 800,000, almost certainly over 900,000 and quite likely over a million. Their deaths were knowingly caused by army officers who had sufficient resources to keep the prisoners alive." So outraged is Bacque by this alleged heinous crime that he has said in an interview that Americans "should take down every statue of Eisenhower and every photograph of him and annul his memory from American history as best they can, except to say, 'Here was a man who did very evil things that we're ashamed of.' "[57]

The author, a Canadian novelist with no previous historical research or historical writing experience, says in his Introduction: "Doubtless many scholars will find faults in this book, which are only mine. I welcome their criticism and their further research, which may help to restore to us the truth after a long night of lies."[58] The Eisenhower Center at the University of New Orleans accepted his invitation. On December 7 and 8, 1990, the Center held a conference to examine the charges. This book brings to print the formal papers given at that conference.[59]

---

56. The number of deaths, especially those in the temporary enclosures on the Rhine, will never be known exactly. But scholars can say with certainty that Bacque's numbers game, based on his interpretation of "other losses," arrives at grossly exaggerated mortality figures. Böhme has estimated that from 3,053 to 4,537 of the 557,000 POWs/DEFs (or 0.6 to 0.8 percent) in the six worst Rhine meadow camps died; see *In amerikanischer Hand: Europa*, 194–205, esp. 203. Although Rüdiger Overmans argues in his essay in this volume that Böhme's figures are generally accurate, Albert Cowdrey and Rolf Steininger believe that as many as 50,000–56,000 POWs may have died. Axel Frohn maintains that Böhme's mortality rates, especially for the Rhine meadow camps, are too low; see his "Schicksal deutscher Kriegsgefangener," 147.

57. Bacque, *Other Losses*, 2; Gulfport (Miss.) *Sun Herald*, March 19, 1990 (Knight-Ridder dispatch).

58. Bacque, *Other Losses*, 4.

59. Stephen E. Ambrose gave a preliminary summary of the conference papers at the American Historical Association's annual conference in New York City at the end of Decem-

Our work—which can be preliminary only, as we have discovered large documentary deposits that need to be fully examined over time—forced us to conclude that when the studies Bacque welcomes are made, scholars will find the sensationalist theses of his book of little use. *Other Losses* is seriously—nay, spectacularly—flawed in its most fundamental aspects. Bacque misuses documents, he misreads documents, he ignores contrary evidence, his statistical methodology is hopelessly compromised, he makes no attempt to see the evidence he has gathered in its relationship to the broader situation, he makes no attempt to do any comparative context, in doing his oral history he puts words into the mouths of his sources, he ignores a readily available and absolutely critical source that decisively deals with his central accusation, and as a consequence of these and other shortcomings he reaches conclusions and makes charges that are demonstrably absurd.

The evidence to support this devastating judgment on Bacque's research and methods appears in the following essays. A few points and documents, however, will be highlighted here.

First, Bacque insists it is a myth that there was a worldwide food shortage in 1945. His "myth" was Eisenhower's nightmare. No food shortage? Eisenhower informed George C. Marshall on February 14, 1945: "I am very much concerned about the food situation. . . . We now have no reserves on the Continent of supplies for the civil population. . . . I find that supplies actually arriving in February will be about 39,000 tons short of our February commitment." On April 25, 1945, Eisenhower informed the Combined Chiefs of Staff (CCS): "Unless immediate steps are taken to develop to the fullest extent possible the food resources in order to provide the minimum wants of the German population, widespread chaos, starvation and disease is inevitable during the coming winter." [60]

These—and many, many similar messages—went out *before* the surrender. After the first week of May, as noted earlier, all of Eisenhower's

---

ber, 1990. In an unprecedented move, historical revisionists, Holocaust deniers, and other supporters of James Bacque disrupted this meeting in an organized fashion. See the filmed footage in the documentary "Rewriting History" by the Canadian Broadcasting Corporation. A published version of the AHA paper appeared as "Ike and the Disappearing Atrocities," *New York Times Book Review,* February 24, 1991, pp. 1, 35–37; see also the unusually large number of printed responses to this article, *ibid.,* April 14, 1991.

60. SCAF 210, February 14, 1945, SCAF 308, April 25, 1945, both in Eisenhower Library, Abilene, Kansas, hereinafter cited as EL. On the postwar food crisis in Germany, see the Tent essay in this volume.

calculations as to how many people he would be required to feed in occupied Germany became woefully inadequate because of the masses of prisoners and refugees.

Basic policy set by the American and British governments was that no food would be brought into Germany, that the Germans would have to feed themselves from existing resources. But to repeat the key request from Eisenhower's cable to the CCS of May 16, 1945, quoted earlier: "In view of the critical food situation in Germany, it is necessary for me to take timely action to meet emergency conditions. It is therefore requested that I be authorized without prior reference to distribute in Germany imported foodstuffs." [61]

No food shortage? This is from the Report of the Military Governor for Germany, July, 1945: "The food situation throughout Western Germany is perhaps the most serious problem of the occupation. The average food consumption in the Western Zones is now about one third below the generally accepted subsistence level of 2000 calories per day per person." The September report declares, "Foods from indigenous sources were not available to meet the present authorized ration level for the normal consumer, of 1550 calories per day." [62]

There is such a thing as common sense. Anyone who was in Europe in the summer of 1945 would be dumbfounded to hear that there was no food shortage.

Even more central to Bacque's accusations is the column headed "Other Losses" in the weekly reports of the U.S. Army's theater provost marshal. It is here that Bacque gets his title, it is here, in the Other Losses column, that he claims to have found a "Missing Million," the prisoners who died of starvation and whose deaths were covered up with the term "other losses." In fact, as Albert Cowdrey's essay in this volume shows, Bacque did not even find a missing *one;* moreover, as Rüdiger Overmans' essay argues with great care, German statisticians never were missing a million German POWs in the West. In addition, Bacque's *only* source for the charge that "other losses" was a cover-up term for deaths has twice repudiated what Bacque claims the man said (the recantation by the aged Colonel Philip S. Lauben is discussed especially in the Cowdrey and Bischof essays).

What, then, *were* the "other losses"? In many cases they were transfers from one zone to another, or between American camps, something that

61. SCAF 396, May 16, 1945, in EL. See also note 14 to this Introduction.
62. Report of the Military Governor, July, 1945, September, 1945, in EL.

Introduction

was regularly done for a variety of reasons, none of them sinister, all properly noted on the documents. But the greatest number of "other losses" is
revealed in the August, 1945, Report of the Military Governor. This is the
critical source, mentioned earlier, that Bacque astonishingly ignores. The
monthly reports are in the Eisenhower Library in Abilene, Kansas; in the
National Archives; and elsewhere. They are a basic source on every aspect
of the occupation, including food shortages and prisoners. Bacque does
not cite them and there is no evidence that he used them.

The August report lists the numbers of DEFs discharged by United
States forces (2,083,500) and those transferred to the British and French
(1,178,415), mostly to be used as labor. The report continues, "*An additional group of 663,576 are listed as 'other losses', consisting largely of
members of the Volkssturm released without formal discharge*" (see Figure 1, a photocopy of the relevant portion of this document).[63]

It takes little imagination to see what happened here. The *Volkssturm*
(or People's Militia) consisted of older men (up to sixty years of age,
mainly World War I veterans) and boys of sixteen or sometimes less.
American and French (see the Overmans essay) guards and camp authorities told the old men to go home and take care of their grandchildren, the
boys to go home and go back to school. This accounts for most, quite
probably all, of Bacque's "Missing Million."

That Bacque is wrong on every major and nearly all his minor charges
seems to us to be overwhelmingly obvious. To sum up: Eisenhower was
not a Hitler, he did not run death camps, German prisoners did not die by
the hundreds of thousands, there was indeed a severe world food shortage
in 1945, there was nothing sinister or secret about the DEF designation or
about the Other Losses column. Bacque's "Missing Million" were old men
and young boys in the militia dismissed early from the American camps;
they were escapees from camps and POWs/DEFs transferred from camp
to camp in Germany and Europe for various reasons.

That still does not answer the question, Did Eisenhower hate the Germans? Certainly he said he did, on a number of occasions, but was he
expressing momentary, war-induced feelings, or a deep-seated hate?[64] Was
his hatred so extreme and his character so monstrous that he could order
readily available food withheld from five million men with the purpose of
starving them to death? Did he have the power to order such a crime? To

63. Report of the Military Governor, August, 1945, in EL (emphasis added).
64. On Eisenhower's feelings toward the Germans, see the Ambrose essay in this
volume.

e. Losses of Manpower. The estimates as to current population in paragraph 1 a exclude POW's and DEF's still held in Allied custody (discussed below in paragraph 1 f) as well as other war losses. Military deaths for all of Germany may be estimated as at least 2,000,000 (Oberkommando Wehrmacht figures to 1 May 1945 were reported as 1,810,071). This would indicate a loss for the American Zone of approximately 400,000 men, not including deaths among those listed as missing. The number of civilian air raid casualties and civilian deaths in concentration camps is not known. An additional manpower loss is through the permanently disabled. The OKW estimates of 700,000 permanently disabled in Germany would suggest a loss in the U.S. Zone of nearly 200,000. This will be increased by the number of permanently disabled among returning POW's and DEF's.

The Military deaths and disabilities, while not a large proportion of the total population, represent a more than proportionate loss in labor productivity because most of the men were in the 18 - 30 age group of the most fit physically. This is of course also the situation in the case of POW's and DEF's.

f. POW's and DEF's. POW's and DEF's held by U.S. Forces (exclusive of holdings in Italy) as of 4 August 1945 numbered 1,610,029. British holdings are estimated at approximately 2,520,000 and French holdings at approximately 925,000. Information is not available as to the number of prisoners held by the Russians. Prior to the collapse of German resistance, 3,000,000 German soldiers were reported as missing on the Eastern Front. It has been roughly estimated that the forces surrendering on collapse might have numbered as high as 2,000,000. Hence, conceivably the Russian holding might be as high as 5,000,000, but in all probability the number is considerably smaller.

POW's and DEF's discharged by U.S. Forces as of 4 August numbered 2,083,500. This includes those discharged, prior to the deployment of Allied troops into their final zones, into what is now part of the British and French zones. It is roughly estimated that about 1,200,000 were discharged into the U.S. Zone. In addition to those discharged by the U.S. Forces, 1,178,415 POW's and DEF's were transferred to the British and French either for subsequent discharge or for work. An additional group of 663,576 are listed as "other losses", consisting largely of members of the Volkssturm released without formal discharge.

The number of POW's and DEF's returning to the U.S. Zone in the near future will depend upon U.S. Theater and UK needs for POW labor units and the number transferred to the custody of the French and other Allies. In addition to holdings prior to V-E Day, the French have requested a total of 1,300,000 men, of whom they have received 562,000. Beginning 1 December 1945, they are to receive the 300,000 POW's held in the U.S. at the rate of 50,000 per month. It is understood that they will receive the additional 427,000 men as they become surplus to the needs of Theater Service Forces. Belgian requests for 45,000 are being met by the transfer of 30,000 men from U.S. holdings and 15,000 from UK holdings. The eventual return of these POW's and DEF's will depend upon the international agreements reached with respect to reparations labor.

The UK holdings are estimated as having less than 200,000 from the U.S. Zone.

It is not anticipated that there will be a return to the U.S. Zone in the near future of prisoners held by the Russians. However, within the last few days discharged Russian-held prisoners have begun to appear in Berlin. The Russian authorities have officially denied that they have permitted the return to Berlin of discharged Prisoners of War. It is recognized, however, that Prisoners of War, mostly disabled and invalid, are sifting into Berlin despite precautionary measures taken.

Working Force in Principal Industries.

a. Agriculture. The U.S. Zone of Occupation is primarily an agricultural area. Nearly 3 million persons out of a working force of about seven million were engaged in agriculture, forestry and related occupations in 1939. The number employed increased during the war, but this included approximately 750,000 foreign workers who replaced Germans in military service and war industry. It is estimated that 300,000 to 400,000 workers were therefore needed, at the time of the

Figure 1. Excerpt from the August, 1945, Report of the Military Governor. The most pertinent portion is the second paragraph under the letter *f*. Photograph of document courtesy of the Dwight D. Eisenhower Library, Abilene, Kansas.

see to it that the policy was carried out? To cover up mass murder for forty-five years? Bacque insists that it is so; we insist that it is inconceivable.

One of Bacque's strongest quotations is a line from one of Eisenhower's letters to his wife, Mamie: "God, I hate the Germans." Bacque seems not to understand that the words were appropriate to the subject, that Ike was by no means unique, and that John Eisenhower printed the letter in his book *Letters to Mamie,* where Bacque found it, without embarrassment. How would Bacque have had Eisenhower sum up his feelings after a letter to his wife recounting all the suffering, destruction, and death he saw around him every day?[65]

Elsewhere Bacque says of Ike that "he felt ashamed that he bore a German name." Bacque cites as his source a personal communication from Stephen Ambrose to Colonel Ernest Fisher. What Ambrose said to Fisher was, "It is rumored that Ike once said, 'I'm ashamed my name is Eisenhower,' but I've never seen it, never used it, and don't believe it."[66] Such twisting of historical evidence—both primary and secondary—is not unusual in *Other Losses.* In the end, Bacque usually resorts to conspiracy theories to salvage his outrageous charges.[67]

The following essays set the larger historical backdrop against which the treatment of German POWs/DEFs at the end of World War II has to be seen. World War II brought death, destruction, and suffering on a scale never witnessed before in history, and the German POWs were included. In reading Bacque's *Other Losses* one would never know that this immensely destructive war was unleashed by the Germans. As General Clay noted, the Germans would have to suffer the consequences for their war of aggression and wholesale slaughter.

65. Dwight D. Eisenhower to his wife, September 19, 1944, in John S. D. Eisenhower, ed., *Letters to Mamie* (Garden City, N.Y., 1978), 210. Operation Market-Garden had just begun when Eisenhower wrote this letter. The full paragraph reads: "You have seen in the papers that two days ago we launched a big airborne attack. Every time I have to order another big battle I wonder how the people at home can be so complacent about finishing off the job we have here. There is still a lot of suffering to go through. God, I hate the Germans!"

66. Bacque, *Other Losses,* 24, 207n36.

67. On Bacque's selective and often faulty treatment of historical sources, see the Villa and Bischof essays in this volume. On the British Tolstoy case, an instructive example of where the writing of "conspiracy history" may lead, see the Barker essay.

I

The United States and the German POWs

Eisenhower and the Germans

Stephen E. Ambrose

I T IS JAMES BACQUE'S contention in his book *Other Losses* that General Dwight D. Eisenhower hated the Germans, to the point that in the spring and summer of 1945 he ordered food and medical supplies withheld from German prisoners in order to starve a million of them to death. According to Bacque, Eisenhower instituted this vengeful policy secretly, on his own, as an act of revenge. In the face of such a charge, it is appropriate to review Eisenhower's evolving feelings toward the German people, the German nation, and the Nazi party.

The family name was originally spelled Eisenhauer. In 1741, Hans Nicol Eisenhauer left his Rhineland home to immigrate to America. He became a farmer in Pennsylvania. He had many progeny; one of them, Jacob Eisenhower (as the name was then spelled), born in 1826, became a Mennonite preacher and farmer. After the Civil War, Jacob moved his family to Abilene, Kansas. He had a full beard, flashing eyes, a stern countenance, and spoke only German. As a boy, General Eisenhower lived with Jacob, but he never learned to speak German, because his father, David, insisted on speaking only English to his sons. But although David had rejected the German language, he was in other ways almost a caricature of the German father. He lived to work; he paid his debts; he seldom displayed any emotion except anger; he was a strict disciplinarian who regularly beat his boys.

General Eisenhower's mother, Ida Stover Eisenhower, was also descended from a Rhineland family that had immigrated to America in the eighteenth century. She was a religious woman, a pacifist, quiet and modest in her demeanor, but a strong person who insisted that her sons grow up with a deep sense of right and wrong.

In sum, Eisenhower grew up in a typical German American household, with no unusual emphasis on his German background, but with some basic German characteristics as an integral part of his environment. In his youth and early career, he had no special interest in Germans or Germany. As a young officer he of course studied the German army—especially after America entered World War I in 1917—but he never got overseas during the war and had no contact with the enemy. He visited the Rhineland in the early 1920s, but only as a tourist on a brief vacation.

By the late 1930s, Eisenhower had been forced by events to think a great deal about Germans, Germany, and the Nazi party. On the day England and France declared war on Germany, September 3, 1939, he wrote his younger brother Milton; in the letter he revealed some of what he had concluded: "It does not seem possible that people who call themselves intelligent could . . . give absolute power to a power-drunk egocentric . . . one of the criminally insane . . . the absolute ruler of eighty-nine million people."[1]

Collective guilt, in short. Having never lived in a totalitarian state, Eisenhower could not imagine how it could be that there was no internal opposition to Hitler. And indeed throughout the war, right to the very end, he had no concern with or interest in the German resistance to the Nazis, partly because he doubted its existence, mainly because he understood that Hitler was indeed an "absolute ruler" more than capable of destroying his opposition. Until they surrendered, he regarded all Germans as the enemy and used every means at his disposal to destroy their ability to wage war.

His anger at the Germans was so great that in May, 1943, when the Germans in Tunisia surrendered to him, he violated the custom of professional soldiers and refused to meet with or shake hands with General Jürgen von Arnim.

As supreme commander, Allied Expeditionary Force, Eisenhower was an agent of the American and British governments, not a policy maker. His orders were to defeat the German forces. Still, his position was so lofty that he sometimes tried to change policy. In January, 1944, he met with President Franklin Roosevelt; among other subjects, he brought up the problem of the postwar occupation of Germany. Eisenhower told the president that the current Allied plan to divide Germany into three zones, one for the Americans, one for the British, and one for the Russians, was a mistake. He felt Germany should not be divided; rather, the military

---

1. Dwight D. Eisenhower to Milton Eisenhower, September 3, 1939, in Eisenhower Library, Abilene, Kansas, hereinafter cited as EL.

government ought to be conducted by a coalition of the Allied forces under a single commander. His reason was less that dismemberment of Germany was wrong, more that a single commander would make administration simpler and would facilitate control of the Red Army's behavior in the areas it occupied. He failed to convince Roosevelt, who said he could deal with the Russians and in effect told Eisenhower to go fight the war and leave the politics to the politicians.[2]

Eisenhower did as he was told. In August, 1944, his armies broke out of their Normandy beachhead and overran France. There was the greatest excitement in the Allied world. People recalled November, 1918, and anticipated a quick German collapse. Eisenhower knew better; he insisted that the Germans would continue to fight until they were incapable of resistance. The theme appears again and again in his letters to his wife. On August 11 he told Mamie, "Don't be misled by the papers. Every victory . . . is sweet—but the end of the war will come only with complete destruction of the Hun forces." In September, when expectation of a German collapse was even higher, he wrote: "I wonder how the people at home can be so complacent about finishing off the job we have here. There is still a lot of suffering to go through. God, I hate the Germans!"[3]

He hated the Germans because they were forcing him to destroy their own country, and because they were continuing to fight long after it was obvious they had no hope of victory, in the process inflicting needless casualties on his own men. As he explained in his memoir of the war, *Crusade in Europe,* "In my personal reactions, as the months of conflict wore on, I grew constantly more bitter against the Germans." He recalled that he signed tens of thousands of letters of condolence to the wives and mothers of his fallen men, and he wrote: "I know of no more effective means of developing an undying hatred of those responsible for aggressive war than to assume the obligation of attempting to express sympathy to families bereaved by it."[4]

At a press conference on August 15, 1944, Eisenhower was furious when reporters asked him how many weeks before capitulation. He said that people who talked that way were "crazy." He reminded reporters that Hitler had absolute power. He predicted that Hitler would end up hanging

2. This issue is discussed at length in Stephen E. Ambrose, *The Supreme Commander: The War Years of General Dwight D. Eisenhower* (Garden City, N.Y., 1970), 387–91.
3. Dwight D. Eisenhower to his wife, September 19, 1944, in John S. D. Eisenhower, ed., *Letters to Mamie* (Garden City, N.Y., 1978), 204, 210.
4. Dwight D. Eisenhower, *Crusade in Europe* (Garden City, N.Y., 1948), 470.

himself, but before he did he would "fight to the bitter end" and most of his troops would fight with him. That was a leap into the mind of the enemy, the highest form of the military art, and he was exactly right.

Eisenhower reminded the reporters that in 1918 the kaiser had reason to hope for a soft peace on the basis of President Woodrow Wilson's Fourteen Points, whereas in 1944 Hitler had only Roosevelt's unconditional surrender demand to contemplate. He had anticipated this problem; in a message to Roosevelt in April, 1944, he had asked the president to clarify the meaning of unconditional surrender "by announcing the principles on which the treatment of a defeated Germany would be based." He said this was highly desirable "in view of the accumulated evidence that German propaganda is interpreting the words of 'Unconditional Surrender' to strengthen the morale of the German Army and people." Eisenhower wanted to emphasize law, order, private property, and the undoubted right of the German people to govern themselves. But Roosevelt, fearful of charges of bad faith after the war criminals were put on trial, declined to make any clarification.[5]

In August, 1944, Eisenhower had a meeting with Henry Morgenthau, Jr., the secretary of the treasury. The two men gave conflicting accounts of the discussion. According to Morgenthau, he got from Eisenhower the idea for the so-called Morgenthau Plan, which called for transforming Germany from an industrial to a pastoral state by removing all her factories, settling factory workers on small farms carved out of the estates of the Junkers, and partitioning Germany. Morgenthau set forth this proposal in a book entitled *Germany Is Our Problem,* which he published in 1945. In October, he sent Eisenhower a copy of the book; Eisenhower thanked him and said he intended to read it immediately.[6] One month later Eisenhower approved the distribution of one thousand free copies of the book to American military officials in Germany. He insisted that free distribution did not "constitute approval or disapproval of the views expressed."[7]

When in 1947 the State Department undertook to write a history of American policy in occupied Germany, it asked Eisenhower to comment on Morgenthau's plan. Eisenhower was emphatic in his reply: "I suggested no plan and never, to anyone, expressed the opinion that Germany should or could become a pastoral state." What he did admit he had said to Mor-

5. Harry C. Butcher, *My Three Years with Eisenhower* (New York, 1946), 644–46; Dwight D. Eisenhower to Walter B. Smith, May 20, 1944, Dwight D. Eisenhower to George C. Marshall, May 27, 1944, both in EL.

6. Dwight D. Eisenhower to Henry Morgenthau, Jr., October 9, 1944, in EL.

7. Dwight D. Eisenhower to Robert Patterson, November 8, 1944, in EL.

genthau in August of 1944 was, however, stern enough: "The German people must not be allowed to escape a personal sense of guilt. . . . Germany's war making power should be eliminated." Certain groups should be punished by Allied tribunals, including leading Nazis, Gestapo, and SS members. Eisenhower recalled insisting that the German general staff be "utterly eliminated," but said he had also told Morgenthau that "in eliminating German war making ability, care should be taken to see that Germans could make a living, else they could become a charitable charge and . . . objects of world pity." [8]

He had little pity for the Germans, especially after early March, 1945, when his armies got across the Rhine and the Germans still would not quit. He wrote Mamie that although the enemy was stretched to the uttermost, "he shows no signs of quitting. He is fighting hard. . . . I never count my Germans until they're in our cages, or are buried!" [9]

To sum up, by the last weeks of the war Eisenhower felt a deep hatred for the Germans. He blamed them for starting the war, for the immense destruction he saw all around him, and for continuing the conflict long after any reasonable people would have quit. The hatred deepened as a result of the sights he saw inside Germany itself. "The other day I visited a German internment camp," he wrote Mamie on April 15. "I never dreamed that such cruelty, bestiality, and savagery could really exist in this world! It was horrible." [10] To George C. Marshall he confessed, "The things I saw beggar description." In one room he saw naked men piled to the ceiling, dead by starvation. "I made the visit deliberately," Eisenhower added, "in order to be in position to give *first-hand* evidence of these things if ever, in the future, there develops a tendency to charge these allegations merely to 'propaganda.'" He insisted that reporters, British members of Parliament, and American congressmen visit the concentration camps to see for themselves, and he sent photographs of the camps to Prime Minister Winston Churchill. [11]

On April 26, Eisenhower received his orders on conducting the occupation of Germany, a document known as JCS 1067 (Joint Chiefs of Staff Paper 1067). It was based on the assumption that all Germans were guilty, although some were more guilty than others. It forbade any fraternization between the occupying forces and the Germans (Eisenhower had already,

8. Dwight D. Eisenhower to Craig Cannon, September 19, 1947, in EL. See also Eisenhower, *Crusade in Europe*, 287.

9. Eisenhower, *Letters to Mamie*, 243–44.

10. *Ibid.*, 248.

11. Dwight D. Eisenhower to George C. Marshall, April 15, 1945, in EL.

in September, 1944, forbidden any fraternization). It called for the auto-
matic arrest of large numbers of Germans who had participated in various
Nazi organizations, and the removal of all Nazis from any public offices
or positions of importance in public and private enterprises. JCS 1067 told
Eisenhower that his most basic responsibility was "to bring home to the
Germans that Germany's ruthless warfare and the fanatical Nazi resistance
have destroyed the German economy and made chaos and suffering inevitable and that the Germans cannot escape the responsibility for what they
have brought upon themselves." [12]

The nonfraternization policy proved impossible to enforce. Eisenhower
said so directly in a June 2 letter to Marshall. There was no way to keep
the GIs from fraternizing with small children; Eisenhower said it was
"simply silly" to forbid soldiers to talk to or give candy bars or chewing
gum to German children. In July, official orders on nonfraternization were
amended to include the phrase "except small children," and ultimately the
nonfraternization policy became a major embarrassment and was quietly
dropped. [13]

Denazification, however, was pursued with sustained vigor, and with
the enthusiastic backing of General Eisenhower. His insistence on its application was so strong that it led to a breakup of his lifelong friendship
with General George S. Patton. In Eisenhower's view, if it was a mistake
to regard all Germans as guilty, it was certainly correct to regard all Nazis
as guilty. In a series of general orders, he directed that no one who had
ever been associated with the Nazi party be allowed to hold any position
of importance in the American zone. His subordinates in the field complained that the policy was unrealistic. General Patton, in command in
Bavaria, was the most outspoken. On August 11 he wrote Eisenhower that
"a great many inexperienced or inefficient people" were holding positions
in local governments as a result "of the so called de-Nazification program." Patton said that "it is no more possible for a man to be a civil
servant in Germany and not have paid lip service to Nazism than it is
possible for a man to be a postmaster in America and not have paid at least
lip service to the Democratic Party, or the Republican Party when it is in
power." He used Nazis to run Bavaria and said that the alternative was
"a bunch of goddamned Communists." [14]

On September 11, Eisenhower wrote Patton a letter that was designed

12. Joint Chiefs of Staff to Dwight D. Eisenhower, April 16, 1945, in EL.
13. Dwight D. Eisenhower to George C. Marshall, June 2, 1945, in EL.
14. George S. Patton, Jr., to Dwight D. Eisenhower, September 11, 1945, in EL.

to set him straight on the issue. "Reduced to its fundamentals the United States entered this war as a foe of Nazism; victory is not complete until we have eliminated from positions of responsibility and, in appropriate cases properly punished, every active adherent to the Nazi party." He insisted that "we will not compromise with Nazism in any way. . . . The discussional stage of this question is long past."[15]

Eisenhower followed up the letter with a personal visit to Patton to emphasize his concern. He said he wanted to extend denazification to cover the whole of German life, not just public positions. He explained that he did not believe the only alternative in Germany was between Nazis and Communists; he believed there was a solid core of decent Germans who were committed to democracy and who should be brought to the fore. As he said in a Frankfurt speech in the fall of 1945, "The success or failure of this occupation will be judged by the character of the Germans 50 years from now. Proof will come when they begin to run a democracy of their own and we are going to give the Germans a chance to do that, in time."[16]

Patton nevertheless kept Nazis in positions of authority. When a reporter asked him at a September 22 press conference why reactionaries were still in power in Bavaria, Patton exploded. "Reactionaries!" he cried. "Do you want a lot of communists?" After a pause, he added: "I don't know anything about parties. . . . The Nazi thing is just like a Democratic and Republican election fight."[17]

The remark caused a sensation. Eisenhower ordered Patton to report to him in Frankfurt. Patton did so. On the day he arrived, Eisenhower's secretary recalled: "General Eisenhower came in looking as though he hadn't slept a wink. I knew at once he had decided to take action against his old friend. He had aged ten years in reaching the decision. . . . When General Patton came in, the office door closed. But I heard one of the stormiest sessions ever staged in headquarters. It was the first time I ever heard General Eisenhower really raise his voice."[18]

Eisenhower relieved Patton, putting General Lucian Truscott in his place. Before Truscott left for Bavaria, Eisenhower called him into his office and told him that the "most acute and important problems . . . were those involving denazification and the handling of those unfortunate persons who had been the victims of Nazi persecution." Eisenhower ordered

15. Dwight D. Eisenhower to George S. Patton, Jr., September 11, 1945, in EL.

16. New York *Times*, October 2, 1945.

17. Peter Lyon, *Eisenhower: Portrait of the Hero* (Boston, 1974), 361, is the fullest account of this press conference.

18. Kay Summersby, *Eisenhower Was My Boss* (New York, 1948), 508.

Truscott to be "stern" toward the Nazis and to give preferential treatment to Jewish displaced persons.[19]

On October 12, Eisenhower held a press conference in Frankfurt. The New York *Times* reported that he spoke "emphatically, and at times bitterly about the Nazis" and insisted that denazification would be carried out.[20] But denazification did not mean the destruction of Germany. In late July, Eisenhower had met with President Harry Truman in Potsdam; there he told Truman that "rehabilitation of the Ruhr was vital to our best interest" and urged Truman to refuse to agree to a program of dismantling German industry. These opinions represented a shift in Eisenhower's thinking, away from a vindictive peace and toward a policy of realism. The shift reflected the influence of General Lucius D. Clay, Eisenhower's deputy military governor. Eisenhower had a high regard for Clay, who was working quietly but effectively to undermine the JCS 1067 clauses that tended in the direction of the Morgenthau Plan. In many long talks with Eisenhower, Clay convinced his superior that in order for Europe to recover from the war, there had to be a German recovery, which in turn had to be based on a revival of the Ruhr because only in the Ruhr could enough coal be produced to meet Europe's needs. Eisenhower had pointed all this out to Truman, but the president nevertheless signed the Potsdam Declaration, which called for definite limits on German production and the actual destruction of much of German industrial capacity. Clay and Eisenhower thought the policy absolute madness.[21]

What the American generals wanted was to promote German democracy. As Eisenhower said, a judgment of how well they had done their job could only be made on the basis of the strength of German democracy fifty years later.

In December, 1945, Eisenhower left Germany to take up new responsibilities as army chief of staff. From then until his appointment in late 1950 as the supreme Allied commander in Europe, he had no direct contact with Germany or Germans. Upon his arrival in Europe in January, 1951, he told a press conference: "When I last came to Germany I bore in my heart a very definite antagonism toward Germany and certainly a hatred for all that the Nazis stood for, and I fought as hard as I knew how to destroy it. But for my part by-gones are by-gones and I hope that some-

19. Lucian K. Truscott, Jr., *Command Missions* (New York, 1954), 508.
20. New York *Times,* October 13, 1945.
21. Jean E. Smith, *Lucius Clay: An American Life* (New York, 1990). Chap. 15. For a discussion of the problems created by JCS 1067 for the American occupation authorities, see Robert Murphy, *Diplomat Among Warriors* (Garden City, N.Y., 1964), 225–85.

day the great German people are lined up with the rest of the free world, because I believe in the essential freedom-loving quality of the German people." [22]

That belief guided his actions. He was an early and strong supporter of the idea of German rearmament, first as a part of an all-European army (the "Pleven Plan") and, after the French Assembly rejected that idea, as an independent army integrated into the North Atlantic Treaty Organization. As president, his policy was to grant full sovereignty to the Federal Republic of West Germany, to support the German army, and to work closely with Chancellor Konrad Adenauer. He gave strong verbal support to the cause of German unity, although only on the basis of free, nation-wide elections.

In Eisenhower's view, if one had to choose between German reunification based on German neutrality and a divided Germany in which West Germany was part of NATO, it was necessary to choose the latter. When the Soviet leaders said they would accept reunification in exchange for neutrality, Eisenhower never believed them. Germany was too powerful, her geographical position too central, for Germany ever to be neutral. He thought that in the long run, the West German economic miracle would be a magnet to the people of East Germany, thus ensuring that when reunification came, it would be on the basis of a free, democratic, market-economy Germany linked to the West. [23]

Meanwhile, Eisenhower was delighted with the progress of the nation he had done so much to bring into being, West Germany. In October, 1954, he agreed with his secretary of state John Foster Dulles' observation that the Federal Republic's transformation from the conquered and ravaged land that was the legacy of twelve years of Nazi dictatorship into a "rehabilitated and equal member of the Western Alliance" with a solid democracy and a booming economy was a "near miracle—a shining chapter in history." [24] When Eisenhower visited Germany in 1959, on the twenty-mile drive from the airport to the American embassy in Bonn the roads were jammed with cheering crowds. It was a moving experience for Eisenhower

22. Press Conference Notes, January 20, 1951, in EL.

23. This issue is discussed at length critically in Anne-Marie Burley, "Restoration and Reunification: Eisenhower's German Policy," in *Reevaluating Eisenhower: American Foreign Policy in the 1950s,* ed. Richard A. Melanson and David Mayers (Urbana, 1987), 220–40. See also Thomas A. Schwartz, "Eisenhower and the Germans" (Unpublished lecture delivered in the Eisenhower Center's Eisenhower Centenary Lecture Series, October, 1990).

24. Burley, "Restoration and Reunification," 237.

to be cheered by the people he had only so recently conquered. Eisenhower told Adenauer it was "astonishing." The chancellor agreed.[25]

In the 1959–1960 Berlin crisis, Eisenhower stood firmly for a free West Berlin. When the Berlin Wall went up in 1961, he called CIA director John McCone and said, "John, isn't there going to be any reaction to this, because I read in the papers that they are starting to build a wall?" McCone replied, "I haven't heard a word about any thought of resistance." Eisenhower said that in his view the written agreements the Soviets had signed on the status of Berlin guaranteed communication between all parts of the city, and that "we had the absolute right to use whatever force was needed to eliminate walls." To his dismay and frequently expressed disgust, there was no action.[26]

This brief review of Eisenhower's feelings toward and relations with the Germans over two decades shows that he had a deep and frequently expressed hatred of the Germans during the war, but that after the conflict ended he began to make a sharper distinction between the German people and the Nazis. Living side by side and working with Germans during the occupation taught him that there were Germans fully committed to democracy. The success of denazification, the emergence of a solid, central core of Germans as the leaders of the Federal Republic, convinced him—as it did millions of Americans—that the Germans were America's strongest and most dependable allies in Europe. He ended up by encouraging German rearmament and reunification, proud of his role in the rehabilitation of West Germany, eager to see East Germany united with the Federal Republic, pleased to be called the German peoples' best friend.

25. Stephen E. Ambrose, *Eisenhower: The President* (New York, 1984), 540.
26. Dwight D. Eisenhower for the record, November 5, 1962, in EL.

A group of young conscripts come down from their hideouts in the Austrian mountains, April 29, 1945. Many Germans surrendered in small groups like this, often overjoyed to make it safely to American captivity.
National Archives photo no. 111-SC-392199

Three German soldiers give up near Kaiserslautern, March 20.
National Archives photo no. 111-SC-203253

By no means did all Wehrmacht troops surrender gladly; these fourteen- and fifteen-year-old boys capitulated only after exhausting their ammunition, still believing that Hitler would find a way to win the war, April 4.
National Archives photo no. 111-SC-203310

American trucks move east as the growing masses of the defeated Wehrmacht head west across the Rhine toward captivity, March 26.
National Archives photo no. 111-SC-202451

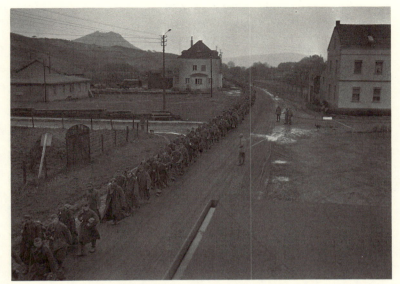

A handful of GIs guard an endless stream of Germans marching through Remagen toward
their temporary POW cages. The date is March 9; the famous Ludendorff Bridge at Remagen had fallen into American hands only two days earlier.
National Archives photo no. 111-SC-202240

Germans fleeing west to escape the Russians used every available means of transportation.
These men from the German Twenty-first Army had just surrendered to the 82d U.S.
Airborne Division near Grabow, Germany, May 5.
National Archives photo no. 111-SC-205636

Civilians joined the Wehrmacht in droves in the mad dash to the west. Here refugees march through "Adolf Hitler Platz" in Ubach, May 10.
National Archives photo no. 111-SC-195034

This German battalion in the picturesque town square of Bad Reichenhall, Bavaria (close to the Austrian border), awaits transfer to a POW camp. Defenses of the nonexistent "Alpine redoubt" in the Bavarian and Austrian Alps had crumbled like a house of cards.
National Archives photo no. 111-SC-207184

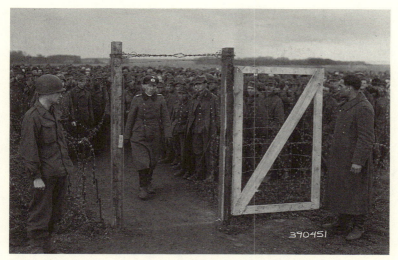

This Wehrmacht officer was designated the 300,000th soldier taken prisoner by the U.S. First Army. He is entering one of the temporary enclosures on the Rhine for screening. Thousands of his comrades await their turn to be processed. "Denazification" procedures held up the quick discharge of millions of German POWs and turned out to be an administrative nightmare for the U.S. Army.
National Archives photo no. 111-SC-390451

The collapse of the Ruhr pocket yielded more than 300,000 prisoners; here are 82,000 initially penned up under open skies in Gummersbach, April 17. Numbers like these overwhelmed the U.S. Army, which at the end of the war had to take care of more than 5 million German POWs, rather than the 3 million for which it had planned.
National Archives photo no. 111-SC-204318

Conditions were also bad in the temporary "cages" outside Kaiserslautern. These Germans surrendered to the U.S. Seventh Army in the Saar and Palatinate areas on the French frontier.

National Archives photo no. 111-SC-203229

Some of the 24,000 German POWs captured by the Seventh Army are massed into the bombed-out medieval town square of Worms. The prisoners ranged in age from fourteen to sixty-two and included everyone sporting a uniform, from regular army to Volkssturm, Hitler Youth, and even German policemen and railroad workers.

National Archives photo no. 111-SC-205482

The worst of the camps were along the Rhine, following the mass surrenders from the Ruhr pocket in April, Remagen (here) being one of the grossly overcrowded temporary enclosures. A few hundred soldiers from the 159th Infantry Regiment ended up guarding over 100,000 German POWs. April 25.
National Archives photo no. 111-SC-204919

When the U.S. 45th Division liberated the Dachau concentration camps outside Munich on April 30, the surviving inmates greeted them joyfully with a self-made American flag.
National Archives photo no. 111-SC-207745

Dachau, May 5. General Eisenhower insisted that reporters and the GIs see the gruesome reality of Hitler's "final solution." American troops left such infernal sights behind with a deep sense of anger, which at times may have produced a backlash in their treatment of German prisoners.

National Archives photo no. 111-SC-205450

Generals Eisenhower, Patton, and Bradley view corpses at a concentration camp near Gotha, April 13.

Courtesy Dwight D. Eisenhower Library, Abilene, Kansas

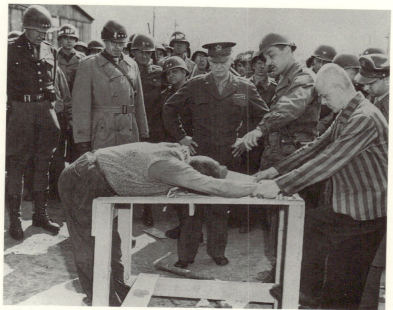

The American generals see a demonstration of Nazi methods of torture near Gotha, April 13. Courtesy Dwight D. Eisenhower Library

The U.S. 80th Division liberated the Ebensee concentration camp in Upper Austria on May 7. In the final months of the war the forced laborers of Ebensee were starved to death at the rate of 2,000 per week. The American soldiers found several rooms full of dead bodies readied for the crematorium.

National Archives photo no. 111-SC-204481

Ebensee was one of the subcamps of the Mauthausen concentration camp system. Ebensee held some 60,000 forced laborers from twenty-five different nations, working for the German rocket program, which late in the war had been relocated to the relatively safe Austrian Alps after the Allies had bombed Peenemünde, the initial V-1and V-2 development site. Half-starved prisoners such as these had to be carefully nourished back to life by the U.S. Army.

National Archives photo no. 111-SC-264842

American GIs captured by the Germans in the Battle of the Bulge in December, 1944, were liberated in half-starved condition in April from the prison hospital at Fuchsmühe. Not all American POWs were treated as badly as these men, although at the end of the war, when German food production collapsed, conditions worsened for many.

National Archives photo no. 111-SC-204898

Hermann Göring surrenders to Major General John Dalquist of the 36th U.S. Infantry Division on the balcony of a hotel in the famous Austrian ski resort of Kitzbühel in the Tyrol.
National Archives photo no. 111-SC-206580

Captain Edward Levy of Denver interviews Hans [*sic*] Goebbels after his capture in Düsseldorf, April 26.
National Archives photo no. 111-SC-231396

SS troops who participated in the slaughter of American GIs taken prisoner during the Battle of the Bulge are lined up. The "Malmedy Massacre" outraged American soldiers and added to their hatred toward Germans; these men may have been beaten by American soldiers.
National Archives photo no. 111-SC-341511

A fifteen-year-old Hitler Youth of the German Nineteenth Army is processed at the U.S. Seventh Army discharge and disbandment center at Aalen, May 11.
National Archives photo no. 111-SC-208956

Two members of the Volkssturm get instructions before being released by Sergeant Werner Neu, 3d U.S. Armored Division, near Elsdorf, March 1. Boys and old men from the Volkssturm such as these were released without discharge by the hundreds of thousands and sent home as quickly as possible after initial screening.
National Archives photo no. 111-SC-204158

German "soldiers" from the Volkssturm, ages fourteen, fifty-nine, and fourteen respectively. These three ended up in the infamous Rheinberg POW temporary enclosure near Düsseldorf, where 89,000 POWs and DEFs were penned up. May 3.
National Archives photo no. 111-SC-390462

The Diplomatic and Political Context of the POW Camps Tragedy

Brian Loring Villa

V OLTAIRE ONCE SAID that history is a pack of lies we practice on the dead. It need not always be that way. Some scholars spend a lifetime studying one subject, something that would not be necessary if they were only inventing the past. But obviously the most sensationalistic efforts at history often fit Voltaire's description, for sensation is most easily achieved by simply wrenching a subject out of its context and discarding, ignoring, or distorting that context. Novel theses, striking revelations, and horrific criminality are easily achievable by such means. It is not always deliberate.

Most professional historians know that they cannot ignore the context or willfully distort it, but an awareness of the ineluctable quality of historical evidence is less present in the mind of the untrained. The frequency with which the basic rules are violated by amateur historians must raise serious questions about the notion that special training for the would-be historian, although useful, is not really necessary. Learning and mastering a context is hard business, not the sort of thing suitable for the dilettante. The difference between history sensitive to the context and that which is not is enormous. Conspiracies have taken place in history, but they abound unnaturally in amateur historical writing because their authors are unwilling or incapable of examining the historical context.[1]

The author wishes to express his thanks to his able research assistant, Richard Wiggers, without whose diligent work and thought-provoking exchanges this piece would not have been, and who is making a study of the legal aspects of the POW question that will add substantially to our understanding of these issues. The author also thanks the Eisenhower Center, most particularly Drs. Ambrose and Bischof, for warm encouragement and support; Dr. Nigel Dennis at the author's faculty; and the University of Ottawa's program of scholarly support for making it possible to devote his energies to this project.
1. My own view on the matter of plots, conspiracies, and evidence is embodied in the

James Bacque's book *Other Losses* illustrates what happens when the context surrounding historical persons and important events is lost. The effect is to give known facts a twist that seems dramatically new in important ways, but this appearance of originality is a little deceptive. For the most part, Bacque's book is not very original at all. When it seems so, the effect is purchased at the price of accuracy. Those parts of *Other Losses* that might rise above a failing grade in an undergraduate term paper are not new. It has long been known that German prisoners of war suffered terribly at the end of World War II, that they died by the thousands after hostilities ceased in the European theater, and that many were required to work as forced laborers for the victors. There are many important dimensions to the POW issue that could be further elucidated, but the main lines of the story have long been known—written up, for example, in exhaustive detail by the German Maschke Commission. Bacque, however, adds two entirely novel propositions, which constitute the principal originality to his work. The first is that the number of those who suffered and died was not in the thousands or tens of thousands, but in the hundreds of thousands. The second is that these deaths were a result of a deliberate extermination policy by Dwight David Eisenhower. To be sure, many POWs did suffer wretchedly during often excessively long detentions, and Eisenhower, by virtue of his office, was formally responsible for whatever happened under his command. But the falsity of Bacque's charges can easily be demonstrated once the context, particularly the decision-making environment, is examined.

Policies, even criminal policies, cannot occur in a vacuum. If a crime is to be alleged, the act and the context must be brought together. Although the average reader of *Other Losses* would never notice it, there was a constellation of authorities to whom Eisenhower had to report his actions. Examining the situation as of May 8, 1945, when his murderous policy is said to have gone into full gear, no responsible historian could ignore the many limitations on Eisenhower's authority that made it impossible for him to carry out an independent policy in Germany. The title he carried was grandiloquent enough: supreme commander; but this was more hyperbole than reality. In modern warfare, theater commanders, like ambassadors, serve largely as glorified mailboxes. Broken down into its constituent components, Eisenhower's office entailed a vast amount of reporting to supe-

methodological appendix to *Unauthorized Action: Mountbatten and the Dieppe Raid* (London, 1989).

riors. Examining these relations one by one, the diligent reader has no difficulty in finding the fault lines in Bacque's thesis.

As the senior United States military officer in the European theater, Eisenhower had to answer to the chief of staff, George C. Marshall. The implications of this obligation for Bacque's thesis are staggering. Bacque uses as evidence of Eisenhower's culpability the fact that Eisenhower seemed to attend to the smallest details in his command, from which Bacque draws the conclusion that, given this apparent style, he must have been deeply implicated in everything his command did.[2] Quite apart from the tendency of most commanders to portray themselves as aware and interested in the finest detail—a pose that rarely corresponds to reality—the fact is that such an image corresponds hardly at all to Eisenhower's style and practice of leadership. He was then, as he would always be throughout his professional career, a generous delegator of authority.

The picture of the hands-on general is rather truer of his superior, Marshall, whose forte and passion was the evaluation of men and their probable performance in command. This austere Virginian was the inheritor of an old and strict code of military professionalism who regarded personal integrity as one of the most important qualities in a commander. Marshall created and staffed the command structure under Eisenhower with men who were as much his candidates as they were Eisenhower's. Even then, he remained ever watchful of his protégé, whose shortcomings he knew as well as anyone. Given this chain of command, by Bacque's reasoning Marshall ought to be implicated every bit as much as Eisenhower. After all, virtually every historian who has studied this period acknowledges that Marshall had Eisenhower's command, Supreme Headquarters, Allied Expeditionary Force (SHAEF), in his purview. Marshall gave SHAEF as much, if not more, attention to detail than did Eisenhower.[3] Ergo, according to Bacque's reasoning, Marshall, too, was a murderer. Is this possible? Bacque, who cares little for exploring the context, does not even raise the question. But if character and personal traits mean anything in the analysis of plausibility, it is a virtual impossibility that Eisenhower could have executed an extermination policy on his own. It is, further, a near-absolute impossibility that Marshall would not have noticed it, let alone that he

2. James Bacque, *Other Losses: An Investigation into the Mass Deaths of German Prisoners of War at the Hands of the French and Americans After World War II* (Toronto, 1989), 162. All references in this essay are to the Canadian edition.

3. Forrest C. Pogue, *George C. Marshall, Organizer of Victory, 1943–1945* (New York, 1973), 35–36, 77, 185, 186–187, and *passim*.

would ever have tolerated it. And what about the scores of officers and millions of soldiers who served under Eisenhower?

If one looks not above, but below Eisenhower, the problems with Bacque's thesis seem no less formidable. Logically enough, Bacque suggests that if Eisenhower had an extermination policy, the staff through which he operated must have been implicated. Bacque charges: "The squalor of the camps came from the moral squalor polluting the higher levels of the army."[4] Perhaps realizing that he already has a thesis involving a massive American conspiracy, Bacque is careful to exclude British officers from any participation or even knowledge of the crime. Although in his vast indictment Bacque has included virtually Eisenhower's entire staff, all the doctors and personnel running the camps, the press who failed to uncover the monstrous crime, and a whole generation of knowing but silent Germans, he has included not a single Briton. But had Bacque given any attention to Forrest Pogue's study *The Supreme Command*—a book he cites in his Bibliography—he would have known that the conspiracy thesis he had stamped out with his amateur's cookie cutter would not work. Pogue's book, it must be pointed out, is absolutely indispensable for anyone studying Eisenhower's role as supreme commander. With even a cursory reading, Bacque would have learned, for instance, that many of Eisenhower's staff officers were British. For instance, Brigadier H. L. Garson, the deputy chief surgeon assisting General W. Kenner during the worst period of the camps, was a British officer. Thus, if a crime involving the health of POWs was committed or acquiesced in by Eisenhower's staff, this Briton must have been deeply implicated. In the decisive first month after the surrender, when the POW camps were set up and the overcrowding and misery were at their worst, British officers proudly served at all levels of Eisenhower's command. In his masterly study, Pogue stresses again and again that SHAEF was a fully integrated Anglo-American command.[5] If there were culpability, Americans and British would share in it.

Bacque did not have to read Pogue's book carefully to realize that the "special relationship" between Americans and Britons characterized the staff of SHAEF; all he had to do was look at the pictures: in slightly more than half the portraits contained therein, the staff officers wear British uniforms. Bacque, one understands, wants a villain in the piece. A complicated modern military bureaucracy such as SHAEF is a tedious subject to

4. Bacque, *Other Losses*, 62.
5. Forrest C. Pogue, *The Supreme Command* (Washington, D.C., 1954), *passim*.

study, unlikely to yield the insidious conspiracy apparently sought by this ex-publisher. Bacque does admit to having found no significant collection of documents on the British and Canadian camps. He seems not to have asked why, but the absence is convenient. He can exclude the British and the Canadians from culpability on the basis of his creative guesswork, buttressed by anecdotal oral testimony. Plainly, he does not understand the integrated nature of Eisenhower's command structure.

The impossibility of Bacque's selective crime thesis—an American but not a British crime—becomes all the more evident when one examines the basic decisions affecting occupation policy. By the power vested in him as supreme commander, Eisenhower set the daily ration levels, not only for the prisoners held by the Americans, but also for those held by the British and Canadians during the crucial first month of the occupation. Bacque does not have a single document, and I know of none, that shows a British or Canadian officer complaining that the ration level set by Eisenhower was too low, or proposing to raise it, in the summer of 1945. Making due allowance for short-term fluctuations, British, American, and Canadian camp commanders were giving essentially the same rations to their prisoners. Here again it becomes evident that the conspiracy, if conspiracy there was, cannot be reduced to the Americans alone.

Bacque builds his indictment of Eisenhower's subordinates, who supposedly acquiesced in Eisenhower's allegedly murderous policy, with a similar disregard for the context. According to Bacque, Eisenhower's staff witnessed the crime in silence, being afraid of implicating their fellow officers or their superiors; in short, they were anxious about keeping their jobs.[6] This may be plausible enough as far as it goes, but that is not very far. To anyone who understands the environment of high command, it is clear that in such circles ambition is rife. The desire to bring down a supremo and his cohorts, and thus step into the shoes vacated, is at least as widespread a motivation as is the cowardice Bacque postulates. In large headquarters, petty staff grievances accumulate by the score, from efficiency ratings insufficiently inflated to medals not received to commands not given. These concerns, often the principal obsession of senior staff, existed even in Eisenhower's surprisingly calm and efficient headquarters. In truth, high command has never been a bucolic pastime.[7] Had Eisen-

---

6. Bacque, *Other Losses,* 165–66, 169.

7. One is reminded of Merriman Smith's interview with Eisenhower in 1962, retold in the first volume of Stephen Ambrose's masterly biography of Eisenhower. Smith commented on Eisenhower's apparent distaste for politics as compared to his military career. Eisenhower

hower committed the crimes Bacque alleges, someone surely would have gossiped, ratted, leaked, or even just hinted. None did. Not even Field Marshal Montgomery. Certainly if there had been a holocaust, it could never have been covered up.

Careful consideration of Eisenhower's staff and his role as Allied commander not only provides the grounds for refuting Bacque's thesis, but it also provides answers to the two central questions Bacque has raised in his own sensational way: Why was it that so many POWs were kept in American hands for so long? And why were the conditions after captivity so abominable? We can take it for granted that some Allied spirit of revenge was at work at the end of the war, especially in the immediate aftermath of the liberation of the Third Reich's concentration camps. The ghastly pictures included in Robert H. Abzug's *Inside the Vicious Heart: Americans and the Liberation of Nazi Concentration Camps* speak powerfully of the spirit of revenge engendered by a bitter war, if we did not already know it.[8]

But the principal explanation for the bad conditions in the German POW enclosures cannot be put down to plain, crude revenge. That would be too simple, not to say simplistic. One has to examine Allied occupation policy, particularly the directives that were given to Eisenhower for him to implement, and consider how they affected the destiny of the prisoners. It was precisely in his capacity as supreme commander that Eisenhower's field of action was most circumscribed. That role gave him many superiors. He had to carry out the decisions of the Combined (Anglo-American) Chiefs of Staff (CCS). He had to execute the directives of the European Advisory Commission (EAC)—an organization, it must be stressed, that included the Soviets. The CCS and EAC issued directives as orders to Eisenhower. The directives were in large part decisions implementing policies of authorities still higher up. The trail leads inevitably to the heads of government, who decided the most important questions of Allied occupation policy. Eisenhower scarcely figured at all in the World War II summit conferences, particularly the conferences at Casablanca,

---

replied: "What the hell are you talking about? I have been in politics, the most active sort of politics, most of my adult life. There's no more active political organization in the world than the armed services of the U.S." See Stephen E. Ambrose, *Eisenhower: Soldier, General of the Army, President-Elect, 1890–1952* (New York, 1983), 96.

8. Robert H. Abzug, *Inside the Vicious Heart: Americans and the Liberation of Nazi Concentration Camps* (New York, 1985), 94 and *passim*. See also that volume's picture essay.

Teheran, Yalta, and Potsdam where the key decisions were made. Ultimately, one must look to this level for the decisions that shaped Eisenhower's working environment and paved the way for the POW tragedy, whose
dimensions Bacque has so grossly exaggerated.

Among these vital decisions, Bacque certainly does understand one,
namely, the unconditional surrender policy formalized at Casablanca. Regarding the obligations the Allies would undertake toward the vanquished,
the policy was unequivocal. Winston Churchill summed it up ably: "If we
are bound, we are bound by our consciences to civilization." [9] That is to
say, the victorious Allies would not be bound by the Geneva Convention
or by international law. Bacque condenses the policy of unconditional surrender by proclaiming that "the disaster in the camps lay coiled under this
term like a snake." [10]

There is more truth in this conclusion than he understands. In 1943 the
unconditional surrender policy seemed innocent enough; certainly it did
not appear as malignant as it would later become. The war had still not
reached its highest pitch of fury, and the Allies had yet to grasp the com-
plex requirements necessary to bring it to an end. Not surprisingly, the
unconditional surrender policy as it was first announced was a comfortably
vague concept. But over the following years it was given content by the
three Allies in the European Advisory Commission set up by the Moscow
Conference (1943). The EAC drafted, among other important postwar
planning documents, the instruments of unconditional surrender while lis-
tening carefully to pronouncements from above. From time to time, the
"Big Three" would blurt out what they thought of the Nazis. As the rheto-
ric became harsher, the terms for the Germans became tougher. In the end
the Allies arrived at their self-arrogation of total sovereignty, being entitled
in their own eyes to a position of total tutelage—they could strip the Germans of all government, indeed of their protection by international law,
and be free to punish them as they saw fit. Had Bacque chosen to follow
these admittedly unexciting EAC debates, he could have learned much. [11]

The idea to treat post–V-E Day prisoners as something other than prisoners of war protected by the Geneva Convention had its vague origins in
the Casablanca statements. But it was given specific form by the EAC,

9. *Parliamentary Debates* (Commons), 5th ser., Vol. 397 (1944), cols. 698–99. See
also Winston S. Churchill, *The Hinge of Fate* (Boston, 1950), 690–91, Vol. IV of Churchill,
The Second World War, 6 vols.

10. Bacque, *Other Losses,* 6.

11. U.S. Department of State, *Foreign Relations of the United States* [hereinafter cited
as *FRUS*], *1944: General* (1966), I, 173, 191–92, 210.

acting on the guidelines provided from above. By the summer of 1944 the EAC had communicated its most important decision to the American government in the context of the "draft instrument of surrender." Washington forwarded it to Eisenhower, whose job it would be to implement the policies of the Big Three as further refined by the EAC. Bacque does not mention the drafts, or even the EAC itself. A crucial year of high-level decision making simply drops from view.

Bacque picks up the story with a cable from Eisenhower to the Combined Chiefs of Staff on March 10, 1945—at a time when Eisenhower's armies were taking thousands of German prisoners daily. In one of the key passages of the book, Bacque presents what he considers to be his central piece of evidence against Eisenhower. "In March, as Germany was being cracked . . . a message signed and initialed by Eisenhower proposed a startling departure from the Geneva Convention—the creation of a new class of prisoners who would not be fed by the Army after the surrender of Germany. The message, dated March 10, reads: . . ." Bacque then quotes the cable *beginning with the third paragraph* ("Although . . ."). The portion quoted goes on to describe the way the prisoners would be classed. On the basis of this cable *as quoted,* the casual reader might think Bacque has some justification for asserting that Eisenhower invented the status of "disarmed enemy forces," as opposed to prisoners of war, in order to take away the rights captured Germans had under the Geneva Convention. As Bacque would have it, only by taking away POW status could a mass killing policy of slow starvation be instituted, as the Convention specifically obligated signatories to preserve the lives of declared prisoners through the provision of adequate food and shelter.[12] Bacque would have us believe that the March 10, 1945, cable points directly to Eisenhower as the creator of this alleged extermination policy, and the quotation seems to support this view. Bacque does not suggest to the reader that the text does not begin with the words he quotes. Given the use made of the quotation, any conscientious historian would indicate to his readers that he is not quoting the full document, either by saying "the message read in part" or by placing an ellipsis to indicate that the opening paragraphs have been deleted from the quoted text. The problem with the omitted paragraphs from Bacque's perspective is that they would make his interpretation untenable. In the omitted text, Eisenhower explicitly refers to the EAC's draft surrender terms, which as early as the summer of 1944 envisioned circumventing the Geneva Convention with a provision that would

12. Bacque, *Other Losses,* 25–26, 29–30.

require the surrendering German commander to accept that his men "shall at the discretion of the Commander in Chief of the Armed Forces of the Allied State concerned be declared to be Prisoners of War." [13] (The words *Disarmed Enemy Forces*—DEF—appeared later as the designation for those not declared prisoners of war.)

Here was the origin of the status that Bacque thinks Eisenhower invented. Eisenhower was merely proposing, in March, to act on the drafts worked out months earlier. If Bacque had simply followed the trail indicated by Eisenhower's cable, he would have found that Eisenhower was not proposing anything startlingly new. All Bacque had to do was look for the EAC draft surrender terms mentioned in the cable—these can readily be found in the standard collection of printed United States diplomatic documents, *Foreign Relations of the United States (FRUS)*, in this case in the volume on the Malta-Yalta conferences. [14] There he would have found that the EAC had not only consciously picked the words "at the discretion," but had also recorded an understanding as to what the words would mean—namely, that a decision to declare the captives prisoners of war "may or may not be taken, depending on the discretion of the respective Commanders-in-Chief. Prisoners of war so declared will be treated in accordance with the standards of international law." [15] In plain English, those not explicitly declared prisoners of war were not guaranteed the Geneva Convention. If a commander in chief decided to grant Geneva rights, an added burden would fall to the Allies, for which no provision was made in the document. So this language suggested that the denial of such rights was to be standard policy.

To repeat, on March 10, 1945, all Eisenhower was doing was asking for authority to implement the terms drafted earlier by his supervisors. It was a typical display of his extreme caution—of his desire to have the confirmed approval of higher authorities for everything he did.

The sequel to the story, following the March 10 cable, emerges no better from Bacque's editing of the rest of the evidence. It is true, as Bacque notes, that the CCS approved Eisenhower's proposed course of action. Yet Bacque seems not to understand their response, for he says the Combined Chiefs urged Eisenhower "not to take in any more prisoners even for labor after VE Day." He adds, "Yet the Army had taken in more than 2,000,000

13. Eisenhower to CCS, March 10, 1945, in SHAEF Signal Log, Eisenhower Library, Abilene, Kansas, hereinafter cited as EL.

14. Report by the European Advisory Commission, July 25, 1944, in *FRUS: The Conferences at Malta and Yalta, 1945* (1955), 110–12.

15. *Ibid.*

DEFs after that." [16] Bacque's thesis amounts to saying Eisenhower was insubordinate. What Eisenhower was proposing was to implement the EAC directive. The CCS were saying not only that they approved of his recommendation, but also that he should not do anything other than what had been proposed; that is, *he should not declare any more captives to be prisoners of war.* The actual wording of the return cable, which Bacque had in hand and cites, is almost peremptory: "It is assumed that you will have no occasion to declare additional Germans to be prisoners of war after the defeat or declaration of Eclipse [end of German organized resistance]." [17] Why not? The explanation seems obvious: the CCS knew that there was not enough food in the European theater to feed the German POWs according to the Geneva Convention, and the chiefs did not want Eisenhower to use the discretion he technically had under EAC decisions to declare subsequent prisoners to be prisoners of war, and assume all the burdens that would have implied. Had Bacque ever cared to look at the original EAC language, he could not possibly have been confused about what the CCS were actually saying to Eisenhower.

The issue, then, was about the status to be accorded to the captured Germans—POW or DEF. It was not, as Bacque suggests, whether Eisenhower should continue to round up and intern German armed forces. The latter was required by Eisenhower's basic instructions, JCS 1067. If the CCS cable of April 26 had been intended to rescind the provisions of JCS 1067, that would have been stated. If Bacque really thinks that Eisenhower was being asked not to take any more prisoners, one would like to know why the CCS did not issue a reminder or clarification when Eisenhower continued to take in more than two million additional DEFs after V-E Day. How did Eisenhower get away with it? Bacque does not even address the problem. It is as if he realizes that it is a nonquestion and that there is little point in pursuing further the implications of a mistaken reading.

The CCS felt so strongly about the necessity of declaring the prisoners to be DEFs, rather than POWs, that after considering Eisenhower's inquiry they promptly cabled Field Marshal Sir Harold Alexander, supreme Allied commander in the Mediterranean, suggesting he take the same steps regarding the German surrenders in Austria. [18] Far from dissenting to this

16. Bacque, *Other Losses,* 58.
17. Combined Chiefs of Staff (CCS) to Supreme Commander, April 24, 1945, CCS 823, in Record Group (RG) 218, National Archives, hereinafter cited as NA. Also SHAEF Cable Log, in EL.
18. CCS to Harold Alexander, Enclosure D-NAF 842 to CCS 823/3, in RG 218, NA.

"murderous" policy, Alexander—a British officer—subsequently asked the CCS for permission to apply the same DEF policy to surrendering German military in Italy as well as in Austria. "In view of the difficulties regarding food and accommodation, it was so decided." [19]

The crucial EAC documents, which Bacque has failed to consult, also make clear what considerations lay behind the original impulse to create a different POW status, and behind the draft surrender terms as they related to the Geneva Convention—the *Soviet Union's refusal to sign the Geneva Convention*. This refusal was disquieting, and Roosevelt, at the insistence of his secretary of state, Cordell Hull, had tried in the summer of 1942 to get the Soviets to sign the convention. In May the president had personally appealed to his White House guest, Foreign Minister Molotov, to this effect. Harry Hopkins, who knew the Soviets better than he is credited with, commented in his personal record of the Molotov-Roosevelt exchange, "You don't have to know very much about Russia, or for that matter Germany, to know there isn't a snowball's chance in hell for either Russia or Germany to permit the International Red Cross really to inspect any prison camps." [20] Molotov, as expected, pronounced the *nyet* for which he was to become famous. Behind the Soviet refusal were a number of considerations closely linked to the secretive nature of the regime, but another major consideration emerged at Teheran: Stalin wanted four million German laborers for an indefinite period (life?). The minutes are silent on this extravagant demand, but Churchill had it very much in mind when it was suggested to him in 1944 that the Germans should be told what they could expect if they surrendered. Knowing Stalin's intent, Churchill doubted anything much could be said that could be reassuring to the Germans.

The Soviet refusal to even consider signing the Geneva Convention created great problems for the EAC. Even a quick perusal of the *FRUS* volumes for 1944 would have revealed this fact to Bacque. The problem was easily stated: how could a single surrender instrument be drafted if a Soviet commander who might take the surrender could not possibly commit his government to accord Geneva Convention rights to German POWs? The only solution was to adopt the lowest common denominator. In this case that meant drafting surrender terms usable for a Soviet commander—terms, in other words, that did not make any promises about POW status.

19. Harold Alexander to CCS, May 2, 1945, Appendix D. to CCS 823/3, in RG 218, NA.
20. Hopkins report of Roosevelt-Molotov meeting of May 29, 1942, reprinted in Robert E. Sherwood, *Roosevelt and Hopkins* (New York, 1958), 558–59.

Although the Soviets feigned not to see the problem, their allies did—as early as March, 1944. When the Soviets drafted a surrender instrument that used the term *prisoner of war* and hence implied Geneva Convention rights, Edward Stettinius, then undersecretary of state, acidly commented: "It would be of interest in this connection to ascertain whether the Soviets propose to accord German prisoners of war the treatment provided by the Geneva Convention, and if not, just what character of treatment they have in mind for them." [21] The point apparently struck home because the instruments as they emerged from the EAC promised nothing, employing awkward and tortured language that made plain the premeditated Allied evasion of the Geneva Convention.

But the Soviets were not alone to blame. Already by 1944, British ministries had decided that they would take advantage of the precedents that had been set by the Germans with Soviet prisoners and the Soviets with German prisoners—they would require German prisoners of war to work for them. The Germans were also working large numbers of French POWs. Why should Germans be treated better? Thus, the EAC terms became convenient for the British and for any other nation that wanted German POW slave labor. By early 1945 the Americans, too, were planning to use German soldiers in ways not accepted by the Geneva Convention, such as in mine clearing. [22]

In April, Stettinius gave a hint of what was in store when he said it might be years before German soldiers were repatriated. Germans were torn between believing Nazi propaganda minister Josef Goebbels, who kept saying that defeat would mean their being hauled away as slaves, and believing what they wanted to believe—that by surrendering to the Western powers they would be assured more humane treatment. After all, the United States and Britain were bound by the Geneva Convention.

Had Bacque taken the time to learn more about the surrenders of World War II, he might have realized that quite apart from the wording of Eisenhower's cable, the "DEF concept" was not Eisenhower's personal invention. Analogous wording occurred in the surrender of German forces in Italy, and had almost prevented that surrender. Bradley Smith and Elena Agarossi have explained in *Operation Sunrise* that the Germans, on hearing the EAC provisions avoiding the conferral of prisoner of war status on the surrendering troops, immediately became alarmed. "What did this

21. Edward Stettinius to John G. Winant, March 3, 1944, in *FRUS, 1944*, I, 191.

22. See transcript of Bedell Smith's press conference of April 21, 1945, reprinted in Harry C. Butcher, *My Three Years with Eisenhower* (New York, 1946), 806–15, esp. 815.

mean? Did the Allies intend to deny POW status to 'all' or 'some' of the men of Army Group C so that they could be exterminated, sterilized, or used as forced labor in Italy, America, or worst of all, in Siberia? Were the Allies planning to exclude large categories of men . . . from the prisoner of war protections of the Geneva Convention?" [23]

Plainly dismayed, the Germans questioned whether they could sign any such surrender. And if they did, would German commanders implement a surrender containing a clause not explicitly according Geneva status to German POWs? Smith and Agarossi have noted that the reading of the terms, as well as the awkward explanation and evasions that followed, amounted to letting the "first scruffy cat" out of the bag. [24] All this, it must be pointed out, occurred under a British commander, General Sir William D. Morgan, who was acting on the authority of Field Marshal Harold Alexander, supreme Allied commander in the Mediterranean theater.

As for Bacque's suggestion that the Combined Chiefs of Staff were only going along with Eisenhower, CCS records do not bear this out. Far from rubber-stamping Eisenhower's suggestion, the chiefs questioned it to the degree of asking for a study by the Combined Civilian Affairs Committee. The CCAC not only concurred with Eisenhower, but also went further than he had proposed: it suggested that the status of *all* German POWs be retroactively lifted after German surrender or collapse. [25] Moreover, when the chiefs ordered Alexander to enforce the same DEF policy regarding surrenders in Austria, the British field marshal, far from raising moral objections to this policy, concurred and followed up with a request to the CCS that he be permitted to apply the same policy to the German surrender in Italy. [26]

Such evidence, besides helping to destroy Bacque's fable of Eisenhower's murderous conspiracy, shatters much of Bacque's portrait of the morally superior British, who supposedly refused Eisenhower's invention of a

23. Bradley F. Smith and Elena Agarossi, *Operation Sunrise in the Secret Surrender* (New York, 1978), 151.

24. CCS Info Memo No. 277, June 7, 1945, in RG 218, NA, and Smith and Agarossi, *Operation Sunrise,* 151–52. Herein lies the explanation, perhaps, for the substitution of the briefer instrument of surrender. See also Arthur L. Smith, *Heimkehr aus dem Zweiten Weltkrieg: Die Entlassung der deutschen Kriegsgefangenen* (Stuttgart, 1985), 25, 137.

25. Report by the Combined Civil Affairs Committee to the CCS, June 2, 1945, Enclosure A to CCS 823/3, in RG 218, NA.

26. Enclosure D-NAF 842- to CCS 823/3, in RG 218, NA. It appears that all German POWs in the Italian theater were in fact declared to be SEPs, the British equivalent of DEFs. See Memo to Chief of Staff, n.d. [*ca.* February 9, 1946], attached to Bevin to C/S, February 28, 1946, 383.6/10, in Box 27, RG 331, NA.

scheme to get around the Geneva Convention.[27] In fact, Bacque's whole statement that the British disagreed with the American DEF policy is woefully mistaken. In the late summer of 1944, British ministries were planning how to utilize German labor for an extended period after the end of hostilities. Indeed, after the war the British, French, and Soviets long used German POW labor contrary to the rules of the Geneva Convention.[28]

Regarding the phrase in a CCS document that Bacque takes to be a major British dissent from American policy, it was nothing of the sort.[29] What the British said, in effect, was that those captives who were to be used for labor outside Germany or outside the theater in which they were captured—particularly those to be used in Britain—would have to be kept as POWs and accorded the treatment such status required. The American position was identical, and the only prisoners the Americans turned over to other powers for use outside of Germany were those who had full POW status. They had to be DEFs or SEPs. This policy excluded the so-called renegades (citizens claimed by the Soviets despite their having served in the Wehrmacht) captured in German uniform, who were stripped of POW status and turned over to the Soviets in complete violation of the Geneva accord, which did not permit looking behind the uniform to identify some other nationality. The complexity of the legal situation regarding who could do what to whom meant that Eisenhower was obliged to run a mixed system of DEFs and POWs, depending on which Allied request was to be met. This caused such confusion in the bookkeeping that his headquarters apparently was never able to sort the numbers out satisfactorily. Bacque, not surprisingly, has no difficulty in seeing the most sinister of motives in this. Neither is it surprising that most British historians with a rudimentary knowledge of Allied POW/DEF/SEP policies have no desire to accent the noble role that Bacque assigns to British policy.

But it must be stressed that it was the Soviets, in their refusal to sign the Geneva Convention and in their vast demands for German labor at Teheran, who first proposed breaking international law and who gave the bad example. Bacque, one suspects, never found the trail pointing in that direction because had he done so it would have obligated him to dilute his indictment of Eisenhower as the inventor of this policy. How far Bacque was willing to go to buttress his case about an American "crime" may be seen in his willingness to cast doubt on the existence of the Russian gulags

---

27. Bacque, *Other Losses,* 25–26, 29–30.
28. WO 32/1121, Public Record Office, London, hereinafter cited as PRO.
29. Bacque, *Other Losses,* 28.

for German POWs; they were, he implies, a myth invented to cover up the American crime. This impression is conveyed largely by innuendo in his description of the dilemma Germans had in locating their missing prisoners presumed to be in Soviet hands. Those who looked to the east, we are told, never came close to understanding the mystery of those prisoners' disappearance. With the flair for drama that so often gets him in trouble, Bacque tells his readers that there would never have been a mystery about the location of the German POWs who ceased to be "if . . . the French and Americans had told the truth about their camps."[30] Bacque not only denies the context, he creates a whole new one at will.

Another major part of the story that escapes Bacque concerns the removal of the Swiss as protecting power over American-held German POWs. The greatest consequence of the Casablanca codification of the unconditional surrender concept was that it gave each ally the right to veto almost any aspect of a surrender, including the critical question of whether any German government was going to be recognized. No doubt the American and British governments had tacitly decided that there would be no German government after the surrender. But one suspects that Eisenhower would have been content to let Fleet Admiral Karl Doenitz' Flensburg government exist for a good while longer had not the Soviets made clear, in May of 1945, that they considered its continued existence intolerable. Whatever Eisenhower might have thought, that settled that.[31]

Germany was left without a central government; it was unable to protect or even to ask others to protect its POWs. Bacque implies it was a unilateral American decision that closed down the Swiss role as protecting power. In reality, that act flowed from an Allied decision—the decision to arrest the Flensburg government—which made it impossible for the Swiss to perform a protecting role as it was then construed. The Swiss, in fact, displayed no desire to continue their role as protector. They, like the United Nations—Canada included—considered that there was no legitimate government in Germany to which the Swiss as protecting power could report.[32]

30. *Ibid.*, 154.

31. Military Mission, Moscow to SHAEF forward, May 7, 1945, SHAEF Cable log, EL. See also Earl F. Ziemke, *The U.S. Army in the Occupation of Germany* (Washington, D.C., 1975), 260–63.

32. This is another case of Bacque's outrageous editing of a document. The Canadian draft he incorrectly identifies as originating with Mackenzie King (*Other Losses,* 71) is dated June 2. What he has excised from his text without the benefit of an ellipsis is, among other things, a recognition from Canadian authorities that "in the present unique situation there can be no protecting power for a Government which does not exist." The Canadian draft Bacque

As a result, responsibility for the welfare of the POWs fell entirely to the Allies, who were bitter about what they found in the concentration camps and too hard-pressed by other concerns to worry very much about the physical well-being of the POWs.

If the unconditional surrender doctrine is what most undermined POW status, and if it is to be attributed to any single person on the Allied side (a dubious historical proposition in itself), it must be Roosevelt who bears principal responsibility for the policy. Bacque, unwilling to dilute his indictment against Eisenhower, refuses to even consider any involvement on Roosevelt's part.[33] Here, more clearly than anywhere else, we see that Bacque is not really driven to his outrageous positions by passionate rage. For if rage were justified, it would surely be justified against Roosevelt and his unconditional surrender policy, under which the tragedy in the camps "lay coiled . . . like a snake," as Bacque puts it. In spite of Bacque's one-sided conspiracy theory, the stubborn truth remains that Roosevelt's decisions and attitudes toward Germany set the stage for the Allied occupation of Germany. Bacque's refusal to deal firmly and directly with the complicated postwar planning landscape invalidates much of his indictment against the lesser figure, Eisenhower.

No less important a constituent of that landscape was the decision, for which Roosevelt bears much of the credit or blame, to try German war criminals all the way down to relatively low ranks. There is no need here to go into the long history behind this decision, made at the highest political levels, but it was firmly in place by the Yalta conference.[34]

The categories of Nazis to be held for possible trial were so vast that they encompassed hundreds of thousands of Germans. Because Nazis were mixed in with prisoners of war, it was impossible to release any POWs until they had all gone through the same complicated process of interrogation and weeding out—a part of the process known as denazification. Some of the highest henchmen of the Nazi regime were posing as privates and corporals; the latter was the rank chosen by Adolf Eichmann.[35] Using the discharge process to screen for possible war criminals was an obvious

---

found is in FO 916/1219, PRO. Dr. Hector MacKenzie of External Affairs drew my attention to this deletion.

33. Bacque, *Other Losses,* 169.

34. Bradley Smith, *The Road to Nuremberg* (New York, 1981); Bradley Smith, *Reaching Judgment at Nuremberg* (New York, 1977).

35. As related by Professor Stephen Ambrose at the December, 1990, International Symposium at the Eisenhower Center.

simplification for the Allied side. But it also meant that the prisoners were kept in "prisoner of war temporary (transient) enclosures" (the military term *cages* is rather closer to the truth) far longer than was originally intended. Bacque, in one of his more preposterous statements, maintains, "The Allies didn't need to imprison soldiers for more than a week or two in order to begin identifying the war criminals."[36] If that were true, the British, who according to Bacque are to be distinguished from the Americans in not having murderous intent, should have processed them much faster. In fact they did not. As Field Marshal Montgomery, who assumed supreme responsibility in the British zone, explained to Anthony Eden on July 8, two months after the surrender, "There are some 2 million men of the German armed forces awaiting discharge to civil life; amongst these are many thousand ardent nazis, who cannot possibly be discharged."[37] Both Eisenhower and Montgomery had to operate under directives of Allied policy on war criminals, a context Bacque sadly neglects.

Eisenhower also had important responsibilities for implementing the labor reparations policy decided at Yalta. While the Soviets hauled the POW slaves away as soon as they were captured, the Western Allies found it difficult to receive their promised quotas. America's allies ultimately required and expected SHAEF to hold the POWs until they were ready to use them. The demands were large. As of June 16, the British wanted 250,000, the French some 2 million, Belgium 45,000, Norway 25,000. It is interesting to observe that Prime Minister Clement Attlee, who presumably represented the interests of working men, insisted on exploiting German slave labor. At Potsdam, where he came to replace Churchill, he also tried to dangle the possibility of more slave laborers (to be drawn from the Western zone) before the Soviets as barter for foodstuffs out of the Soviet zone. As he said on July 21: "Any labor needed to exploit the eastern areas should be made available from the rest of Germany including released army forces. They should be directed to such places as they can work most usefully. The allies should not be confronted by an impossibly difficult [food] situation."[38] Thus, Attlee bargained for the most he could get for the tragic captives. Eisenhower, as the supreme Allied commander, had to

36. Bacque, *Other Losses,* 145.
37. Bernard Montgomery to Anthony Eden, July 8, 1945, and enclosure, in Rohan Butler, M. E. Pelly, assisted by H. J. Yasamee, eds., *Documents on British Policy Overseas,* Ser. I, Vol. I, *The Conference at Potsdam, July–August, 1945* (London, 1984), 69.
38. Minutes Plenary Meeting, July 21, 1945, in *FRUS, Diplomatic Papers: The Conference of Berlin (Potsdam)* (2 vols.; 1960), II, 203–14.

see that there were adequate numbers of German POWs on hand to meet at least some of these political requirements. Since all the Germans in Italy had been denied POW status, they could not be used for this purpose. By default, Eisenhower and Montgomery were forced to meet Allied labor demands from their prisoner-camp holdings. While the exact terms and totals required were worked out, millions of prisoners were kept waiting in confinement. The process dragged on for many months after V-E Day. It was complicated by the fact that the French, whose demands were the greatest after the Soviets, could accept only so many at a time. As time-tables were posted, taken down, and reworked, the prisoners languished in the supposedly temporary camps and cages along the Rhine. When they were finally assigned to an Allied power, they began their long stretch of involuntary servitude. This sad labor reparation policy is barely touched by Bacque.

Bacque not only fails to trace Allied occupation policies back to the Big Three and EAC meetings of 1943 and 1944, but he also fails to carry his story forward far enough. Had he done so, he would have found that the harsh Allied exploitation of POW labor continued long after Eisenhower had returned to the United States. At the end of 1946, there were still some 600,000 German POWs in French hands and 400,000 in British. The Soviets were estimated to be holding 3 million. Bacque, anxious to preserve the credibility of his thesis about a morally superior British approach, says in his text that the British rapidly discharged their "surrendered enemy personnel" (SEPs), until there were only 68,000 in the spring of 1946. The other shoe is discreetly dropped in an endnote indicating that Bacque has excluded POWs from his count and that at the time, "the British had around 400,000 prisoners of war at work in the British Isles." [39] This is the sort of double-entry bookkeeping Bacque asks his readers to believe was a peculiarly American vice; in an effort to create and maintain an illusion of American malevolence and British benevolence, he has resorted to it himself.

One central point needs to be stressed: the policy most responsible for keeping German prisoners of war from returning to their homes was the labor reparation policy, in the elaboration of which the British government was deeply implicated and from which that government attempted to profit beyond 1946. Eisenhower's "complicity," if that is what it should be called, consisted largely in implementing orders in 1945: he understood

39. Bacque, *Other Losses,* 139, 227 n 22.

that he had to hold sufficient numbers of German prisoners to satisfy the wants of the Allied powers who had requested labor reparations. The record shows Eisenhower asked the Combined Chiefs of Staff to begin general disbandment at once; failing that, he wanted to be told the minimum number of prisoners that had to be kept for labor reparations.[40] He was shocked by the magnitude. But it should be noted that the Americans ceased using ex-POWs for labor at the end of 1946—at a time when, in addition to the 400,000 held by the British, 600,000 were held by the French, while the Soviets were estimated to be holding 3,000,000.[41] If one recognizes these fundamental facets of Allied occupation policy, Bacque's theory simply collapses.

Orders issued to Eisenhower also explain the policy of trying to limit as much as possible the activity of the Red Cross, the American Friends Service Committee, and other welfare organizations operating within Germany. Bacque admits that Chief of Staff Marshall ordered Eisenhower to keep the Quakers from operating in occupied Germany during the summer of 1945. But even in conceding this he makes it appear that Marshall had no motive save to agree with his commander in the field, the presumed architect of the policy.[42] This is not true. If one goes to the policy directives drafted for Eisenhower in September of 1944 by Morgenthau's Treasury as well as the State and War departments, one finds the initial traces of the policy in question: "Representatives of civilian agencies of the U.S., U.K., and U.S.S.R. governments shall not participate [in activity in Germany] unless and until you consider such participation desirable. Representatives of the civilian agencies of other Allied Governments or of UNRRA may participate only upon your recommendation and the approval of the Combined Chiefs of Staff."[43] The last phrase seems to indicate the preference that Eisenhower not invite the civilian agencies in. By the time the final presurrender revision of JCS 1067 was sent to Eisenhower in April, 1945, American policy had hardened and Eisenhower's discretion was further limited: "Pending the formulation in the Control Council of uniform policies and procedures with respect to inter-zonal travel and movement of civilians, *no civilians* shall be permitted to leave or enter

40. SCAF 432, June 4, 1945, in 387.4/1, Box 51, RG 332, NA. See also Bacque, *Other Losses*, 58.

41. Department of State, *Occupation of Germany: Policy and Progress, 1945–46* (Washington, D.C., 1947), 15.

42. Bacque, *Other Losses*, 81.

43. Directive to SCAEF, September 22, 1944, in Department of State, *FRUS: Malta-Yalta*, 143.

your zone without your authority."[44] All of Germany was in fact under sequestration. Through the big holes in Bacque's line of argumentation one can see that this was Allied policy as well. Bacque notes that the British and French implemented similar policies. Yet Bacque deduces from the relatively minor differences in the dates when the policy was relaxed a wholly different, indeed murderous, intent by the Americans.[45]

Another important question Bacque gets wrong is who prevented the importation of large amounts of food into Germany. Bacque leaves the reader with the firm impression that this was a policy created by Eisenhower and his staff—they refused to allow food into Germany so that they could carry out the alleged extermination policy. Bacque creates the impression that in order to justify lower food imports, and thus starve the POWs, SHAEF deliberately underestimated the number of POWs, the basis on which rations were demanded.[46] Once again he willfully stands history on its head. In Bacque's tortured analysis, Eisenhower's problem was trying to find ways of reducing food imports so he could starve the prisoners.

In fact, Eisenhower faced the reverse problem. He desperately tried to persuade his superiors to allow him to import food. Here, for instance, is what JCS 1067 said on the subject in the fall of 1944: "German import requirements shall be limited to minimum quotas of critical items and shall not, in any instance, take precedence over the fulfillment of the supply requirements of *any* liberated territory."[47] One does not need to know much about the misery expected in the countries liberated from brutal German occupation and the impossibility of fulfilling their food requests to realize that the directive contained in JCS 1067 amounted to a virtual ban on imports for Germany. The final presurrender revision allowed Eisenhower to import supplies only to the extent that was unavoidably necessary "to prevent starvation or such disease and unrest as would endanger these [Allied] forces."[48] This was the famous "disease and unrest" formula that allowed Eisenhower to fulfill the obligated food needs of lib-

44. JCS 1067/6, in *European Advisory Commission: Austria, Germany* (1968), 486, Vol. III of *FRUS, 1945* (emphasis added).

45. Bacque, *Other Losses,* 82; Conférence Internationale de la Croix-Rouge, *Rapport du comité international de la Croix-Rouge sur son activité pendant la seconde guerre mondiale, 1er septembre 1939–30 juin 1947* (Geneva, 1948), III, 441–47

46. Bacque, *Other Losses,* 52–55, 61, 165.

47. Relief Directive, September 22, 1944, in *FRUS: Malta-Yalta,* 154 (emphasis added).

48. Directive to Commander in Chief, JCS 1067/6, April 26, 1945, in *FRUS, 1945,* III, 494, 497–98.

erated Europe long before giving the minimum to the Germans. JCS 1067 also ordered Eisenhower to take no action that would allow basic living standards in Germany to rise above those of any existing neighboring United Nations.[49] The conditions in some of these countries, such as the western USSR and Poland (to which German conditions were to be *depressed*) beggars imagination. The way the Soviets conceived the possibilities was revealed at Potsdam, a tranquil island that could only be reached by passing through zones of horrific destruction. When Churchill asked Stalin how Germany was going to pay for reparations, Stalin replied succinctly, "There is much fat in Germany."[50] One wonders where, other than at that table.

Just in case Eisenhower did not understand how tough he was supposed to be, another clause made clear that as regards food imports for civilian relief, he had power only to "estimate the requirements." This was another way of saying that he had to have higher authority for any imports under this category. Bacque never once cites JCS 1067 in his notes, although he quotes Clay and others to the effect that it was the fundamental policy governing the American occupation of Germany.[51]

Even if one could pardon Bacque's choosing to ignore JCS 1067, the basic directive for anyone trying to understand Allied occupation policy in Germany, the fact remains that he had many other documents in hand which, read reasonably, explain in a perfectly straightforward manner the context within which Eisenhower was operating. Such a document was a June 5 SHAEF report by Lieutenant General A. E. Grasett, which Bacque takes as proof that Eisenhower could get the food if he wanted. "There was no doubt in Grasett's mind," Bacque asserts, "that the wheat was there to be requisitioned." According to Bacque, it was not requisitioned—from which the reader draws the natural conclusion that there was a crime, and deduces complicity by Eisenhower's staff, who knew the real situation. Once again Bacque misrepresents a document. In his survey of the food situation, Grasett recorded how Eisenhower had to plead for the importation of food (a point not mentioned in this section of Bacque's narrative) and how the British and American chiefs of staff, acting as the CCS, had granted permission for importation of a limited quantity of flour (also not mentioned by Bacque here) while expressly denying the importation of any

49. *Ibid.*
50. Minutes, July 25, 1945, in *FRUS, Potsdam*, II, 390.
51. Directive, in *FRUS, 1945*, III, 494; Bacque, *Other Losses*, 30–31.

other foodstuffs.[52] Incidentally, this is another case of Bacque's ignorance about the proper identity or functions of the personnel involved. In this case Eisenhower's officer in charge of civil affairs—Eisenhower's G-5 and assistant chief of staff—was Lieutenant General A. E. Grasett. If anyone was guilty by silence or complicity in the so-called starvation policy, it had to be he. Grasett was Canadian-born, serving in the British army.

Here then was a food policy dictated by the Anglo-American chiefs, implemented by a Canadian-born general in the British Army. In spite of the facts, Bacque construes a picture of an alleged American extermination policy spearheaded by a man psychologically troubled by the burden of his German roots! Bacque did have a document in his hands specifying the restrictions on Eisenhower's freedom of action. But he avoided mentioning those relevant portions that would have cast great doubt on his central thesis. If there had been an extermination policy, it would have been Allied policy—not Eisenhower's—for all the key directives came from decision-making levels above him. But, of course, there is no evidence of an extermination policy. It is all a figment of Bacque's imagination and careless misconstruction.

This is not to deny the validity of Bacque's hunch that the policy dictated by Eisenhower's superiors and implemented by SHAEF may have been infused by some desire for revenge, disguised as stern justice. Yet there is ample evidence that it was also motivated by practical and moral considerations of greater import. A rudimentary knowledge of just the root issues in the European situation of 1945 might have been instructive to Bacque. That there would be a struggle for influence between East and West for the hearts and minds of Europeans was already evident. Britain, primarily, but also the United States, wanted to have friendly liberated governments that would eschew the policies then deemed in London to be "extreme left." But the problem was that the liberated governments the Western Allies had set up in Western Europe, reluctantly including the participation of some Communists, were tenuous and fragile. They faced nearly insuperable problems in supplying food, clothing, and housing. There was likely to be a dramatic shift to left or right depending on who seemed to have a solution to the pressing needs of the citizens. As the fate of Europe hung in the balance, the question of civilian relief became paramount.

52. Bacque, *Other Losses,* 30–31; A. E. Grasett to Bedell Smith, June 8, 1945, in Box 37, Walter Bedell Smith Collection of World War II Documents, EL.

Churchill carefully explained all this to his ambassador in Washington, instructing him to discourage any inclination in the Americans to fritter away scarce Allied resources. Writing on July 6, 1945, Churchill warned:

> We hope that after the French elections in November a reasonably strong and moderate Government will emerge which will be easier to deal with than the present government. We must support this government and help it rebuild France. But this future will depend largely on its success in dealing with economic problems. Meat, coal and means of transport are going to be desperately short during the winter, and the resulting hardships might bring about serious internal disturbances. To guard against this it is important for the United States and the United Kingdom to do all in their power to help the French get supplies from abroad—especially coal and meat. Failure to do so may not only entail collapse of a new French Government but lasting ill feeling between France and the United States and United Kingdom. Material help is what France will need, not kind words. . . . The position in Holland and Belgium resemble that in France. The governments need outside economic help if they are to survive and to retain the confidence of their people. Italy. . . . A new and promising government has just been formed [the Parri government] which must be given every help. Otherwise Italy might swing violently to the Left. Coal is the crying need, but Italy must also be helped with food and raw materials.[53]

Churchill might have added that the situation was not very different in Britain, where, with elections coming, he could not run the risk of being accused of having depressed British consumption for the sake of improving the fate of the defeated Germans, a concern voiced to Eisenhower on May 15. The implications of such concerns are nowhere noted by Mr. Bacque.[54]

The political requirements of the victors and what might be called the future "Western satellites," added on top of the burden imposed by a swollen army of occupation, millions of displaced persons, and ethnic Germans fleeing from the east, not to speak of the prisoners, put an enormous strain on Allied supply pools and transportation facilities. All needs could not be met in full. So some had to be sacrificed. Not surprisingly, the British and Americans chose to meet the needs of their clients, the liberated governments, before the needs of the defeated Germans. This was Allied policy. As Sir William Strang explained to the burgomaster of Hamburg, a recognized "good German," the situation was brutal: "If there was not enough to go 'round, and there certainly was not, the needs of the liberated

---

53. Winston Churchill to Lord Halifax, July 6, 1945, in Butler and Pelly, assisted by Yasamee, eds., *Documents on British Policy Overseas,* Ser. I, Vol. I, pp. 4–5.
54. *Other Losses,* 50, 213n1.

territories which had suffered under German occupation must first be met, and among others from German resources. Our military government was doing its best to place the German administration and economy upon a tolerable basis. But the sufferings of the coming winter would have to be faced." [55]

British policy paralleled that of the Americans in other important ways as well. Bacque makes much of Eisenhower's nervousness at disclosing to the American public how severe occupation policy was. [56] British fears were quite similar. The published briefing paper for the British delegation to the Potsdam conference, to which Bacque could easily have had access, explained how the British public was to be sold on a tough occupation policy: "To the extent that Germany's needs are met, our Allies, and perhaps ourselves, will go short. The fact is that by her action Germany has placed all the liberated countries in a condition of serious fear and want. Her population can now only be saved from the most dire consequences at the expense of [the] political and economic needs of our allies. One must hope that the British public will be made and kept aware that the responsibility for all this lies at the door not merely of the nazi leaders but of the whole German population." [57] British officials did not want the public pleading for the defeated before the needs of the liberated had been met. American policy was the same.

Given Allied policy and the orders to Eisenhower that flowed from it, given the complaints of the liberated countries whose insistent refrain was that their minimum standards were not being met, what amazes this author is how hard Eisenhower tried to get decent quantities of food and supplies to the vanquished. The historical context is the opposite of what bedevils Bacque, who can think of no other reason for the denial of supplies than Eisenhower's willful cruelty.

Perhaps there is evidence hidden somewhere that may change the context as historians presently understand it. The evidence that is available clearly points to the conclusion that within the constraints of Allied policy, which were considerable, Eisenhower tried to alleviate the fate of the vanquished. He had no secret policy to aggravate it. According to Bacque, quoting General Robert Littlejohn, the deadly conditions in the camps were created by "strenuous efforts." Need it be added that anyone going back

55. William Strang to Anthony Eden, July 11, 1945, in Butler and Pelly, assisted by Yasamee, eds., *Documents on British Policy Overseas,* Ser. I, Vol. I, pp. 192–97.

56. Bacque, *Other Losses,* 81.

57. Potsdam Briefing Paper, E. L. Hall-Patch, July 12, 1945, in Butler and Pelly, assisted by Yasamee, eds., *Documents on British Policy Overseas,* Ser. I, Vol. I, pp. 217–18.

to the documents to find this purported confession of an extermination policy by one of Eisenhower's principal staff officers will find nothing even faintly suggestive of it? Bacque has simply distorted the context beyond all recognition.[58]

To sum up the conclusions reached in this paper, the decisions that fated hundreds of thousands of German soldiers to languish for months and even years in Allied camps were not Eisenhower's, but Allied occupation policy forged in a spirit of understandable severity toward those who had plunged Europe into unfathomable misery. The Allies, not Eisenhower, decided to feed the captives minimum rations and provide them with only minimal clothing. Nor was it Eisenhower's policy that led to the destruction of a central German government. Nor was it his decision to screen all POWs for possible war crimes or to hold them for labor reparations. If, as Bacque says, the key question was why the prisoners were not simply released, the answer is to be found in the vast and complicated political and diplomatic context of the 1943–1945 period—which Bacque ignores. Part of his apparent mystification may be the product, pure and simple, of historical ignorance. On some occasions, however, it seems to be the product of misrepresentation of the documents. What else, if not a determination to win his case, led him to suppress key portions of the evidence, such as in his excision of all mention of the EAC in his discussion of Eisenhower's March 10 cable on the DEF decision?

But perhaps the most important shortcoming is Bacque's failure to understand that from the military point of view, it was in Eisenhower's interest to release as many of the prisoners as possible. He wanted to get them back to work, to make them fend for themselves, and thus conserve his precious resources for needs that had higher priority. Allied decisions sanctioned a vast war-crimes trial procedure (criticized by many as not being vast enough), an even vaster denazification process, and finally, the use of POWs for involuntary labor. These were the principal decisions that dragged out the process of discharging the prisoners. These were the policies that perpetuated the nightmare of the camps.

Bacque stumbled across the evidence of Eisenhower's desire to release the prisoners. Bacque had in hand a cable from Eisenhower of June 4 asking, once again, that he be given wide discretion to release prisoners, saying it was "imperatively necessary" to arrange for their "early disposal." Bacque reports that this cable utterly puzzled him: "It is hard to understand what prompted this cable," Bacque writes. "No reason for it

58. Bacque, *Other Losses,* 169.

is evident in the massive cable traffic that survives in Abilene, London and Washington."[59]

In fact, the cable he quotes, which he says stumped him, gives the explanation in the section he neglected to quote. It was imperative to effect general disbandment of German POWs and DEFs, Eisenhower explained, because it was "necessary to relieve Allied forces of the burden of feeding and maintaining the former and supervising the administration of the latter."[60]

To an objective researcher with an open mind for the evidence—wherever it might lead—a serious effort in the archives would have cleared up many of Bacque's mysteries. But little more than a year after he began work, he was sending out the manuscript for review. No doubt the title of the article in *Saturday Night,* accompanying the first public exposé and explaining Bacque's research travels, must be unintentional in its irony, but it sums up the truth quite well: Bacque was in search, *Saturday Night* proclaimed, of "A Story He Didn't Want to Know!" *Saturday Night* also observed that Bacque had gone to Europe in search of his "first big international book" and that his motives were "not entirely pure: he'd been a publisher before becoming a novelist, he knew that 'scandalous revelations' sold books."[61] What should be clear from this review, and what I hope to make clearer still in my book on the controversy, is the fact that Bacque's method guaranteed that he would attain this goal. He certainly found something big, and surely sales and royalties have reached totals far higher than any debutant historian could ever have dreamed. What he did not find was the truth. It can never be found by anyone who fails to set out carefully the context, which is to be found in a mass of documents. But that would take years of research and would hardly produce best sellers.

59. *Ibid.,* 58.
60. SCAF 432, June 4, 1945, in 387.4/1, Box 51, RG 332, NA.
61. *Saturday Night,* September, 1989, p. 43.

A Question of Numbers

Albert E. Cowdrey

OW MANY GERMAN PRISONERS died in the transient camps established by the American army along the Rhine River in the spring of 1945?[1] The question is basic to James Bacque's *Other Losses,* but its importance goes beyond current scholarly debates, and its ultimate solution must be of interest to the still-unwritten history of World War II's least remembered victims: the prisoners of war of all nations.

Scholarly studies of the German prisoners have been either reticent or baffled by the question of how many prisoners actually were taken in the West. The official history of the U.S. Army surgeon general, although denouncing in scathing terms the conditions that existed in the transient camps, confesses that the author, a Medical Corps general, found a reliable total of prisoners impossible to obtain, either from contemporary records or from surviving officers whom he interviewed. Photographs of the great prison pens, some of which held more than 100,000 inmates at times, suggest the practical impossibility of counting the enormous, gray-clothed, faceless masses as new arrivals continually were added and others were taken away to permanent camps in France. The contradictions between various reports pointed out by the Medical Corps historian suggest that officers detailed to count their captives estimated their numbers, and that

1. On the German prisoners of war, see Kurt W. Böhme, *Zur Geschichte der Kriegsgefangenen im Westen* (Bonn, 1963) and *Die deutschen Kriegsgefangenen in amerikanischer Hand: Europa* (Munich, 1972); James B. Mason and Charles H. Beasley, "Medical Arrangements for Prisoners of War En Masse," *Military Surgeon,* CVII (1950), 341–43; and Stanhope Bayne-Jones, "Enemy Prisoners of War," in *Special Fields* (Washington, D.C., 1969), 372–401, Vol. IX of Medical Department, *Preventive Medicine in World War II,* 42 vols. A substantial first-person literature by former prisoners also exists; see, for example, Fritz Mann, *Frühling am Rhein, Anno 1945: Das Drama der deutschen Kriegsgefangenen im Lager Remagen-Sinzig* (Frankfurt am Main, 1965).

the estimates agreed on little except the general dimensions of the captive army.[2]

Questions regarding the number of deaths have also been treated with caution by scholars. The German authority Kurt W. Böhme cites the official total of 15,285 reported by the American theater provost marshal but also reprints communications from former prisoners that suggest unrecorded deaths occurred in the American transient camps, in numbers that varied widely from one man's recollections to another's.[3] The surgeon general's history ventures no overall estimate, but confines itself to a contemporary study that reported precise totals and rates of death and sickness during a six-week period between May 1 and June 15, 1945. I will say more about this study later.

Bacque departs in striking fashion from this cautious approach grounded in sharply conflicting documentary evidence and recollection. Declaring that "without the Big Number of deaths in the camps, there could be no history of the camps," he alleges that Dwight D. Eisenhower deliberately helped to cause the deaths of 800,000 to 1 million German prisoners, which he alleges took place in the American and French camps.[4]

His method of reaching the Big Number therefore deserves examination. He asserts that roughly a million German prisoners—the "Missing Million"—disappeared from European theater of operations (ETO) records between two reports issued on June 2, 1945.[5] In the first, the grand total of prisoners "in U.S. custody, ETO" is given as 2,870,400, and in the second, "Total PWs on hand in COM Z" is given as 1,836,000. But the Communications Zone (COM Z) was a subordinate command of the ETO, and its total omitted the million or so prisoners held by the armies and army groups. Moreover, both reports state exactly the same number of prisoners for which the ETO is responsible overall—3,193,747. To judge by these documents, there was no Missing Million. There was not even a Missing One.

In seeking for those who supposedly died, Bacque makes the central claim of his book: that "Other Losses," a column found in some American prisoner-status reports, represents a "body count" of dead POWs. He asserts that those recorded in the column died of disease while undergoing

---

2. Bayne-Jones, "Enemy Prisoners of War," 387.

3. Böhme, *Zur Geschichte der Kriegsgefangenen im Westen*, 95, 122–28.

4. James Bacque, *Other Losses: An Investigation into the Mass Deaths of German Prisoners at the Hands of the French and Americans After World War II* (Toronto, 1989), 142. All references in this essay are to the Canadian edition.

5. Conveniently reproduced in Bacque, *Other Losses*, 52–53.

slow starvation. Even at first glance, this interpretation appears dubious, for the daily and weekly totals fluctuate wildly—except, of course, in the cumulative totals Bacque reproduces in his book—rather than assuming the typical form of a bell-shaped epidemic curve. Consider the Seventh Army's totals for June 3–9, 1945:

June 2	2,107
June 3	2,558
June 4	813
June 5	0
June 6	510
June 7	0
June 8	115
June 9	189,949[6]

Bacque's novel interpretation appears to arise from the fact that *losses* is an ambiguous word. To the common man it may mean casualties, but to a personnel officer it means those who depart from a particular unit or command, by whatever means. A number of footnotes in the reports themselves indicate that the second meaning is correct, for they show that hundreds of thousands of "other losses" were in fact transferees from one American command to another.

Thus, on the ETO Weekly PW and DEF Report for August 14, 1945, 132,374 prisoners in the Other Losses column receive the following footnote: "II Corps Enclosures (132,262) turned over to U.S. Forces, Austria" (Figure 1). This is a substantial number. Even more pointed are two daily reports, "Status of Disarmed Enemy Forces," for June 9 and June 10, 1945. The Seventh Army Report shows in the column Other Losses that on the first date 189,949 prisoners, and on the second date 76,598 prisoners, were "Transferred to Third Army." The equivalent Third Army report shows in the column Gains that on June 9, 189,949 prisoners, and on June 10, 76,598 prisoners, were "Transferred from Seventh Army" (Figures 2 and 3).[7] If Bacque counts the losses as deaths, should he count the exactly equal numbers of gains as births?

Aggregating 398,809 prisoners, these records alone expose the fallacy of the supposition that gives the title to Bacque's book. Since the records

6. Weekly PW and DEF Reports, File No. 383.6/1–3, in Box 26, SHAEF G-1 Administrative Section, Decimal File, 1944–45, RG 331, National Archives, hereinafter cited as NA.
7. *Ibid.*

HEADQUARTERS
UNITED STATES FORCES
EUROPEAN THEATER
G-1 Division

Date ___14 August 1945___

WEEKLY PW & DEF REPORT

AS OF 2400 HRS. 4 August 1945

	PREVIOUS ON HAND	GAINS	DISCHARGED DURING WEEK	DISCHARGED TO-DATE	TRANSFERRED DURING WEEK	TRANSFERRED TO-DATE	OTHER LOSSES	BALANCE ON HAND
EASTERN MIL. DISTRICT	449,107	48,623	53,804	1,377,081	7,157	7,157	132,374**	304,395
WESTERN MIL. DISTRICT	86,144	69,188*	4,843	201,465	1,778	46,753	25,952	122,759
SEC/TOR	350,700		311	311	23,453	23,453		326,936
TOTALS	885,951	117,811	58,958	1,578,857	32,388	77,363	158,326	754,090
			Prisoners of War					
TSFET	811,875							501,493***

NOTE:

* - PW total of 66,392 included with DEF total as of 3 August.

** - II Corps Enclosures (132,262) turned over to U.S Forces, Austria.

*** - No report received as yet giving breakdown for week.

Distribution:

General XXXX Bevans
Col. Lauben
Col. Negrotto G-3
Major Lustig, G-1 USFET (Rear)
Lt Col. Petitc, G-1 USFET (Main)
Major McCaskey, PWR G-2 USFET (Main)
Capt. Truelock, Army Gd Div, USFGCC

Information Control Division, USFET (Main)
SGS, Stats Section, USFET (Main)
G-3 War Room, USFET (Main)
G-4 War Room, USFET (Main)
Theater Provost Marshal, Hq TSFET
APO 887, U.S Army
Att: Chief of PW Div.
File.

15 1115

Figure 1. August 14, 1945, Weekly PW [POW] and DEF Report for the European theater of operations. *Source:* Weekly PW and DEF Reports, 383.6/1-3, in Box 26, Decimal File, 1944–45, Administrative Section, G-1 Division, General Staff, SHAEF, RG 331, NA.

REPORT OF STATUS OF DISARMED ENEMY FORCES

SEVENTH ARMY

DAILY

Date	Gains	Dschgd	Trfd	Other Losses		Balance
		NO FIGURES AVAILABLE PRIOR TO JUNE 1				
TO JUNE 1	395,428	354		2,382		392,692
JUNE 2	2,210	343		2,107		393,452
3	3,733	521		2,553		393,106
4	6,375	678		813		397,990
5	5,277	1,394				341,873
6	13,630	2,993		510		352,000
7		2,210				349,790
8	3,889	4,008		115		349,556
9	884	781		189,949	1	159,710
10	1,231	1,300		6,874		
10				76,598	1	76,269

Note 1 - Transferred to Third Army

15 1188

Figure 2.   Daily Report of Status of Disarmed Enemy Forces, June 1–10, 1945, Seventh Army. Compare numbers of prisoners "Transferred to Third Army" June 9 and 10 with numbers received by Third Army those dates (Figure 3). Source: See Figure 1.

Date	Gains		Dschgd	Trfd		Other Forces	Balance
To May 19	772,758		34,646			13,838	724,274
May 20	47,447		26,345			6,949	738,427
21	42,817		21,988			3,114	756,142
22	16,696		25,544			25	747,269
23	12,759		30,502			128	729,398
24	12,240		26,346			1,538	713,754
25	4,436		27,076			2,846	688,268
26	16,720		33,005			10,837	661,146
27	5,375		33,836			2,377	630,308
28	11,194		25,630			21,320	594,552
29	5,740		24,806			2,580	572,906
30	14,629		34,942			1,340	551,253
31 June	19,108		19,828			929	549,604
1	3,768		21,244			6,673	525,455
2	3,200		21,188			2,056	505,411
3	3,486		25,058			11,339	472,500
4	7,282		11,755			158	467,869
5	14,067		16,127			640	465,169
6	7,892		11,287			9	461,765
7	6,142		16,201			3,110	448,596
8	5,369		15,534			2,232	436,199
9	12,111						
9	189,949	1	19,761			1,377	617,181
10	68,253						
10	76,598	1	11,072			3,141	747,819
	15 1186						

Note 1 - Transferred from Seventh Army.

Figure 3. Daily Report of Status of Disarmed Enemy Forces, May 20–June 10, 1945, Third Army. *Source:* See Figure 1.

are contained in a file at the National Archives from which several items are reproduced in *Other Losses,* it is unclear how Bacque could have failed either to see these documents or, if he saw them, to understand their significance to the book he was writing. "Other Losses" was an accounting category, one of whose components was prisoners transferred within the American army. Other notes show just as clearly that the column "Transferred," which also appears in the POW status reports, referred to transfers from American to other Allied commands.

Further documents turned up by Stephen Ambrose and others have subsequently revealed that "other losses" also comprehended escapees and Volkssturm members (that is, citizen militia) who were turned loose without formal discharge (Figure 4).[8] In short, it was a catchall category, whose random fluctuations marked the shuffling about and release of prisoners. Hence the fact that the reported numbers changed so drastically from day to day and week to week.

Bacque cites as sole authority for his own interpretation the word of one witness, retired colonel Philip Lauben. Lauben's own account of his interview with Bacque is revealing:

> I am 91 years old, legally blind, and my memory has lapsed to a point where it is quite unreliable. . . . Often during my talk with Mr. Bacque I reminded him that my memory has deteriorated badly during the 40 odd years since 1945. Mr. Bacque read to me the USFET POW figures for discharge and transfers to other national zones. It seemed to me that, after accounting for transfers and discharges, there was nothing left to make up the grand total except deaths and escapes, i.e.: the term OTHER LOSSES. I was mistaken. . . . many POWs were transferred from one U.S. Command to another U.S. Command. This left one with a loss and the other with a gain.[9]

As if all this were not enough, there is another simple but utterly telling point to consider: as Professor Arthur Smith discovered in the American military governor's monthly reports (which Bacque never studied), the total number of the catchall category "other losses" climbed to over 2 million by late 1946. According to Bacque's logic, this would mean that not a mere million, but *two* million German prisoners died because of American

---

8. See, for example, Report of Status of Disarmed Enemy Forces, 12th Army Group, June 1–6, 1945, USFET SGS Classified General Correspondence, 1944–45, File No. 383.6/3, Box 50, RG 332, National Archives.

9. Philip S. Lauben to David S. Hawkins, March 6, 1990, copy supplied by Colonel Lauben to the U.S. Army Center of Military History, Washington, D.C., hereinafter cited as CMH.

mistreatment—which fully brings to light the manifest absurdity of his reasoning.[10]

Bacque's methodology is all too often as slipshod as his logic. For example, during long periods the column Other Losses completely disappears from the records, calling forth a remarkable display of ingenuity from Bacque. To fill the gaps, he "computed the number of deaths by applying the death rate given in Army statistics for another period to the known number of prisoners on hand."[11] Leaving aside the question of whether the rate for one period is applicable to another, the "rate given in Army statistics" turns out on examination to be a rate invented by Bacque himself.

In July, 1945, the ETO surgeon issued a standard report on Essential Technical Medical Data. It included a brief section on the health of prisoners of war in the Advanced Section, Communications Zone (ASCZ), during a six-week period, May 1 to June 15, 1945.[12] The material was later copied—not entirely correctly—into a manuscript medical history that Bacque uses extensively.[13] The report concentrated on a very bad period in the lives of the prisoners, when shelter was absent, few or none of the Wehrmacht personnel had as yet been discharged to civil life, and the official ration was cut.

A table appended to the report showed the number of hospital admissions for disease, battle and nonbattle injuries, the number of deaths, and the calculated rates per thousand per year—that is, the number of prisoners out of every thousand who would have taken sick or been injured or died if the morbidity or mortality rate existing during the six weeks of the study had continued for a year; this is standard in military medicine. The table also compared the health of prisoners with that of American forces in the theater, showing that the former were much worse off (Figure 5).[14]

The ETO report contained one serious and very evident typographical error: it gave the average strength of POWs in the ASCZ camps as 70,000, during a period when individual camps held more than that number. The nature of the error is clear from the table, which explicitly records not a sample, but the "Number of Admissions and Death Rates Per 1000 Per Annum For Prisoners of War in ACSZ Enclosures . . . During Six Week

10. See "Rewriting History," *Fifth Estate* (CBC), 1991.

11. Bacque, *Other Losses,* 179.

12. Photocopy in CMH.

13. [Sanford V. Larkey], "Administrative and Logistical History of the Medical Service, European Theater of Operations" (manuscript history), XIV, 88–91.

14. The table is also reproduced in Bacque, *Other Losses,* 188.

REPORT OF STATUS OF DISARMED EN FORCE

THIRD ARMY

DAILY

Date	Gains	Dschgd	Trfd	Other Losses	Balance
To May 19	772,758	34,646		13,838	724,274
May 20	47,447	26,345		6,949	738,427
21	42,827	21,988		3,114	756,142
22	16,696	25,544		25	747,264
23	12,759	30,502		128	729,398
24	12,240	26,346		1,530	723,754
25	4,456	27,076		2,846	688,868
26	16,720	33,005		10,837	661,146
27	5,375	33,836		2,377	630,308
28	11,194	25,630		21,320	594,552
29	5,740	24,806		2,580	572,906
30	14,629	34,942		1,340	551,253
31	19,108	19,828		929	549,604
June 1	3,768	21,244		6,673	525,455
2	3,200	21,188		2,056	505,411
3	3,486	25,058		11,339	472,500
4	7,232	11,755		158	467,869
5	14,067	16,127		640	465,269
6	7,892	11,287		9	461,765

A- GAINS Column shows all receipts from whatever source; surrender, stragglers, transfers, etc.

B- TRANSFERRED Column shows only personnel transferred to British Custody. None have been made to French or Russians to date.

C- OTHER LOSSES Column shows all losses other discharge or transfer to custody of another nation; i.e., normal attritions, desertion, release without discharge of volkssturm personnel and civilians, etc.

REPORT OF STATUS OF DISARMED ? ?Y FOR

NINTH ARMY

DAILY

DECLASSIFIED
E.O. 12356, Sec. 11
AND 760099
By RB/BC NARA, Date 7/31/??

Fig 4

Date	Gains	Dschgd	Trfd		Other Losses	Balance
TO MAY 19	684,385	500				683,885
20	20,694	878			2,162	701,459
21	18,531	1,430			6,189	712,371
22	7,556	2,622	330,396	1	4,934	382,975
23	2,509	2,625			644	381,207
24	1,592	2,399			1,721	378,721
25	3,723	4,213				378,231
26	646	6,471			47	372,359
27	544	2,732	60,414	1		309,519
28	200	7,707			446	301,566
29	4,283	4,730	11,457	2		289,452
30	45,191	3,569			1,943	329,031
31 JUNE 1	722	2,396	28,209	1		298,577
1	2,554	3,812			601	298,318
2	2,854	5,078	26,446			269,040
3	2,232	4,527				267,452
4		1,061			1,357	265,034
5	657	5,424				260,267
6	3,584	2,656			1,421	259,774

A— GAINS Column shows all receipts from whatever source; surrender, stragglers, transfers, etc.

B— TRANSFERRED Column shows only personnel transferred to British Custody. None have been made to French or Russians to date.

C— OTHER LOSSES Column shows all losses other discharge or transfer to custody of another nation; i.e. normal attrition, desertion, release without discharge of Volkssturm personnel and civilians, etc.

Figure 4. Daily reports, Status of Disarmed Enemy Forces. May 20–June 6, 1945, Third and Ninth armies. Definition of "Other Losses" circled on one copy by author. In the first line of this definition "other discharge" clearly should read "other than discharge." *Source:* Classified Correspondence, 1944–45, Secretary General Staff, USFET, RG 332, NA.

TABLE I

Comparison of Number of Admissions and Death Rates Per 1000 Per Annum
For Prisoners of War in ASCZ Enclosures and ETO Troops (Less UK)
During Six Week Period Ending 15 June 1945.

	ADMISSIONS				DEATHS			
	P. O. W.		U.S. TROOPS		P. O. W.		U.S. TROOPS	
	Number	Rate Per 1000	Number	Rate Per 1000	Number	Rate Per 1000	Number	Rate Per 1000
Disease	345,324	4,235	155,785	551	2,754	34.2	161	.6
Non-Battle Injury	37,713	468	31,070	110	98	1.2	919	3.2
Battle Casualty	20,105	250	2,204	8	16	.2	82	.3
TOTAL	403,142	5,003	189,059	669	2,868	35.6	1,162	4.11

Figure 5. Table appended to European theater of operations surgeon's report on Essential Technical Medical Data. *Source:* U.S. Army Military History Center, Washington, D.C.

Period Ending 15 June 1945." The 345,324 hospital admissions could hardly refer to a sample of 70,000 prisoners; in six weeks, every man would have had to be admitted to a hospital almost five times, and if the sample was representative, the whole command would have counted almost 3.5 million admissions, far beyond the power of the supporting hospital to admit. (By way of comparison, the total of all admissions—battle, nonbattle injury, and disease—for all American soldiers in the European theater for the whole war amounted to only 2.7 million.) Finally, all calculations in the table are done on the basis of 700,000 prisoners, which is, by the way, a highly plausible average strength for the command over the period of the study.[15]

The conversion is simple: divide the number of sick or dead for six weeks by 42 days to get the average for one day; multiply by 365 to get the average for a year; and divide by the number of thousands to get the average per thousand per year. Any reader with a hand calculator can verify in a few minutes that the rates given in the table are without any significant error and that they are based on a population of 700,000, not 70,000.

Yet Bacque appears utterly baffled by this material. In attempting to carry out the arithmetic I have just described, he omits dividing by the number of thousands—in other words, he calculates "per year" but not "per thousand." Unable to reach figures even resembling those in the table, he tries to find the number of prisoners by dividing the rate per thousand per year into the number of hospital admissions for six weeks and multiplying by a thousand. Thus he derives the meaningless number 80,583, which he believes to be the "real number" of prisoners in what he construes as a sample.[16] This flight of fancy serves no purpose but to introduce still another layer of confusion into the discussion.

His reading is in the same state as his 'rithmetic: he imagines that the number of accidental deaths for six weeks, plainly labeled as 98 on the chart, represents a *projection* "from six weeks to an annual figure of 98." He divides 98 by 52 weeks, multiplies by 6, and finds that by his calculation 11.308 men died during the period of the study. Having arrived at this utterly irrelevant figure, he dismisses it on the ground that human beings die only in whole numbers. In short, instead of attributing the result to his

15. The strength of the camps was about 776,000 during May; the strength during June has not been ascertained, but is known to have fallen drastically because of mass discharges begun during that month. See Earl F. Ziemke, *The U.S. Army in the Occupation of Germany* (Washington, D.C., 1975), 293.

16. Bacque, *Other Losses*, 187.

own misunderstanding, he takes it as proof that the numbers in the chart are false. He also takes, from another table, a total of the chief causes of death by disease and expects it to equal a total of all causes of death. And he invents, by methods I am not able to follow, a "second survey of 560,899 prisoners" from the whole cloth, apparently because he is unable to reconcile the rates in the table shown in Figure 5 with his imaginary figure of 80,583.[17]

In the end he concludes that the death rate in the camps was about 30 percent a year, and uses this invented death rate to calculate the absent "other losses," opening the way to the Big Number his project demands. By contrast, the Army Medical Department calculated correctly that the death rate for one year, had the conditions of May 1–June 15 continued, would have been 35.6 per *thousand,* or 3.56 percent.

If Bacque accepted personal responsibility for the 30 percent figure, he would at least be assigning blame where it properly lies. But he does not. Instead, he has asserted that the U.S. Army Medical Corps recorded a 30 percent death rate; noting that "the Theater Provost Marshal [reported] 2,276 [deaths], for a death rate of only 1.4 percent per annum," he asks: "Can anyone believe that? Or would you sooner believe the evidence quoted in the book from the U.S. Army Medical Corps? Their six-week survey in May to June in the better camps [*sic*] containing over 80,000 people [*sic*] showed the death rate was 30 percent per year [*sic!*]." [18]

As I have said elsewhere, it seems strange to me that Bacque was content with a Missing Million. By such methods as these, he might equally well have proved the existence of a Butchered Billion.

Perhaps *Other Losses* has gotten as far as it has because so many scholars and journalists either are or believe themselves to be mathematically illiterate. Although perfectly capable of adding a tip to a restaurant bill, and even of balancing a checkbook, victims of the literary tradition tend simply to throw up their hands at the sight of numbers, believing that they cannot possibly understand them. Yet the mathematical blunders of *Other Losses* are elementary. One turns from them feeling only embarrassment for the author who naïvely grounds his thesis upon them.

So much for arithmetic. On a human level, it is quite shocking enough that, on average, one man of every two in the ASCZ camps was admitted

17. ETO, Essential Technical Medical Data, July, 1945, Inclosure No. 11, Table 1, in CMH; Bacque, *Other Losses,* 191.
18. Washington *Times,* March 5, 1990.

to the hospital once in six weeks; the sick rate of more than 4,000 per 1,000 per year is comparable to that of Americans in the worst malarial pestholes of Guadalcanal and New Guinea in early 1943, at the medical low point of the Pacific war. Bacque's failure points to the fact that the definitive history of the German prisoners, using all available records and employing rational mathematics, has yet to be written. Let us hope that it will not remain so for long.

Whoever attempts that history will face the genuinely difficult question of numbers with which this essay opens—how many German prisoners in the American transient camps actually did die? (I am assuming that deaths in the permanent camps were far more likely to be recorded.) So disorderly are the records, and so disorderly were the times that produced them, that I cannot answer the question. But it seems to be that there are several suggestive parameters.

As noted above, Böhme reports that the European theater of operations provost marshal listed a total of 15,285 prisoners who died in American hands. In 1950 the *Suchdienst* (Tracing Service) of the German Red Cross reported that 100,000 members of the Wehrmacht remained missing on the western front, a number that included both battle losses and deaths in prison camps.[19] In 1974, the German Red Cross reported that of the 1,743,000 missing in action (MIAs) for both eastern and western fronts, 2.35 percent, or about 41,000 men, were last reported in western Germany, where all the transient camps were located.[20]

It is reasonable to assume that, in addition to the reported deaths, some prisoners died in the transient camps during the period prior to or immediately after the end of the war whose deaths went unreported in the chaos of the time. Böhme gives abundant anecdotal testimony to support the supposition. How is it possible to estimate the number? I suggest that the number of unrecorded deaths that must be added to the theater provost marshal's figure of recorded deaths cannot be larger than the Red Cross figure for all those last reported as missing in action in western Germany. That is, the total number who died unrecorded in American camps cannot

19. "Es kann lediglich ausgeführt werden, dass anlaesslich der Maerz-Registrierung im Jahre 1950 100.000 Westverschollene gemeldet werden. Unter diesen Westverschollenen verbergen sich sowohl die im Kampf gefallened Soldaten, wie auch die im Kriegsgefangenschaft verstorben sind." Dr. H. Kalcyk, Abteilungsleiter, Deutsches Rotes Kreuz, Generalsekretariat Suchdienst München, to Albert E. Cowdrey, November 11, 1989, in CMH.

20. Chart, "Die Wehrmachtverschollenen nach dem Land ihrer letzten Nachricht von der Truppe[,] von 1734000 Verschollenen," in Deutsches Rotes Kreuz–Suchdienst, *Nachforschung nach den Wehrmachtsverschollenen des Zweiten Weltkrieges* (Munich, 1974).

exceed 56,285, and—since this figure would assume that all or virtually all died in camps rather than in the last battles—the correct total is probably very much smaller.

The maximum number of 56,285 would constitute about 1.1 percent of the total number of German prisoners held by the United States at the peak in the spring of 1945; that rate agrees well with Böhme's intuitive suggestion of 1 percent for deaths of prisoners held by the Western powers. By way of comparison, only .7 percent of Americans held as POWs by the European Axis powers died.[21] If subsequent study shows that such a differential existed, the effect of the age and condition of the prisoners when taken and the support their nations were able to provide them in captivity will have to be considered as contributory factors.

Nevertheless, a full study of the surviving records dealing with the POW camps of the Allied powers in the spring and summer of 1945 will, I have no doubt, offer a sobering corrective to any remaining illusion that in World War II all the inhumanity was on one side. I venture to predict that such a study, carried out seriously by a competent scholar, would convict some or all of the Allied governments of failure to abide by their treaty obligations, and some or all of the Allied armies of failure to observe their own regulations regarding the treatment of prisoners of war.

Indeed, the admittedly preliminary work of both German and American scholars to date has shown precisely this. But when the deaths have been tallied as well as possible, no trace of James Bacque's Big Number will be found.

21. Bernard M. Cohen and Maurice Z. Cooper, *A Follow-Up Study of World War II Prisoners of War* (Washington, D.C., 1953), 15. By way of contrast, between 34 and 38 percent of Americans held by the Japanese as prisoners died; about two-thirds of Russian prisoners held in Germany appear to have died; and the proportion of Germans captured on the eastern front who died has been estimated as high as 80 percent.

II

Germany in 1945 and German POW Historiography

Food Shortages in Germany and Europe
1945–1948

James F. Tent

FOR THOSE WHO experienced living conditions in Europe at the end of World War II and in the immediate postwar years, one of the more constant and vivid recollections is of a preoccupation with hunger. Acute food shortages were simply a fact of life at the end of the most destructive war in history, and all the peoples of Europe, from the North Cape to the Peloponnesus, from Belfast to the Urals and beyond, experienced them. Until now, no one had thought to challenge this fact of life of 1945, accepting hunger as simply a given; certainly no one had contended that food was abundant. Yet, denying the obvious, Canadian novelist James Bacque makes precisely that claim in his 1989 study, *Other Losses*.

This claim stems from Bacque's main thesis: that General Eisenhower, embittered by German wartime conduct, deliberately created such harsh conditions for captured personnel that more than a million of them died in American and French custody. Other scholars can deal more authoritatively with that allegation. This essay, which derives from a forthcoming examination of humanitarian relief efforts in postwar Europe, addresses the issue of food shortages at the end of the war.

Dismissing the notion of a worldwide food shortage, Bacque states early in his study: "There was a lot more wheat available in the combined area of western Germany, France, Britain, Canada and the USA than there had been in the same physical area in 1939." Bacque then lists extensive surpluses in wheat in the United States, Canada, and even France, adding that the area of Germany coming under Western Allied control had a population that was 4 percent smaller than it had been before the war. For good measure, shipping and distribution of food should have been no problem, Bacque says, since Allied shipbuilding had more than replaced all losses in the war and, according to him, 93 percent of French railway trackage was intact by May, 1945, when American military demands on railroads had dropped to 70 percent of the levels of the previous winter.[1]

This optimistic assessment is based largely upon a private report by a friend of President Roosevelt's, Sam Rosenman; diary entries by an Eisenhower staffer, Brigadier General Everett Hughes; and the author's interpretations of statistical figures on wheat and corn production provided in recent general statistical works by Brian R. Mitchell.[2] By using selective evidence and selective statements by two eyewitnesses, the author concludes that the world food shortage at the end of the war was essentially a myth created by Eisenhower to serve his own sinister end—the starving of German troops.

Even as he makes such statements, Bacque concedes some remarkable and ominous developments in the last nine months of the war. "As the British and Canadians fought their way into Holland," Bacque writes, "starvation began to threaten Dutch civilians trapped behind German lines."[3] In this instance, however, the author cites the information in order to establish a revenge motive by Eisenhower when the Germans were finally at his mercy.

It would have been inconvenient for Bacque to draw other conclusions from the stark facts of that time. It is left to the reader to make the connections that cry out against Bacque's claims. For example, the population of the three Western zones of Germany that was supposedly 4 percent smaller in 1945 than in 1939 was, Bacque concedes, experiencing an "influx of refugees from the East." That influx consisted of at least 10 million Germans, perhaps as many as 13 million—no one really knows for sure because of the chaotic conditions that prevailed. As for those Dutch civilians trapped behind German lines, the magnitude of the problem could easily

1. James Bacque, *Other Losses: An Investigation into the Mass Deaths of German Prisoners of War at the Hands of the French and Americans After World War II* (Toronto, 1989), 24–25, 208n43.

2. Brian R. Mitchell, *European Historical Statistics, 1750–1975* (London, 1981) and *International Historical Statistics: The Americas and Australasia* (London, 1983). It is instructive to examine the statistical evidence provided by Bacque's main source, Mitchell. For example, in *European Historical Statistics,* 250–72, the figures on output of main cereals, potatoes, and sugar beets in western European nations show an unmistakable, often sharp, downward trend in the course of World War II, especially in 1944. They also indicate a slow recovery after the war. Bacque's claim that French wheat production in 1944 exceeded consumption by 500,000 tons might be true. It is also decidedly at variance with overall trends in western European food production. That production was by far the most important factor affecting the Europeans' diet after the war.

3. Bacque, *Other Losses,* 24. All references in this essay are to the Canadian edition.

escape the lay reader. Reports in March, 1945, to Eisenhower's Supreme Headquarters, Allied Expeditionary Force (SHAEF) from the International Committee of the Red Cross stated in the strongest language that "the plight of the 4,500,000 inhabitants of the three western provinces will become absolutely catastrophic and desperate from May 15, 1945." On an individual basis, the tragedy that was unfolding before Allied eyes "is given," the report continued, "by statistics according to which the caloric content of a Dutch workingman's rations have scarcely exceeded 500 a day since December 10, 1944." [4] The situation for the Dutch was so extreme that in a rare act of cooperation, the German occupation authorities allowed Allied aerial drops of food and medicine to civilians in late April, 1945.

Recommended dietary allowances (RDA) for human beings are the subject of considerable discussion even today despite extensive nutritional studies since World War II. Bacque claims that the "minimum to maintain life for adults lying down, doing no work but self-care, varies from 1,800 to 2,250 calories per day, according to various experts." Bacque's source, convenient for him but not for the reader, proves to be a conversation with Dr. A. B. Miller in the Department of Preventive Medicine and Biostatistics at the University of Toronto. Most readers would deduce from such information that the average human being would require some 2,000 calories per day simply to stay alive. [5]

Bacque admits that various factors, such as the individual's level of activity, clothing, and general health, as well as exposure and the ambient temperature of the environment, have an effect. Other factors he does not include are body size, pregnancy, lactation by nursing mothers, and significant variations in nutritional needs for infants, children, adolescents, and the aged. An abundant literature concerning nutritional needs is readily available to the lay reader, and even a casual perusal of it will indicate the complexity of the factors involved. [6]

---

4. Harry L. Coles and Albert K. Weinberg, *Civil Affairs: Soldiers Become Governors* (Washington, D.C., 1964), 830, Vol. VI of subseries *Special Studies* of *United States Army in World War II*. This volume, part of a series that is widely available to the public, gives extensive and graphic eyewitness reports and statements about the terrible deprivations of peoples in the liberated areas and in the areas still under German control. Bacque could hardly be ignorant of this information. He consulted the series extensively in his researches and cites individual volumes in his own work. To be sure, he does not cite this one.

5. See Bacque, *Other Losses,* 25; see also 207 n 40.

6. For a widely available explanation of human nutritional needs, see the Washington-based National Research Council, ed., *Recommended Dietary Allowances* (9th ed.; Washington, D.C., 1980), 16–30. It demonstrates the complexities involved in establishing minimum

What is pertinent to this discussion on postwar hunger is that dietary levels lower than the 1,800- to 2,000-calorie minimum do not lead immediately to starvation. If they did, then only the citizens of a few isolated nations such as Switzerland and Sweden, which were almost alone in being above the 2,000-calorie mark on the Continent after the war, would have escaped hunger edema of massive proportions. Patently this did not happen in postwar Germany. This is not to say that a majority of the German population, and for that matter of most other European states, escaped malnutrition. They experienced it in good measure. In this respect the plight of the Dutch civilians cited above was the most extreme, in Western Europe at least, and if uncorrected would have led to their rapid starvation. Hence the unique relief measures undertaken by the Allies with German acquiescence toward the end of the war.[7]

So too, in varying degrees, the peoples in all the liberated areas and areas still under German occupation were feeling the pinch of genuine hunger in the sixth year of the war. For example, Belgium, although it was directly astride the supply routes for many of the Allied forces once the port of Antwerp was open, found its import and distribution system drastically affected by the war effort. An early United Nations Relief and Rehabilitation Administration (UNRRA) report of July 30, 1945, described the situation of the previous ten months: "At the time of liberation in September–October [1944], the average ration was approximately 1450 calories. It is now over 2000 calories. This improvement was made possible by a good harvest, importation of food products by SHAEF and by less food being held by farmers in agricultural producing regions." Not just

---

and recommended levels. For example, the 1,800- to 2,000-calorie minimums it outlines are adequate only if fat, sugar, and alcohol levels are lower than is normal in a typical American diet. Such was indeed the case in postwar Europe. Other sources demonstrate the ongoing debate over nutritional needs. See, for example, John F. Cunningham, ed., *Controversies in Clinical Nutrition* (Philadelphia, 1980), 1–52.

7. A SHAEF report on the food situation in Western Germany from June 1, 1945, explained briefly why normal consumers in occupied Germany were receiving 1,550 calories per day: "This was considered by nutritional experts as the minimum necessary to maintain health on an emergency basis for a period not to exceed six months." The same report also conceded that the chaotic conditions of postwar Germany did not permit even that minimum. "Actually, ration scales have been substantially below this level," the report admitted. See "The Food Situation in Western Germany as of 1 June 1945," 7, in 430.2, Records of the Allied Operational and Occupation Headquarters, World War II, SHAEF, G-4, RG 331, National Archives (hereinafter cited as NA).

Belgium but most other liberated areas were still struggling nearly two months after the war to raise civilian diets above 2,000 calories.[8] Inevitably, German civilian rations would be lower than those of the liberated peoples.

German civilian rations had held relatively constant during the war, remaining well above 2,000 calories until the last full year of the conflict. Inevitably, the scale dropped as food-producing regions outside Germany fell into Allied hands while at the same time disruptions in production and distribution within Germany sharply increased. Initial U.S. military government reports in the American zone in Germany in the summer of 1945 showed wide discrepancies in ration distributions, whereby citizens in larger cities usually fared worse than those in rural areas. One summary noted that just prior to V-E Day the normal consumer's daily caloric intake was only 1,050, and that after V-E Day it dropped to 860 calories per day. The picture was confusing because of the wide fluctuations from place to place and because unofficial intakes were usually higher than the official scales. Initially, some advance units of the U.S. Army, in a kind of victory celebration, had even opened up German food warehouses to liberated Allied prisoners, foreign workers, and displaced persons. However, the reality soon dawned that such caches and stockpiles, although they might look imposing, were hopelessly inadequate given the general condition of the population. Overall, the picture was grim. In the spring of 1945, the German population as a whole was existing on rations that in the long run would not sustain life.[9]

News of the dire food situation was hardly confined to American offi-

8. UNRRA Council Meeting, London, July 30, 1945, pp. 3–4, in Box 25, 080 UNRRA, Adjutant General Files, 1945–46, Office of Military Government (U.S.) for Germany, RG 260, Washington National Records Center, Suitland, Maryland (hereinafter cited as WNRC), NA.

9. Section "Medical and Health Affairs," Office of Military Government Report No. 1, August 20, 1945, p. 2, in Records Pertaining to Medical Conditions in Western Europe, Public Health and Public Welfare Branches, Civil Administration Division, RG 260, WNRC, NA. This initial report showed average intakes between 1,150 and 1,730 calories daily even though official rations were set at anywhere between 400 and 1,100 calories. *Cf.* OMG Report No. 2, September 20, 1945, Section "Medical and Health Affairs," 3, which indicated, on the basis of five U.S. survey teams investigating in fifteen cities over a ten-week span in the summer of 1945, that actual consumption was averaging 1,600 calories per day, although in some places it had dropped as low as 800. The report also noted the discrepancy between average actual consumption levels and the lower official consumption rates. The author wishes to thank John Gimbel for timely advice in locating these records.

cials in Europe. A Combined Civilian Affairs Committee sent a summary of the military governor's July, 1945, report directly to the Joint Chiefs of Staff in Washington. It was circulated as document JCS 1517 and minced no words: "The food situation in western Germany is perhaps the most serious problem of the occupation. Average consumption is now about one-third below the generally accepted subsistence level of 2000 calories per day." [10]

Relative to the general population in Europe, captured German soldiers fared reasonably well in terms of nutrition during much of the war. For example, most Germans captured during the Normandy campaign were shipped to Great Britain and issued a daily ration of 3,612 calories whether they worked or not—the same level as that supplied to American troops. German prisoners on the Continent received the same rations or even slightly higher, except that nonworking prisoners received 20 percent less food. Most worked. On December 7, 1944, that ration was reduced from 3,860 to 3,258 calories. Nonworkers received 10 percent less. In April, 1945, a much larger reduction occurred, bringing German POW consumption down to 2,000 calories for the first time. A report from Colonel Wendell H. Griffith, SnC, chief of the Nutrition Branch, Division of Preventive Medicine, Office of the Chief Surgeon, European Theater, explained why the change took place. "These ration decreases were the result," he said, "of the disparity between tremendous numbers of captured prisoners and the relatively small stocks of available foodstuffs." The reduction brought captured German personnel down to the same level that the Allies were attempting to provide for displaced persons and others whose survival depended upon support from the advancing armies. [11]

10. Germany, August 20, 1945, p. 6, in 319.1, CCAC, Records of the Joint Chiefs of Staff, RG 218, NA. A forthcoming dissertation by Otto Burianek at Emory University, "The Politics of Rectification: The U.S. Army and Displaced Persons in Munich, 1945–1951," will give detailed evidence of the chaotic food situation in occupied Germany and of the army's frantic efforts to find enough of it to bring DP rations up to 2,000 calories per day in the spring and summer of 1945. Burianek to author, February 28, 1991, in possession of author. Future research on hunger in postwar Europe should include investigation of Record Group 407, Office of the Adjutant General, Administrative Services Division, Foreign Occupied Area Reports, Special Reports, Germany, U.S. Zone. WNRC archivists Richard Boylen and David Pfeiffer, to whom the author is indebted, indicate that this collection alone encompasses over one hundred archival boxes of pertinent material.

11. Medical Department, U.S. Army, ed., *Special Fields* (Washington, D.C., 1969), 390, Vol. IX of *Preventive Medicine in World War II,* 42 vols. The reader can gain a comprehensive picture of the treatment of Axis prisoners in Allied hands from Chap. 6, "Enemy Prisoners of War," by Stanhope Bayne-Jones, M.D., 341–418. The fact that German prison-

Griffith's Nutrition Branch had conducted surveys of German prisoners in American custody in February and March, 1945. Examination of 800 prisoners chosen from work camps and enclosures indicated some noteworthy trends. "The results showed that the nutrition of prisoners who had been in American hands for 50 days or more was satisfactory and considerably superior to that of newly captured Germans. This indicated that the POW ration in use during the early part of 1945 was superior to the ration of the German Army." By the following summer, however, conditions for captured Germans were considerably less favorable, as shown by a second survey by Nutrition Branch. "The 2000 calorie ration was found to be insufficient for German prisoners under 21 years of age and for others who were classed as nonworkers but whose caloric needs were significantly increased by fatigue duties, calisthenics or marching. The 2000 calorie ration was adequate for individuals who were inactive in fact." The report also noted that the German civilian ration issued to disarmed forces "varied from 1200 to 1500 calories at that time and was inadequate. This was especially true because there was no opportunity for the men in the enclosures to supplement their rations as German civilians were able to do from gardens, household supplies, etc." Far from being sanguine about the deteriorating conditions for German prisoners, the nutritionists were blunt in describing the alarming downward trend. Their August, 1945, survey "disclosed evidence of very extensive malnutrition among prisoners of war and disarmed enemy elements in the large enclosures maintained by the Third and Seventh U.S. Armies and by the Communications Zone. There was a lack of uniformity in the ration scales in various areas, and the caloric scales averaged below 2,000. There was consistent evidence of insufficient amounts of riboflavin and nicotinic acid in the prisoner-of-war diet." The report accounted for these developments by referring to the previous surveys, which had "shown that the standard German Army ration had been deficient in riboflavin and nicotinic acid for some time.

---

ers received such generous rations until the last weeks of the war caused hard feelings. Colonel Griffith noted in his report the effect such disparities caused. "The earlier rations supplied nonworkers were in accordance with the Geneva Convention and were in excess of the actual requirement of the prisoners," he stated. "This original policy was bitterly criticized by allied civilians because nonworking prisoners had more to eat than allied workers." For Griffith, the disparity brought with it a logical development at the end of the war: "Following the German surrender in May, 1945, practically all the prisoners held by the Armies inside of Germany were classified as 'disarmed forces' and their subsistence became the responsibility of the civilian food distribution."

Superimposed upon this deficiency intake of fairly long standing was the variable period of severe deprivation of all nutrients during the final weeks of active campaign and in the forward POW enclosures." [12] In short, by the summer of 1945, German military personnel were subsisting on the same meager diet as German civilians and Europeans as a whole.

For Eisenhower and SHAEF, who had long been aware of these trends, the impending crisis in Europe was ominous, but they also received warnings from the War Department in Washington that the dimensions of the crisis went well beyond Europe. "Official notification has been received from the War Department," a SHAEF memo to senior commanders of March 24, 1945, read, "that the world-wide food shortage will necessitate a substantial reduction in amounts of certain critical items to be shipped to this theater." The explanation for these measures was unambiguous: "Recent major military activity in other theaters has placed a heavy drain upon dehydrated potato stocks in the U.S." For the planners deficiencies in precisely those food stocks so early in the growing season had serious consequences. "The situation," the memo continued, "as it applies to dehydrated potatoes is one which extends throughout the entire food kingdom." The memo then detailed measures that the senior commanders were to institute immediately in order to cut down on consumption, wastage, pilferage, spoilage, or any other factor that might necessitate sending further supplies from North America. Unless such savings were effected, the directive concluded, the diet of Allied personnel in the theater would simply have to be lowered. The document was issued "By Command of General Eisenhower." [13]

The reason for such stringent measures is clear. The Allies faced continuing commitments to sending huge quantities of supplies and food to the Mediterranean theater, where disruptions in worldwide commercial

12. *Ibid.*, 390–91. The Nutrition Branch report was correct, but also slightly misleading in stating that the German prisoners' ration scale was below 2,000 calories. In fact, it was 1,500 calories, as confirmed by a report from Major General Archer L. Lerch after his inspection of all concentration camps and internment camps in the European theater. See "Inspection of Concentration Camps and Other Internment Camps in the European Theater of Operations," Lerch to Commanding General, Army Service Forces, June 9, 1945, in 383.6, Army Service Forces, Control Division, 1945–1946, Records of Army Headquarters, RG 160, NA. Lerch noted that conditions in Nazi concentration camps were "beyond description," those in German camps for Allied personnel were abominable, and those for Germans in Allied custody were generally superior.

13. Memo by Brigadier General R. B. Lovett, "Conservation of Food," June 9, 1945, p. 1, in Box 22, U.S. Group Control Council (hereinafter cited as USGCC), Adjutant General (AG) Files, RG 260, WNRC, NA.

shipping made the nations of that region totally dependent upon Allied transport. The Italians and Greeks—to name only two peoples—were also experiencing severely reduced rations. Extensive crop failures had occurred in all of Africa and in India in the summer of 1945 because of drought. The China-Burma-India theater drained resources further, but it was in the Pacific that vast operations were building up in the spring and summer of 1945 as the Americans closed in on the Japanese home islands. The Pacific theaters had consistently placed high demands on shipping and had caused frictions among competing theater commanders through much of the war. Operations Coronet and Olympic, the amphibious assaults being prepared against Japan for the autumn of 1945 and the spring of 1946, were expected to dwarf the demands of even the Normandy invasion. All planners, whether they knew about the Manhattan Project or not—few did—acted on the assumption that unprecedented quantities of shipping, military stores, and foodstuffs would be expended later that year and the next. There might be surplus wheat harvests in North America in 1945. Getting that surplus to Europe and elsewhere was another matter.

SHAEF planners looking ahead to the postsurrender phase in occupied Germany had ample warning that they faced awesome problems and responsibilities. With victory they would assume responsibility for a hostile population in excess of 50 million Germans in the three Western zones. In May, 1945, immediately following the armistice, a British agricultural expert, Sir William Gavin, investigated conditions in northern Germany at Prime Minister Churchill's request. Gavin was blunt in assessing the bleak prospects for the German people. His report was immediately forwarded to Eisenhower at SHAEF. "German organizations must make known the critical food situation which they have brought upon the whole world," he wrote, "and that in the unlikely event of any surplus becoming available *they will inevitably be last on the list to get it.* Even England within a few weeks of victory has had to reduce her own rations which were already lower than most Germans received during the war." [14]

Under no illusions as to the extent of the food crisis and the limited means to combat it, Gavin had some concrete recommendations. The Germans would have to grow as much of their own food as possible, given the fact that outside supplies were not going to be forthcoming. "The only way the German people can avoid starvation conditions," he wrote, "is for

14. Memo by Sir William Gavin, "Report on Visit to Germany," June 9, 1945, p. 1, in Box 22, USGCC, AG Files, RG 260, WNRC, NA (emphasis added); hereinafter cited as Gavin Report.

the organisations to ensure that supreme efforts are made to grow more potatoes and bread corn for direct human food and far fewer crops to convert to meat." Gavin admitted that the Germans were themselves aware of the problem. They had been moving in that direction ever since the mid-1930s, a process that had been accelerated during the war. Therefore, there were limits on how much more could be accomplished. "Every little garden and piece of land that I saw is growing potatoes and vegetables," Gavin noted.[15]

The outlook was hardly cheering, especially since the Nazi leadership had used up so much of Germany's resources and reserves in its irrational determination to fight on. For example, the Germans had distilled vast quantities of seed potatoes to produce alcohol for V-2 rockets. Coal reserves, a key element in German industrial recovery, had disappeared from the entire industrial pipeline, making fertilizer plants, along with all production facilities, inoperable. German farmers could expect little or no commercial fertilizer for at least a year and probably two. Farm machinery was run down or destroyed, and fuel for tractors was nonexistent. In some areas devastation from fighting plus heavy minefields planted by the Wehrmacht inhibited farming operations. Manpower was in drastically short supply because most able-bodied men were in uniform in the last weeks of the war. Protein and fats were especially scarce. Fishing fleets were either destroyed or immobilized by the mine-infested waters of the North Sea. In the spring of 1945 the Rhine River ran clean for the first time in generations, and with good reason: no factories were left operating to pollute it. Thus, in a multitude of ways, the signs were there to see. Germany's society and economy were disintegrating in the last months of the war.[16]

Another report, one selectively quoted by Bacque, emanated from Lieutenant General A. E. Grasett for SHAEF in June, 1945. Like the British report, it depicted the awful conditions in Germany in stark terms. Bacque quotes Grasett as saying that the "present food situation in Western Germany is critical. It is estimated however, that the 630,000 tons of im-

15. Gavin Report, 7. Gavin's report referred only to the immediate postsurrender period. For an excellent, detailed study of food production problems, especially in the British zone, in the period 1944 to 1948, see John E. Farquharson, *The Western Allies and the Politics of Food: Agrarian Management in Postwar Germany* (Leamington Spa, Eng., 1985).

16. For a reliable overview of the state of the German economy and industry from the moment of defeat to the beginnings of recovery in approximately 1947, see Werner Abelshauser, *Wirtschaftsgeschichte der Bundesrepublik Deutschland, 1945–1980* (Frankfurt am Main, 1983), 13–45.

ported wheat will meet the minimum food needs of German civilians prior to the next harvest." The impression gained is that abundant food stocks not only could be shipped to Europe, but in fact were being shipped, seemingly without undue effort. The world food shortage was, Bacque insinuates, obviously a contrived shortage.[17] However, the situation was hardly as easily remedied as Bacque's description of the situation implies. The reader can best draw his own conclusions from the report (see Appendix A).

The responsible American official in Germany, General Lucius D. Clay, who was fated to grapple with food shortages in the occupied zones for three years—far longer than General Eisenhower—gave an entirely different explanation about food shortages and the 600,000-plus tons of wheat cited by Bacque. "The need to provide food and thus prevent disease and unrest in the population behind the battle lines was recognized throughout the war," Clay recorded in his memoirs, "and SHAEF had brought to Germany for this purpose 600,000 tons of grain. The supply was not to be used lightly, because we did not know where and how more could be obtained for the forthcoming winter. . . . The provision of an adequate supply was more than a humane consideration. We expected German reserves to be low and to be faced with a difficult period. To make the best of the situation we had brought seeds into Germany with us, even though we recognized that it was too late for extensive additional planting." Clay then recounted the many impediments to increasing domestic production, such as lack of fertilizer and farm machinery. Needless to say, the 600,000-ton grain reserve disappeared quickly. Clay continued: "We divided the SHAEF stocks, although they had been purchased almost entirely with our funds, keeping 300,000 tons and sending 250,000 tons to the British and 15,000 tons to the French Zone. I agreed to this transfer because Germans in the British and French areas were existing on a ration lower than in our zone, and starving Germans wherever located would delay the accomplishment of our objectives."[18]

In late June, 1945, Clay observed that conditions in Western Europe as a whole were not recovering quickly. In a confidential letter to Assistant Secretary of State John J. McCloy, he stated: "If we look at conditions in France we will find that after a year under no political restrictions, France has achieved only a very limited return to its normal economy. Under po-

---

17. See Bacque, *Other Losses*, 59–60, 215 n27.
18. Lucius D. Clay, *Decision in Germany* (New York, 1950), 263–64.

litical restrictions and with far greater destruction, the return in Germany will be much more difficult."[19]

This is not to say that Clay considered his role as that of a social welfare official for the German people. "I feel that the Germans should suffer from hunger and from cold as I believe such suffering is necessary to make them realize the consequences of a war which they caused," he wrote to McCloy. "Nevertheless," he continued, "this type of suffering should not extend to the point where it results in mass starvation and sickness."[20] Moreover, the ration scale of 1,550 calories, a meager ration to be sure, was a level at which the British had arrived independently of the Americans, and had instituted earlier. Clay's distinction between punitive ration levels and an actual starvation diet is important here. The 1,800-calorie minimum posed by Bacque would not lead immediately to starvation. Neither did the 1,550-calorie level established by the Allies. However, Clay was about to receive an unpleasant surprise. Neither he nor anyone else was aware at the end of the war how long it would take to resolve the food crisis brought about by the world's most destructive conflict.

In March, 1946, when it became apparent that food shortages were going to pose long-term headaches for the occupying powers, Clay cabled a civil-affairs expert, General John Hilldring, about food developments since July, 1945. Clay urged uniform food policies in the Western zones. "In July of last year," he told Hilldring, "prior to the establishment of quadripartite machinery, I personally urged both the British and French representatives here to consider food resources to belong to Germany as a whole, with a view to developing a common import program. This was turned down emphatically by both the British and the French, and hence was not presented in quadripartite machinery. . . . It is also interesting to remember that British zonal authorities established this ration scale [1,550 calories per day] in their zone without consultation with us and two months before we did."[21]

Clay was well aware that the Germans, lacking the ability to feed themselves and now unable to produce exports to pay for imported food, were in a tight spot. "I thought the situation was so serious in November 1945," he wrote, "that I made a hurried trip home to discuss it with government

19. Jean Edward Smith, ed., *The Papers of General Lucius D. Clay: Germany, 1945–1949* (2 vols.; Bloomington, 1974), I, 41.

20. *Ibid.*, 41–42.

21. *Ibid.*, 177.

officials and to ask personally for their assistance in increasing the food supply. I found that the world shortage in grain resulting from war dislocation had placed heavy demands on the United States. Everyone was sympathetic, but German needs could not be given a higher priority than those of the countries allied with us in our war effort."[22] Clay was a keen observer of trends in the Washington political and military establishments, as well as being intimately informed on conditions in Europe. He had no difficulty in accepting the realities of severe food shortages on a global basis. After all, it was his responsibility to manage the affairs of the one people most directly affected by the effects of that shortage in the West, namely, the Germans.

Fortunately for all, the winter of 1945–1946 was an especially mild one in Europe and so did not affect the public health of the German population as much as originally feared. An Anglo-French-American Combined Nutritional Committee (CNC) had formed up by order of the respective military governors in the summer of 1945 and had periodically conducted surveys. Their findings of late February, 1946, gave a hint of bleak optimism despite the general misery: "The medical evidence has satisfied the Committee that although some degree of malnutrition exists in Germany, there is at present no important incidence of nutritional disease constituting a major Public Health problem in the three zones. The principal limitation to minimally adequate nutrition is the shortage of calories." To be sure, that news was grim enough, but at least people were not literally starving or succumbing in significant numbers to hunger-related diseases.[23]

Although American public opinion had supported punitive occupation policies toward the Germans at the end of the war, the harsh realities of such a policy when implemented brought increasing attention from the public media to the problem, and pressure from church-related and charitable groups began to grow in the fall of 1945 to alleviate the distress overseas. Such groups as the Cooperative of American Remittances to Europe (C.A.R.E.), the American Friends Service Committee, the Catholic Relief Services, Unitarians, Mennonites, and others clamored for action, and in December, 1945, President Harry Truman allowed them to form an umbrella group, the American Council of Voluntary Agencies (ACVA),

22. Clay, *Decision in Germany*, 265.
23. Report of Combined Nutrition Committee, February 20, 1946, p. 1, in Box 144, German Correspondence, Famine Emergency Committee, Hoover Presidential Library (hereinafter cited as HPL), West Branch, Iowa.

which he then sent to Berlin in the new year to confer with General Clay. By this time Eisenhower had returned to Washington and had no further direct responsibilities for the Germans.

The ACVA delegation's first meeting with Clay was not harmonious. Disagreements developed immediately on how best to proceed. The ACVA members, with long experience in raising charitable aid, wanted to launch operations with their own personnel in Germany and urged Clay to allow them to earmark some of the funds for specific groups on the grounds that donors were likely to contribute more if they could identify with specific recipient groups in Germany. Clay felt differently. He wanted to leave the distribution fully in German hands because he considered that they had administered aid efficiently to date. He disagreed strongly with earmarking aid. Moreover, he expressed concern that large numbers of Allied nationals working in Germany would take away scarce accommodations and food from German mouths. Unstated, but a factor in Clay's reasoning nonetheless, was his distaste for carpetbaggers. A native Georgian, he had inherited that post–Civil War southern prejudice from his parents, and in occupied Germany made a concerted effort to reduce the size of the American military government as early and as drastically as he could.[24]

Eventually—that is, a year later—the disagreement was resolved when Clay relented and allowed American civilians to function in American-occupied territory under an umbrella organization, the Committee of Relief Agencies Licensed to Operate in Germany. Bacque's interpretation of these disagreements is singularly hostile and focuses—erroneously—on Eisenhower as the culprit.[25] It was primarily Clay, for the reasons just given, who made the decision to bar civilian relief personnel from Germany for the time being.

Mounting concern about the continuing world food shortage and an actual food crisis in central Europe almost one year after the war prompted President Truman in the new year to draw a distinguished American out of retirement. Former president Herbert Hoover, in eclipse since his defeat by Franklin Roosevelt in 1932, became chairman of Truman's Famine Emergency Committee and personally undertook a worldwide survey of food shortages from February to May, 1946. He had achieved fame after World War I in organizing relief, especially in Europe and Russia. Now, a

24. For an examination of the frictions encountered between Clay and American charitable groups, especially the Quakers, see James F. Tent, "Simple Gifts: The American Friends Service Committee and the Establishment of Neighborhood Centers in Occupied Germany," *Kirchliche Zeitgeschichte*, II (Spring, 1989), 64–82.

25. See Bacque, *Other Losses*, 80–82.

quarter of a century later and in advanced age, he undertook a nearly identical mission.[26]

The statistics in Hoover's report to Truman provided sobering news. Worldwide, but excluding the great exporter, North America, demands for cereal imports totaled not quite 14.5 million tons for 1946. Yet, supplies available totaled only 10.9 million tons. Since cereals supplied 85 percent of emergency diets, this gap was an especially serious one. Hoover offered various suggestions for increasing supplies through new sources, "through additional loans of cereals from early crop countries which may not themselves have annual surpluses, through substitution of other cereals for wheat and rice; and as a result of conservation up to this time."[27]

The implications from Hoover's report did not take long to materialize in Germany. The official—and punitive—ration of 1,550 calories per day could only be continued briefly into 1946. Then reserves and shipments began to falter. Clay recounted what happened next. "But in February, 1946, it [the ration] resumed its downward trend and reached its low-point in our zone in May–June, 1946, about 1,180 calories per day for the normal consumer. In March, the evidence of suffering was real and led me . . . to cable General Eisenhower and personally ask the latter's support in obtaining relief." Eisenhower assented, and growing awareness of the acute shortages among key leaders such as Truman, as well as among the public, allowed accelerated shipments to Germany that summer.[28]

As Hoover's report implied, there were no magical solutions to the problems at hand, and true to the situation, none was forthcoming. By the end of 1946, Truman received a report containing both good news and bad news from his agriculture secretary, Clinton P. Anderson. He passed it along to his famine expert, Hoover. "Fortunately for this country and for the world," Anderson related, "American farmers produced record crops of both wheat and corn again in 1946." A major problem, one that Bacque ignores, was how to get those record harvests to those who needed them most.

26. A widely available and detailed account of Hoover's activities after World War II, including hunger relief, is Gary Dean Best, *Herbert Hoover: The Postpresidential Years, 1933–1964* (2 vols.; Stanford, 1983); see esp. II, 286–306. Equally illuminating and even more detailed about the plight of the German population during the three-year food crisis after World War II is Louis P. Lochner, *Herbert Hoover and Germany* (New York, 1960), 170–201.

27. Herbert Hoover to Harry S. Truman, May 13, 1946, in Box 239, Truman Correspondence, 1946–47, HPL.

28. See Clay, *Decision in Germany,* 265.

"The situation with regard to transportation and shipment is not at all favorable," Anderson stated, "with transportation apparently the limiting factor this year on our total shipments of grain for food use abroad." Anderson then went into considerable detail on the situation, citing not only trouble with shipping and labor. In the real world, officials such as Anderson, Clay, Eisenhower, and Hoover had to grapple with those irksome bottlenecks that plague all such operations. For Anderson, "Looming constantly larger in the whole picture is the very serious shortage of box cars to move wheat from local elevators to terminals, and to move both wheat and flour to ports for shipment. Records show that the number of freight cars available to move grain in recent weeks has been running about 14 percent below a year ago, and the situation was not good last year." [29] If overland transportation was a problem for the Americans as they struggled to replace aging, war-weary rolling stock, then it paled in comparison with the problems the Europeans, and especially the Germans, were facing at the same time. German industry, including the crucial pacesetter, coal production, had experienced some recovery from the end of 1945 to the end of 1946. Then bad weather combined with the breakdown of worn-out rolling stock made it impossible to move bulk items such as coal to where they were needed. Germany's shaky economic recovery collapsed immediately—striking evidence of the importance of coal. In parallel with this general downturn, the food crisis sharpened in that terrible winter of 1946–1947. [30]

In the midst of those ominous developments, Truman asked Hoover to make a second worldwide survey in early 1947. Hoover agreed, but he had some new advice for Truman now:

> I feel, however, that such a mission, to be of real value and helpful to you and the country, should be somewhat broadened out. It will come as a great shock to our people that the American taxpayer for a second year must expend huge sums to provide food for the enemy peoples. Therefore, it seems to me that this

29. Clinton P. Anderson to Harry S. Truman, November 26, 1946, pp. 1–2, in Box 239, Truman Correspondence, 1946–47, HPL. Truman agreed emphatically with Anderson, listing transportation as the key limiting factor for grain exports that year. See attached Truman letter to Hoover, November 29, 1946.

30. See Werner Abelshauser, *Wirtschaft in Westdeutschland, 1945–1948: Rekonstruktion und Wachstumsbedingungen in der amerikanischen und britischen Zone* (Stuttgart, 1975), 133–38 with respect to food, 138–47 with respect to coal production. Abelshauser notes that the failure to deliver stocks of coal from the Ruhr district immediately led to a sharp decline in overall industrial output in both the British and American zones.

mission to accomplish its purpose must also include inquiry into what further immediate steps are possible to increase their exports and thus their ability to become self-supporting, what possibilities there are of payment otherwise, and when charity can be expected to end. Without some such inclusive report, the Congress and the taxpayer are left without hope.[31]

Coming as it did at the moment when the Cold War was crystallizing and Germany's future role in world affairs urgently required clarification, when Secretary of State George Marshall's economic-recovery plan for Europe was incubating, Hoover's advice to Truman fell on receptive ears. Hoover made his second survey, and with his help an ambitious child-feeding program was instituted in German schools in April, 1947—to cite just the German experience—to protect the youth from the worst effects of the shortages. Despite far slenderer resources, the British had also issued supplemental rations to children in their zone starting in 1946. The programs were coordinated with the merging of the two zones into Bizonia in 1947.[32]

The provision of special programs and ration supplements for children is only one example of how the Allied authorities attempted to cope with the ongoing shortages. By the spring of 1947, and thereafter to the end of the military occupation, the number and variety of supplemental programs expanded to the point that some observers asked with only slight irony if there were any normal consumers—that is, those consuming 1,550 calories per day—left in the British and American zones. The reason for such "generosity" was based above all upon pragmatism. Malnourished Germans were less productive, and without increased productivity and a revived economy the Western zones of Germany would continue to pose a significant economic burden upon the occupying powers, as Hoover and others had already pointed out.[33]

The real end to the food shortage came only in the summer of 1948, when the revival of the European economies, Western Germany's included, became apparent. The return to an export economy, institution of a workable currency for West Germans, reknitting of the crucial transportation arteries, adequate production of the most vital raw material, coal, plus sufficient quantities of fertilizer, seed, and so on allowed the Germans

31. Hoover to Truman, January 19, 1947, in Box 239, Truman Correspondence, 1946–47, HPL.
32. See Farquharson, *Western Allies and the Politics of Food*, 230–31.
33. *Ibid.*, 231–42.

to help themselves far more effectively. To be sure, charitable aid continued for some time, but the crisis in food finally came to an end three years after the conclusion of World War II.

James Bacque might be willing to relegate the world food shortage to the category of myth. Few others will do so. Perhaps he can try the interviewing techniques that he employed in writing *Other Losses*—namely, putting words in the mouths of selective eyewitnesses. However, there is an excellent chance that today's survivors among the 400 million Europeans in general and the 70 million Germans in particular who experienced conditions at war's end will remember that they had little of anything to put into their mouths in the aftermath of widespread destruction.

German women give food and water to some of the thousands of POWs captured by U.S.
8th Division near Milspe, April 18.
National Archives photo no. 111-SC-204943

The 8th Division distributes K rations, the standard U.S. Army emergency rations, to German POWs captured at Remscheid, April 19.
National Archives photo no. 111-SC-204455

POWs dug holes for shelter during the wet and cold spring weeks of 1945. The U.S. Army
provided tents to them as soon as possible, but for the first few weeks of captivity they
suffered greatly. Rheinberg, May 3.
National Archives photo no. 111-SC-206200

German POWs who deserted their Baltic Sea ports rather than risk capture by the Russians
dig a well for water at a temporary camp of the 82d Airborne division, May 11. Bacque,
using this very photo to help make his case in *Other Losses* (Los Angeles, 1991), mis-
identifies the activity as digging "earth holes for shelter."
National Archives photo no. 111-SC-206673

The first weeks after the unconditional surrender were the worst for the German prisoners, and the Sinzig enclosures on the Rhine were as bad as any. May 12. Note that many of the photographs in this section were taken at a time when, according to Bacque, the POWs were starving to death in vast numbers. Thus it is instructive to compare their general observable physical condition (hungry though many of them undoubtedly were) with that of men who truly have been starved—for example, the Ebensee concentration camp survivors pictured earlier.
National Archives photo no. 111-SC-205048

Due to the large numbers of captives, conditions improved only slowly for them in May and June, 1945. This is an officers' compound at the transient camp at Ludwigsburg, where 35,000 officers and men were kept temporarily. May 28.
National Archives photo no. 111-SC-206574

German POWs shave and clean up in a small stream near Büderich, another of the notorious temporary enclosures on the Rhine, holding some 21,000 prisoners. May 3.
National Archives photo no. 111-SC-206201

Büderich, May 3. German POWs line up for water.
National Archives photo no. 111-SC-390464

A German priest holds Catholic services for German POWs at the U.S. 75th Division's holding camp near Plettenberg, May 8; such services were not permitted by the German Wehrmacht during the war.
National Archives photo no. 111-SC-206436

Germans taken prisoner in the Ruhr pocket are given K rations in an open field by the U.S. Army near Gummersbach, April 19.
National Archives photo no. 111-SC-392187

German POWs unload a train filled with K rations for the prisoners of Rheinberg, May 3.
National Archives photo no. 111-SC-390463

Representatives from each company pick up bread at one of the POW enclosures, May 12.
There was only enough for one loaf of bread for every twelve men.
National Archives photo no. 111-SC-392239

German women POWs eat rations in an enclosure at Remagen, while others line up for sick call, April 25.
National Archives photo no. 111-SC-203854

German POWs in an 82d Airborne temporary enclosure use their own field kitchens to cook food distributed by the Americans, May 11.
National Archives photo no. 111-SC-392234

By the beginning of 1946, when the initial chaos of the spring and summer of 1945 had been overcome and most POWs/DEFs had been discharged, the German prisoners remaining were housed in wooden barracks and fed three meals a day. Lunch here at the 166th Labor Service Company compound in Mannheim, January 16, 1946, consisted of soup, bread, and coffee. Prisoners who were working received more food than those who were not.
National Archives photo no. 111-SC-227618

Some of the 35,000 prisoners taken by the 3d U.S. Division and penned up in the Bad Aibling airport in Bavaria before V-E Day.
National Archives photo no. 111-SC-206067

Bad Aibling again, some eight months after the airport photograph was taken. The masses of POWs/DEFs had been processed; life in the camp had improved greatly for those who remained in captivity. This is POW enclosure No. 26, February 1, 1946. The inmates were put to work rebuilding Germany.
National Archives photo no. 111-SC-227620

The Germans built up incredibly elaborate tracing services after the war to try to learn the whereabouts of every missing prisoner. Few were left unrecorded. The tracing (or search) services compiled albums of more than a million missing POWs. Since the Soviets did not abide by the Geneva Convention, information about POWs held in the East usually came by word of mouth via comrades fortunate enough to come home early. Although more than a million German POWs were missing, only few were "lost" in these carefully kept German statistics. In other words, had "a million" died in American camps, the German tracing services would have raised hell long before Bacque.
Courtesy German Red Cross Tracing Service, Munich

(Top) A woman discovers the picture of her grandson in an album of the Red Cross Tracing Service. (Bottom) Another grandmother writes down data from an album to report to her in-laws.

Both courtesy German Red Cross Tracing Service, Munich

The tracing services made inquiries about specific cases of missing POWs among German POWs returning from Soviet camps, here in Friedland, 1948. A number of routine questions were asked: Do you know him? Did he die in the war? Did he die in the POW camp? Is he still alive in the camps?
Courtesy German Red Cross Tracing Service, Munich

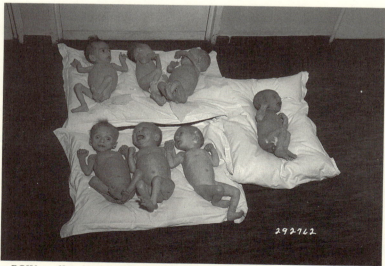

German POWs suffered grievously, but so did German civilians, especially babies, during the severe food shortages of 1945 to 1947. Here seven German infants picked at random from sixty such cases at the Catholic children's hospital in Berlin show malnutrition in various stages. October 25, 1947.
National Archives photo no. 111-SC-292762

Between 1945 and 1948, the Germans utilized every available spot to grow vegetables in order to improve their scanty diet. Here Berliners harvest potatoes in the Tiergarten, formerly the "Central Park" of Berlin, with the ruins of the Reichstag in the background, October 21, 1947. The food crisis eased after 1948 when rations started to become adequate again.
National Archives photo no. 260-MGG-80-1

The bitter reality of hunger in central Europe after the war ended: German children looking for scraps in garbage cans. Western Germany, fall, 1945.
Courtesy American Friends Service Committee Archives, Philadelphia

An eight-year-old German boy in Berlin eats a lunch of potato soup.
National Archives photo no. 306-NT-879-42

Bread sustained the population. Near Bamberg, a happy boy gives his little sister a ride along with some precious loaves of bread, April 8, 1946.
National Archives photo no. 111-SC-233293

Food was still very scarce in Germany as late as 1948. Here the *Gretna Victory* is greeted by residents of Bremen, March 9, 1948. The ship carried 3,000 tons of food donated by residents of Washington, Oregon, Idaho, Montana, and Alaska.

National Archives photo no. 260-MGG-468-3

German Historiography, the War Losses, and the Prisoners of War

Rüdiger Overmans

HOW MANY GERMAN SOLDIERS really died in American captivity after World War II? This question is provoked by James Bacque's book. The reader might think that a figure could be found quite quickly because the Germans, and especially the Wehrmacht, are well known for their exactness. However, no clear, definite result is to be found, and speculations about Wehrmacht losses have ranged from 3 to 7 million dead.[1]

At first sight this wide variation is quite surprising. In order to show why it exists and to establish what one can say for sure about the history of the German POWs, one first must ask what sources exist in Germany and what results can be obtained from these. In this essay I will first give a short overview of the history of the German POWs following World War II, based mainly on German literature and those sources German authors have used for their publications, and then compare the theses of James Bacque and the findings of German historiography.

The Administrative Side: Censuses, Registrations, Searches for POWs and Missing Persons

First of all, some clarifications. In World War II there were civilian as well as military captives. In many cases the Allied military authorities were not

---

The titles of books are cited in the original. The references to Bacque are from the German edition, with the corresponding pages of the Canadian edition cited parenthetically. The following conventions and abbreviations are used: Deutsches Reich—Germany within its extended borders up to 1945; West Germany—the Federal Republic of Germany within its borders of 1949–1990; East Germany (GDR)—the former German Democratic Republic; Federal Republic (of Germany)—Germany as reunified in 1990.

1. Rüdiger Overmans, "Die Toten des Zweiten Weltkrieges in Deutschland," in *Der Zweite Weltkrieg,* ed. Wolfgang Michalka (2d ed.; Munich, 1990), 858–73 (here 859).

aware whether a prisoner was military or civilian. Despite this ambiguity, this essay will be limited to the military prisoners.

In military statistics, all soldiers no longer available are designated as "losses," including not only those killed in action, missing, wounded, or captured, but also those discharged in good health for personal or other reasons.[2] Sometimes—primarily in Anglo-American statistics—a distinction is made between soldiers killed in action and soldiers killed by disease or accident. German records often do not allow this distinction, so in the following all soldiers who died during the war or afterward in captivity are designated as "losses."

There is a further vagueness concerning the term *missing*. In Anglo-American statistics, all soldiers who go missing from their units are registered in this category, and if one of the "missing" returns, the overall number of missing will not be reduced. The reappearance will be recorded as "returned to duty." For this reason a single soldier can be recorded as "missing" several times and all the same return home in good health. In the following, the German definition is used—that is, a soldier is recorded as missing only for that period of time in which his whereabouts is uncertain. Uncertainty as to the actual fate of missing persons also leads to the odd result that a soldier may be regarded as missing by his own side and his relatives, while being registered by the enemy as dead or captured. For these reasons the category "missing" constitutes an element of uncertainty in all quantitative analyses.

A further lack of clarity may result from the terms *Wehrmachtangehöriger* (member of the Wehrmacht), *soldier,* and *German,* which are far too simply set on the same footing. The Wehrmacht included noncombatant employees (such as civil servants and workers) as well as soldiers, and some of these were women (for example, the *Wehrmachthelferinnen*). During a deployment, not only the members of the army, navy, and air force were regarded as soldiers, but also the members of the Waffen SS (Armed SS) and the Volkssturm.[3] Many ethnic Germans from other coun-

2. One strange example is the so-called *Fürsten Erlass* (Prince Decree) of May 19, 1942. Hitler distrusted the aristocracy so much that he discharged them from the Wehrmacht, sending officers home in the middle of the war. See Rudolf Absolon, *Wehrgesetz und Wehrdienst, 1935–1945* (Boppard am Rhein, 1960), 350. Numerically more significant were those 2 million discharged from military service because they were needed as workers in the weapons industry. See Burkhart Müller-Hillebrand, *Der Zweifrontenkrieg* (Darmstadt, 1969), 253, Vol. III of Müller-Hillebrand, *Das Heer,* 3 vols.

3. The Volkssturm was the "people's militia," a kind of National Guard (U.S.) or Home Guard (U.K.), but made up of young boys, old men, and disabled men.

tries and foreigners from all over Europe served in these units—especially the Waffen SS.[4] From parts of France and Luxembourg people were called up into the Wehrmacht. Additionally, it should be kept in mind that Austria and parts of Czechoslovakia and Poland were included within the *Grossdeutsches Reich* (Greater German Empire) until the capitulation, although their inhabitants were not regarded as Germans after the end of the war. Many numerical discrepancies can be attributed to the use of these terms without exact definitions. In the following, all "prisoners of war" should be understood as being both soldiers and Germans unless otherwise noted (I nevertheless appreciate that this procedure may result in some inaccuracies).

Finally, there is the relationship among Prisoners of War (POWs), "disarmed enemy forces" (DEFs), and "surrendered enemy personnel" (SEPs). The difference is mainly a legal one and of little relevance here; thus the terms are treated as synonyms.

Wartime Sources

Quantitative information about the Wehrmacht—especially about POWs and the missing—are available from different sources. Although losses were counted by the Wehrmacht, the recording system was not as accurate as is often assumed, and it broke down as a result of the collapse of the Third Reich. Thus the last (nevertheless incomplete) report is from the end of January, 1945.[5] The subsequent gap is particularly serious, since the battles from mid-1944 to the capitulation were the heaviest of the whole war. The Wehrmacht kept files on individuals as well as statistical records. Thus all information about an individual's movements and fate (such as transfers, injuries, discharge, disappearance, death) was collected by the *Wehrmachtauskunftstelle* (WASt, the German Armed Forces Inquiry Of-

---

4. There were many ethnic Germans from eastern and southeastern Europe, as well as people from northern and western Europe (for example, the Netherlands and Scandinavia).

5. An internal analysis by the OKW in 1944 showed that the recording system had not worked even for the light casualties taken in the short campaigns of 1939–1940. In the French campaign, for example, 26,455 soldiers were recorded as killed in action, whereas by August, 1944, the number had been corrected to 46,059 dead. See OKW/AWA/WVW(V), Az t 61, gKdos vom 30.8.1944, Betr.: Statistik der Menschenverluste im Kriege, RM 7/807, Bundesarchiv-Militärarchiv, Freiburg im Breisgau, hereinafter cited as BA-MA. In the final report, army losses on the eastern front and navy losses are incomplete. OKW/WFSt/Org (Vb), Nr. 743/45 g.K. vom 14.3. 1945, Beurteilung der personellen und materiellen Rüstungslage der Wehrmacht (Monatsmeldung) Januar 1945, RM 7/819 D, BA-MA. This report was published with some transcription errors in Percy E. Schramm, ed., *Kriegstagebuch des OKW, 1940–1950* (Frankfurt, 1961), 1509–11.

fice), a large organization with several thousand employees in the last years of the war.

The WASt also received information from the enemy: because Germany had signed the Geneva Convention of 1929, it was obliged to communicate the names of captives in German hands to the International Committee of the Red Cross (ICRC) in Geneva, which passed this information to enemy states; in return, the ICRC gave the names of German POWs to the WASt. This exchange operated between Germany and the Western Allies, but not with the Soviet Union, as the latter had not ratified the Geneva Convention.

There was a third source of information for the WASt. If a disabled serviceman wanted to get a disability pension or special health treatment, he needed certification from the WASt. Likewise, widows or children of deceased servicemen who wanted to apply for special pensions (such as war widow's or war orphan's pension) needed certification. Their applications made it possible for the WASt to compare its information with those of the next of kin. The WASt obtained information from and supplied information to all administrative authorities as well as next of kin and therefore possessed the most exact information of all.

Some limitations on this gathering of information must be considered. Often, several months passed from the capture or death of a soldier to the registration of the event. Further, the WASt was responsible only for the Wehrmacht. The Waffen SS, numerically the most important military organization after the Wehrmacht, and all other paramilitary organizations had their own registration offices.[6] For all these reasons the last surviving WASt report, of February 28, 1945, is reliable as regards cases registered to that point of time, but incomplete as regards the total losses.[7]

From the foregoing it can be seen that there are no complete German casualty statistics from wartime. Nevertheless, the existing ones are not worthless; their incomplete figures are the minimum in many cases, even though they do not give comprehensive figures.

Soon after the capitulation, the Allies' realization of the unsatisfactory

6. The *Auskunftsstelle für Kriegsverluste der Waffen-SS* (Waffen SS Inquiry Office) was located in Bamberg. All its files were destroyed at the end of the war. Paramilitary organizations included the *Organisation Todt,* the *Reichsarbeitsdienst,* and the *Nationalsozialistisches Kraftfahrerkorps.*

7. WASt/Gruppe I an Abteilungsleiter OKW/AWA/WVW, geheim vom 5.3.1945, Betr.: Verluste der Wehrmacht (H.M.L.) nach den bei der Wast bis February 28, 1945, stat. erfassten Meldungen, RW 6/v. 550, BA-MA. See also Helmut Wolff, *Die deutschen Kriegsgefangenen in britischer Hand. Ein Überblick* (Munich, 1974), Vol. XI, Pt. 1 of the Maschke Commission, 4–5.

state of statistical affairs prompted them to require the Oberkommando der Wehrmacht (OKW) to investigate Wehrmacht losses. The results of this investigation and other studies produced after the war by high-ranking former German officers are available, but they are all based on these incomplete Wehrmacht statistics and completed by making estimates.[8]

Postwar Registrations and Statistics

In the aftermath of the war the Allies were as interested in statistics on Wehrmacht losses as historians are today, but all German efforts to work out what had happened to the soldiers were regarded as attempts to reorganize the Wehrmacht.[9]

For the Germans, clarification of the fate of the Wehrmachtangehörigen was essential for several reasons. First and most important was the reunification of families. At the end of the war millions of civilians were being evacuated from bomb-wrecked cities or were fleeing from the Red Army. Additionally, there were millions of displaced persons (DPs), as well as the first soldiers returning from captivity and searching for the address of their next of kin, POWs trying to send messages from captivity, and relatives of the Wehrmachtangehörigen asking after their fathers and sons.

Very soon private, governmental, and ecclesiastical tracing services began to appear in all four zones of occupation. At first their work was hindered by the Allies' distrust of them and by their own fragmentary nature as small, regionally based organizations with different responsibilities and methods of procedure.[10] Nevertheless, in West Germany a unified tracing service with offices at local level gradually emerged.

The early piecemeal efforts proving insufficient, as early as 1947, the first official registration took place, first in Bremen (January, 1947), then in the rest of the U.S. zone (spring of 1947), then in the British zone (summer of 1947), and finally in the French zone (1948)—but not in the

8. OKW/WFSt/OrgAbt (H) Nr. 2084/45 vom 19.5. 1945, Betr.: Besuch bei Oberst Barsukow am 15.5. 18–19 Uhr, RW 44 I/58, BA-MA; OKW/WFSt/OrgAbt(Heer), Nr. 5815 vom 19.5.1945, Betr.: Gesamtverluste des Heeres (einschl. Waffen-SS und Luftwaffe im Erdeinsatz) in der Zeit vom 1.9.39–1.5.45, RW 44 I/58, BA-MA. The three most important studies are: *A Study of the Employment of German Manpower from 1933–1945*, compiled at GMDS by a combined British, Canadian, and American staff between 1945 and 1947; Burkhart Müller-Hillebrand, *Personnel and Administration*, Foreign Military Study, U.S. Historical Division (Königstein, 1948); and Burkhart Müller-Hillebrand, *Statistical Systems*, Foreign Military Study, U.S. Historical Division (Königstein, 1949).

9. Kurt W. Böhme, *Gesucht wird . . . Die dramatische Geschichte des Suchdienstes* (Munich, 1965), 18.

10. *Ibid.*, 38–68.

Soviet zone. Returning soldiers were registered in 1948. The results lose some of their value because of the lack of data from the Soviet zone and the time between the various registrations—a time during which there were millions of repatriations. Furthermore, we have only incomplete information about missing ethnic Germans.[11] The considerable resentment among the German population to registration carried out under Allied control helps explain why the figures are numerically incomplete. Despite this, the results add to the pool of information concerning the POWs and the missing.

Because the first registration had proved to be unsatisfactory, on December 21, 1949, the West German government decided to hold a second registration, which took place in March, 1950—unfortunately, only in West Germany. The registration was carried out by the *Statistisches Bundesamt* (Federal Statistical Office) and the *Deutsches Rotes Kreuz* (DRK), the German Red Cross. The former was responsible for statistical evaluation; the latter used questionnaires to complete the tracing indexes but also made its own statistical analyses.[12]

Because of their geopolitical limitation, the results do not extend to all members of the Wehrmacht but only to those living in West Germany. Furthermore, the results cannot be compared with the registrations of 1947–1948 as regards the missing because they show only those still missing in 1950, neither those who returned from captivity in the intervening period nor those who had been added to missing lists. However, the most important results of this registration are not the total figures for missing persons, but the breakdowns of the German Red Cross analyzing missing persons according to year of capture, region of disappearance, and custodial power.

The names of 1.4 million missing persons resulting from the registration were compiled into thirty-eight volumes on 8,341 pages. At thousands of *Kameradschaftstreffen* (comradeship meetings) of former soldiers and at other meetings, investigations were conducted on the basis of these lists of missing persons.[13] In the period from February, 1951, to October, 1958, alone, the tracing services carried out a million interviews with former soldiers in order to collect information about the fate of the missing. In addition, soldiers returning from captivity were interviewed. Starting in

11. *Ibid.*, 108; Gerhard Reichling, "Eine grosse Aufgabe der amtlichen Statistik," *Deutsche Suchdienst Zeitung,* special issue (February, 1950), 4; Arthur L. Smith, *Heimkehr aus dem Zweiten Weltkrieg: Die Entlassung der deutschen Kriegsgefangenen* (Stuttgart, 1985), 70.
12. Reichling, "Grosse Aufgabe," 4.
13. Böhme, *Gesucht wird,* 120–22.

1958, supplementary volumes were printed that included photographs of the missing, and these volumes were used in 2.7 million interviews. The tracing services also tried to get information by displaying posters with photos and names, and by publishing lists of names in newspapers and on radio.[14] (Among the photographs in this volume are some showing these tracing efforts.) The millions of items of information were collected in card indexes. As a result of these endeavors, the search concentrated on the missing in the East—that is, on those soldiers who had last fought on the eastern front and were now assumed to be in Soviet captivity. On that front whole divisions and armies had been captured completely—such as the Sixth Army at Stalingrad—and there had been no communication from the soldiers since. There were rumors of secret POW camps from which no messages could be sent. "Where are the lost millions?" and "Where are the vanished divisions?" were questions voiced often. The whereabouts of the missing in the East remained unclarified for a longer time than the whereabouts of other groups of POWs for the following reasons:

1. The Soviet Union had not ratified the Geneva Convention of 1929; therefore, there was no regular correspondence with the POWs during the war.
2. For propaganda reasons, such letters from POWs in the Soviet Union as did reach Germany were nevertheless not delivered.
3. After the war the Soviet Union behaved more restrictively as regards mail than did the other Allies.
4. Even when a next of kin had received mail from a POW in the Soviet Union, the difficulty in communication within Germany in these years hindered the dissemination of the news.

As a result of the public concern about the "lost millions," certain aspects of the history of the POWs, especially those held in the Soviet Union, were investigated to a degree to which they would not otherwise have been, and this is of considerable importance for researchers today.

Over the years the resources of the tracing services were pooled and responsibilities clearly assigned to different offices. The Munich DRK-Suchdienst (German Red Cross Tracing Service) took responsibility for civilian missing and family reunification; the Arolsen International Tracing Service became responsible for displaced persons and concentration-camp victims; the Munich Kirchliche Suchdienst (Ecclesiastical Tracing Service) worked for the victims of the expulsion from the eastern territories; and

14. *Ibid.*, 89, 122, 222; Smith, *Heimkehr*, 75.

the successor of the WASt became responsible for Wehrmachtangehörige and paramilitary organizations and the issue of official certificates. All these organizations continue to function today and exchange their information regularly.

After Allied mistrust had subsided, the former WASt—now the Deutsche Dienststelle—was able to start functioning properly again.[15] Under first American, then French, supervision, it was now responsible for registering the fate of all German participants in the war, irrespective of whether they had been Wehrmachtangehörige. In contrast to wartime, the organization was no longer responsible for non-Germans (such as Austrians, Alsatians, and *Fremdvölkische*), a group numbering not thousands, but more than a million soldiers.[16] Over and above this, it was difficult for Germans of the former eastern territories and East Germany to get in touch with the Deutsche Dienststelle.

Even after the successful reunification of a family, information about wartime service remained important in West Germany. As in the Deutsches Reich, there were various social benefits for former Wehrmachtangehörige. Length of active service increased the level of pensions. There were also special health treatment and pensions for soldiers disabled in the war. Soldiers returning home received reintegration grants. Even today, ethnic German immigrants from Eastern Europe need only provide evidence that a close relative served in the Wehrmacht in order to prove their nationality. Finally, Wehrmacht membership was important even in those less fortunate cases in which soldiers failed to return home. If a widow wanted to get a war widow's pension or to remarry, her husband had to be declared dead. If the estate of a dead soldier was to be inherited or if the successors to an estate included a missing soldier, death had to be certified.[17] Certification could only be issued by the Deutsche Dienststelle.

For these purposes all administrative authorities passed information to the Deutsche Dienststelle. As the date of death was important for deciding the level of pensions as well as the order of succession to an estate, the Deutsche Dienststelle and the courts (which had to issue the death certificates) sought to determine the fate of the deceased as accurately as possible. Therefore, not only did they collect information, but they were also

15. The full name is *Deutsche Dienststelle für die Benachrichtigung der nächsten Angehörigen von Gefallenen der ehemaligen deutschen Wehrmacht* (German Office for Information of Next of Kin of Former German Wehrmacht Casualties).

16. *Fremdvölkische* were foreigners who were not ethnic Germans, such as French, Dutch, and Scandinavians.

17. Smith, *Heimkehr*, 72.

obliged to make their own investigations. For these reasons there is a large pool of information in West Germany about the individual fates of former soldiers; the card index of the Deutsche Dienststelle is presumably complete—at least for the territory of West Germany—but statistical analyses have never been made.

Both war deaths and judicial declarations of death were recorded in an official register that, although relating only to West Germany (excluding the Saarland and West Berlin), nevertheless gives interesting breakdowns of the distribution of deaths over a long period of years. It also contains separate statistics of civilian deaths. (The situation in East Germany was totally different. Unlike West Germany, the GDR furnished no special benefits for veterans or widows, and consequently had no registration systems for these purposes.)

All these efforts show that, out of humanitarian reasons, much was achieved in the postwar period toward revealing the fate of POWs and missing persons. Insofar as the information exists, it therefore has a high degree of reliability.

What do the card indexes of the tracing services contribute to the inquiry at hand? The efforts of the tracing services were aimed at discovering the whereabouts of missing persons or providing certification of periods of military service, injuries, deaths, and so on. The primary concern was therefore the fate of individuals, not statistical analysis. Yet even though the available figures were originally gathered for other purposes, they could be usefully adapted to a quantitative analysis. (Such an analysis of the card indexes of the tracing services remains to be carried out; undoubtedly it would yield interesting and detailed information.)

Despite the individualistic orientation of the tracing services, more general information—about how many soldiers were in the custody of which country, how many were dead, and how many were still alive—was not only of importance to the public, but was also needed by the newly constituted German authorities, on the one hand for general planning purposes, on the other hand for making formal requests for release of POWs. As early as 1946 the states (at this time there was no central governmental body) had attempted to set up a POW office that would deal with all questions of repatriation. In 1947 an *Ausschuss für Kriegsgefangenenfragen* (Committee for POW Questions) was set up at the *Länderrat* (States Council) of the American zone of occupation.[18] The Ausschuss assigned the *Friedensbüro Stuttgart*—a forerunner of the later West German Foreign

18. *Ibid.*, 65–68.

Ministry—the task of assessing the fate of POWs.[19] The memoranda, still available today, provided the basis for the West German government's requests for repatriation of POWs. In December, 1950, the West German government managed to persuade the UN Commission for Social and Humanitarian Affairs to set up an *ad hoc* commission for POWs. The task of this body was to clarify the fate of German POWs, and above all those missing in the East. At the commission's first session, in January, 1952, the West German government presented to it a documentary report compiled by the DRK-Suchdienst from confidential reports and assessments. Up to the last session of the UN commission, in 1955, the documentation was updated several times.[20] All these documentary reports from different authors give detailed and interesting information, but like other publications they deal only with those not yet repatriated. Any statistical overview that could be obtained from them would extend neither to all POWs and missing nor to the entirety of the Wehrmacht.

The lack of an exact figure for repatriated soldiers prompted the West German government to register this group separately in the 1961 census. Unfortunately, these data are incomplete, since they are restricted to West Germany, and even there they cover only those repatriates who were still alive in 1961, ten to fifteen years after their return.[21]

A last source that should be mentioned here consists in the numerous reports in medical journals on the state of health of repatriates, the consequences of illnesses related to captivity, and associated topics, but these are not discussed further in this essay.

Reports and Documentation

In the preceding section, measures taken to clarify the fate of the soldiers were described; in the following, special emphasis will be given to literary and historiographical attempts to describe the events.

The captivity of POWs naturally preoccupied the German public. A vast

19. The full name is *Deutsches Büro für Friedensfragen* (German Office for Peace Questions); it was located in Stuttgart.

20. Erich Maschke, "Deutsche Kriegsgefangenengeschichte: Der Gang der Forschung," in Erich Maschke et al., *Die deutschen Kriegsgefangenen des Zweiten Weltkrieges: Eine Zusammenfassung* (Munich, 1974), 4, Vol. XV of Maschke Commission; Smith, *Heimkehr,* 61–68; Böhme, *Gesucht wird,* 152–53, 156–61. Examples of updates are Deutsches Rotes Kreuz–Suchdienst, ed., *Lagerverschollenenliste* (2 vols.; Munich, 1953), and Federal Republic of Germany, ed., *Missing Members of the Wehrmacht: Stand 30.6.1954* (7 vols.; N.p., n.d.).

21. "Heimgekehrte Kriegsgefangene, Zivilinternierte, und Zivilverschleppte," *Statistische Monatshefte Baden-Württemberg,* No. 4 (1964), 104–105.

number of publications deal with the situation of captives in Eastern Europe, but there are others, too. In those concerning the Western captives, the *Rheinwiesenlager* ("Rhine meadow camps") are mentioned with particular frequency, not only because the conditions were intolerable, but also because the discrepancy between German expectations of America and reality was especially great. Besides books, including some on conditions in the Rheinwiesenlagern, there are also numerous articles in repatriate periodicals and newsletters. These contain horrifying accounts from camps in which the Americans were accused of fatal mistreatment of German POWs.[22]

Although the conditions in the camps were a matter of public knowledge and debate, on a purely quantitative scale it was the situation of POWs in the East, rather than those in the West, that aroused the main concern. On the basis of these sources, but with even greater help from unpublished materials, more comprehensive reports were made. The first, starkly describing the situation, were the aforementioned memoranda of the Friedensbüro Stuttgart from 1949. In these memoranda, for example, the French figures on the number of mortalities in the French camps were already criticized as too low. Similarly, between 1954 and 1962, the DRK published a four-volume account of the history of the POWs.[23] These reports contain much information that has since been confirmed or stated in more detail.

After preparatory investigations beginning in 1957, in 1959 the *Bundesministerium für Vertriebene, Flüchtlinge, und Kriegsgeschädigte*

22. See, for example, Emil Blum, *Kriegsgefangene in Frankreich: Dokumente der Deutschen Evangelischen Kirche* (Tübingen, 1948); [?] Buff, "Kriegsgefangene am Niederrhein," *Nachrichtenblatt Kameradschaftsbund 6. Panzerdivision,* No. 12 (1965), 8–13; Herbert Michaelis and Ernst Schraepler, eds., *Das Dritte Reich: Der militärische Zusammenbruch und das Ende des Dritten Reiches* (Berlin, n.d.); Fritz vom Hellweg, *Rheinwiesen, 1945* (Wuppertal, 1951); Manfred Hornung, *PW: Tatsachenbericht über die Kriegsgefangenenlager der westlichen Verbündeten des 2. Weltkrieges* (Vienna, 1959); Hansheinrich Thomas and Hans Hofmeister, *Das war Wickrathsberg: Erinnerungen aus den Kriegsgefangenenlagern des Rheinlandes. Gemeinsam erlebt und dargestellt* (Minden, 1950). See also "Das Geschick Hermann Noacks: Ein Zellenkamerad berichtet über entsetzliche Grausamkeiten," *Der deutsche Fallschirmjäger,* No. 3 (1952), 3, and "So starb mein Mann," *Der deutsche Fallschirmjäger,* No. 4 (1952), 1. There is a dissertation that concerns itself exclusively with the literature of captivity in American camps; see Volker Christian Wehdeking, "Der Nullpunkt: Uber die Konstituierung der deutschen Nachkriegsliteratur (1945–1948) in den amerikanischen Kriegsgefangenenlagern" (Doctoral dissertation, University of Stuttgart, 1971).

23. Maschke *et al., Zusammenfassung,* 4; Smith, *Heimkehr,* 64; DRK-Suchdienst, ed., *Zur Geschichte der Kriegsgefangen* (4 vols.; Munich, 1954–62).

(Federal—that is, West German—Ministry for Exiles, Refugees, and War-Injured) set up the *Wissenschaftliche Kommission für deutsche Kriegsgefangenengeschichte* (Scientific Commission for the History of German POWs). Dr. Erich Maschke was soon appointed head of this commission, which operated for sixteen years.[24] When the first volume went to print in 1962, the project consisted of five researchers, seven specialists with experience in the tracing services, six clerical assistants, student assistants, and free-lance workers. Although these numbers decreased as the collection of data became more complete up to the disbandment of the commission, obviously this was no casual exercise, but a major scientific undertaking.

The documentation is of a correspondingly considerable scale. As well as some 45,000 reports, there are 200,000 completed questionnaires and hundreds of tape recordings. The catalog numbers stretch to 1,800—filling forty-eight meters of shelf space, excluding photographs, tape recordings, and printed material.[25] Thirteen authors set down their conclusions and findings in a total of twenty-two volumes, part-volumes, and supplements. The documentation is characterized by its effort to avoid any evaluation or accusation; for example, there is no summarizing table of the losses. Nevertheless, the fact that there were shortcomings in the POW camps is addressed by the authors—irrespective of whether the wrongs occurred in American, French, or Soviet custody. After publication of the first two volumes, the West German government decided against further publication for fear of endangering East-West relations, and instead restricted access to the ensuing volumes to limited groups. Besides governmental bodies, the qualified users included university libraries both at home and abroad, so the material has always been available to researchers.[26] Since the 1970s the series has been publicly available; its results have found their place as an accepted standard in the literature, but have never been subjected to a critical assessment.

In the years following the series' public release, little was heard about

24. Maschke *et al.*, *Zusammenfassung*, 4–11. Contrary to what Bacque claims, this commission's work was not simply "a series of books . . . in which the authors attempted to trace the history and fate of German prisoners of war in the two world wars." James Bacque, *Der geplante Tod: Deutsche Kriegsgefangene in amerikanischen und französischen Lagern, 1945–1946* (6th ed.; Frankfurt, 1990), 234 n 28, similarly 152 (*Other Losses*, 225 n 29, 128).

25. Record Group B 205, BA-MA. To convey an impression to the reader: these extensive records are almost twice the volume of the records collected by the States Council of the American Zone of Occupation during its period of operations from 1945 to 1949.

26. Maschke *et al.*, *Zusammenfassung*, 34–37.

the story of the POWs in the West—although I should mention the 1985 monograph by Arthur Smith on the return of the POWs, *Heimkehr aus dem Zweiten Weltkrieg,* published by the Institute for Contemporary History, which widely supports the findings of the Maschke Commission. Also noteworthy is the recently published collection of four firsthand accounts of captivity, *Kriegsgefangenschaft,* edited by Wolfgang Benz and Angelika Schardt.[27]

Although there are abundant statistics and publications in certain areas, such as the Maschke documentation on the POWs, no comprehensive and accurate work exists on the fate of all soldiers, that is, including the dead and the discharged. This does not mean that we are unable to come to concrete conclusions. The available materials do indeed allow us to subject theses to a partial check, and where applicable, to reject these theses. What this statement really means should become clearer in the following.

The Fate of the Prisoners of War

So far the questions have been what sources exist, how they came into existence, and in what ways they are limited. The following will show what these sources have to say. I will seek to give the reader a brief insight into the course of events of greatest importance for the discussion, as well as an overview of the figures.

Wartime Losses

The best-known source on German losses is *Beurteilung der personellen und materiellen Rüstungslage der Wehrmacht (Monatsmeldung).*[28] According to this source, up to January 31, 1945 (the last date for which a report is available), the Wehrmacht had lost nearly 4 million men (See Table 1). When distribution by theater of operations is taken into account (Table 2), it is apparent that about two-thirds of the losses—as far as they can be assigned to particular fronts—occurred in the East.

---

27. Arthur Smith, *Heimkehr,* and Wolfgang Benz and Angelika Schardt, eds., *Kriegsgefangenschaft: Berichte über das Leben in Gefangenlagern der Alliierten von Otto Englebert, Kurt Glaser, Hans Jonitz, und Heinz Pust* (Munich, 1991). See also the popular account Paul Carell and Günter Böddeker, *Die Gefangenen: Leben und Überleben deutscher Soldaten hinter Stacheldraht* (Berlin, 1980). The literature on German POWs in the Soviet Union is more comprehensive. See, for example, Albrecht Lehmann, *Gefangenschaft und Heimkehr: Deutsche Kriegsgefange in der Sowjetunion* (Munich, 1986).

28. Translation: "Assessment of the State Personnel and Material Equipment of the Wehrmacht (Monthly Report)."

Rüdiger Overmans

Table 1
Wehrmacht Losses up to January 31, 1945

Service	Dead	Missing*	Total
Army	1,782,798	1,646,316	3,429,114
Navy	60,029	100,256	160,285
Air Force	158,572	156,132	314,704
Total	2,001,399	1,902,704	3,904,103

*Including POWs.
Source: Beurteilung der personellen und materiellen Rüstungslage der Wehrmacht (Monatsmeldung) Januar 1945, RM 7/810 D, BA-MA. Specifications for the army include those for the Waffen SS. See OKW/WFSt/Org (Vb), Nr. 743/45 g.K. vom 14.3.1945.

Table 2
Dead, Missing, and POWs by Theaters of Operations

Service	East	All Others	No Assignment*
Army	2,124,352	831,128	502,709
Navy	9,676	139,484	11,125
Air Force	102,142	163,707	52,278
Total	2,236,170	1,134,319	566,112

*Not assigned to any particular front.
Source: Beurteilung der personellen und materiellen Rüstungslage der Wehrmacht (Monatsmeldung) Januar 1945, RM/810, BA-MA. Specifications for the army include those for the Waffen SS; in the original figures 17,015 soldiers of the army are not shown; they were added without assignment. See excerpt from OKW/WFSt/Org (Vb), Nr. 743 g.K. vom 14.3.1945.

These were the last, albeit rather incomplete statistics. After the surrender the OKW was required to submit a balance of losses; unfortunately, only the figures for the army survived. These figures (see Table 3) also include land deployments of the air force.

From Table 1, one can see that the navy and air force losses together came to 14 percent of the number of army losses. If that percentage is extrapolated to Table 3, it seems probable that complete figures would show a further 300,000 dead and 400,000 missing. Thus, the probable total losses of the Wehrmacht amounted to 2.3 million dead and 3 million missing—altogether, 5.3 million soldiers.

The next question is how many of these personnel were in captivity at

140

Table 3

Total Losses of Land Forces* up to May 1, 1945

Losses	Dead	Missing	Total
Up to Dec. 31, 1944	1,757,000	1,610,000	3,367,000
Jan. 1—May 1, 1945	250,000	1,000,000	1,250,000
Total	2,007,000	2,610,000	4,617,000

*Including the *Luftwaffenfelddivisionen*.
Source: OKW/WGSt/OrgAbt (Heer), Nr. 5815 vom 10.5.1945, Betr.: Gesamtverluste des Heeres, RW 44I/58, BA-MA. All figures have been rounded.

the time of the capitulation. Even if all those registered as missing ended up alive as POWs, the number of POWs could not have exceeded 3 million, of whom some 2 million would have been in the East (Table 2), leaving approximately a million prisoners for the Western Allies in the time before capitulation. This calculation, albeit crude, brings out one aspect of the matter that will become even clearer later on: considering the 11 million or so captives held in June–July, 1945, the vast majority of the POWs did not fall into Allied hands over the long course of hostilities, but only toward the very end, around the time of the capitulation.

In the first postwar years one of the foremost experts on the subject, former general Burkhart Müller-Hillebrand, attempted a quantitative assessment of the movement of personnel through the Wehrmacht (see Table 4). For an idea of how many soldiers might have been captured in total, the following categories from Table 4 should be considered:

Soldiers as of May 1, 1945	7,590,000
Wounded and sick in military hospitals	700,000
Total	8,290,000.

Adding together the earlier estimate of about 3 million soldiers missing up to May 1, 1945, and the estimate of something over 8 million active or wounded soldiers still available for capture by the Allies as of the same date produces a maximum possible total of just over 11 million soldiers who might have been captured by the Allies. Of these 11 million, many may already have been killed in action, so the real number of captive soldiers—calculated on Wehrmacht statistics—was probably lower. And when the roughly 8 million soldiers as of May 1, 1945, are compared with the 3 million, it becomes yet clearer that by far the greater part of the soldiers were captured in a brief period around the time of the capitulation.

Table 4

Movement of Personnel Through the Wehrmacht

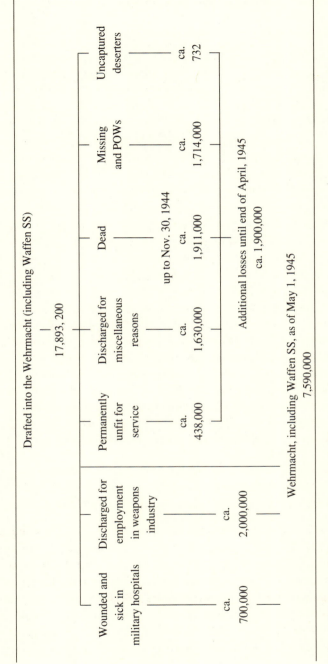

Drafted into the Wehrmacht (including Waffen SS)

17,893,200

Wounded and sick in military hospitals	Discharged for employment in weapons industry	Permanently unfit for service	Discharged for miscellaneous reasons	Dead	Missing and POWs	Uncaptured deserters
ca. 700,000	ca. 2,000,000	ca. 438,000	ca. 1,630,000	ca. 1,911,000	ca. 1,714,000	ca. 732

up to Nov. 30, 1944

Additional losses until end of April, 1945
ca. 1,900,000

Wehrmacht, including Waffen SS, as of May 1, 1945
7,590,000

Source: Müller-Hillebrand, *Der Zweifrontenkrieg*, 253.

POWs in Allied Hands: An Overview

On the basis of investigations into the number of prisoners held in custody in all the countries involved, the Maschke Commission came to the conclusion that about 11.1 million soldiers ended up as POWs. Not included in that number are those who were briefly taken into custody as members of the Volkssturm or on other grounds, and who were released without formal discharge.[29] An exact calculation was difficult for several reasons. Since the infrastructure of the Wehrmacht was no longer intact, there were no exact Wehrmacht data for the number of its troops or their region of deployment. Further, in the final days of the war many units had tried to save themselves from the Red Army by falling into Western hands. The Allies, however, had decided that German troops should be surrendered to those against whom they had last fought. The American command kept to this agreement by delivering such soldiers to the Soviets, but the British accepted the surrender of whole units from the eastern front and designated them British captives. Doubtless many individual soldiers also managed to remain in the supposedly kind hands of the American forces, but for units that were captured as a whole this was not possible, and thus the total number of troops from the eastern front remaining in American custody was limited.[30] Yet another complication is that not only were prisoners handed over to the Soviets, but also captives were exchanged among the Western Allies, with the consequence that later official inquiries about which country had held prisoners could receive varied answers from the ex-POWs, further clouding the statistics.

All these problems are taken into account in Table 5. The data are based on estimates from internal and published reports of the custodial powers, neutral organizations (YMCA, ICRC, and others), and German tracing or inquiry offices. Reports of press agencies, specialist scientific journals and monographs have also been taken into account. In some details the figures vary from the official data of certain custodial powers.[31]

29. Sometimes everyone who wore a uniform was arrested, including foremen, railroad stationmasters, and postmen.

30. Kurt W. Böhme, *Die deutschen Kriegsgefangenen in sowjetischer Hand: Eine Bilanz* (Munich, 1966), 34–45, Vol. VII of Maschke Commission; Kurt W. Böhme, *Die deutschen Kriegsgefangenen in amerikanischer Hand: Europa* (Munich, 1973), 65, Vol. X, Pt. 2, of Maschke Commission.

31. Contrary to Bacque's charge, the Maschke Commission did not limit itself to figures from the Western Allies. For a comprehensive list of sources, see Werner Ratza, "Anzahl und Arbeitsleistungen der deutschen Kriegsgefangenen," in Maschke *et al., Zusammenfassung,* 188–89.

Table 5
Total Numbers of German Prisoners of War

Country	Captured	Transferred	End Quotas	Country
USSR	3,155,000		3,060,000	USSR
		25,000	25,000	Czechoslovakia
		70,000	70,000	Poland
Yugoslavia	194,000		194,000	Yugoslavia
USA	3,800,000		3,097,000	USA
		5,000	5,000	Luxembourg
		667,000		
		31,000		
			64,000	Belgium
Britain	3,700,000		3,635,000	Britain
		33,000		
		7,000	7,000	Netherlands
		25,000		
France	245,000		937,000	France
Totals	11,094,000		11,094,000	

Source: Werner Ratza, "Anzahl und Arbeitsleistungen der deutschen Kriegsgefagenen," in Maschke *et al., Zusammenfassung,* 207–208.
Note: Some smaller custodial powers are not included; POWs from North Africa are excluded; exchanges of POWs according to wartime agreements are not shown.

These figures from the Maschke Commission once again make it clear that about 11 million soldiers were captured. Indeed, the total of about 11.2 million POWs (including those from North Africa) is very similar to the 11 million-plus that the Wehrmacht data indicate were missing or captured. Since not all the missing did get into captivity, however, there is a discrepancy, but it can be explained by the considerable number of noncombatants and/or nonmembers of the Wehrmacht who were taken prisoner. For the following discussion of the Bacque theses, it is important that these two separate estimates of roughly 11 million are good enough to exclude the possibility of further millions.

Of interest here is not only the total number of POWs, but also the distribution according to dates and regions. For the sake of simplification in Table 6, only those figures important for the Bacque theses receive separate columns. First, what of the reliability of these figures? It is noticeable that the numbers in certain columns (for instance, the Soviet Union) appear to be precise to the last digit, whereas in others (such as the USA) they are

Table 6

Numbers of German Prisoners of War in Foreign Custody

Year/ Quarter	USSR	USA Abroad	Britain Abroad	France	Other Countries	Totals
43/I	167,371	—	27,730	—	1,897	196,998
II	156,315	—	29,755	—	19,972	206,042
III	192,494	—	33,040	—	88,747	314,281
IV	197,355	—	33,820	—	122,760	353,935
44/I	238,488	—	34,660	—	130,172	403,320
II	373,372	—	36,660	—	145,321	555,353
III	557,274	153,000	62,630	—	251,348	1,024,252
IV	559,142	178,300	109,065	—	428,356	1,274,863
45/I	1,067,640	313,000	197,485	52,507	459,688	2,090,320
II	2,040,744	2,591,500	2,122,975	142,279	689,636	7,587,134
III	1,862,258	3,400,000	2,151,235	448,958	858,881	8,721,332
IV	1,448,724	2,200,000	349,385	705,006	808,675	5,511,790
46/I	1,319,733	1,000,000	532,750	676,631	698,938	4,228,052
II	1,261,576	690,700	439,255	675,354	636,895	3,703,780
III	1,131,979	381,300	309,485	634,402	628,914	3,086,080
IV	1,072,808	72,000	258,635	587,745	593,875	2,585,063
47/I	1,020,805	38,250	203,520	552,970	549,212	2,364,757
II	968,323	—	142,230	512,313	485,348	2,108,214
III	896,935	—	67,420	450,579	446,029	1,860,963
IV	841,649	—	61,250	358,195	335,272	1,596,366
48/I	760,556	—	53,200	241,660	252,850	1,308,266
II	616,296	—	29,650	137,995	171,230	955,171
III	554,629	—	11,670	79,488	127,120	772,907
IV	501,855	—	—	23,609	64,900	590,364

Source: Ratza, "Anzahl und Arbeitsleistungen," in Maschke, *Zusammenfassung,* 194–97, 200–201.

Note: The columns USA Abroad and Britain Abroad include all prisoners in the custody of the countries but not held in those countries themselves; they include, in particular, those POWs held in Germany. The Soviet numbers include those prisoners in Joachimstal. Data prior to 1943 are omitted since the number of those prisoners was less than 100,000. Data after 1948 are omitted since after this time the only POWs were in custody in Eastern Europe. The totals are calculated according to the individual data in the original statistics. Due to mistakes, Ratza has slightly different totals for the quarters 45/III, 45/IV, and 47/IV.

clearly rounded. This somewhat surprising feature can be explained as follows. The table is taken from the Maschke Commission's summary volume (XV), where the figures have been lifted from the volumes devoted to each country. In the latter volumes data are not given for every date; thus, in order to enter the data into a unified table, it was naturally necessary to interpolate and extrapolate averages for each quarter. The figures therefore correspond, by and large, to those in the following tables, but are not identical.

What was already presumed the case with regard to the Wehrmacht statistics becomes even more apparent here: the vast majority of soldiers entered into captivity at around the time of the capitulation, particularly so with the Western Allies. After this peak period the numbers for the four Allies decrease unsteadily and quite differently.

In the case of the Soviet Union, the number of captives had already started rising sharply by mid-1944 as a result of the collapse of the Central Army Group and the encirclement battles in the Balkans. In the first quarter of 1945, immediately before the main collapse, the number of Soviet captives had already risen to more than half of the later maximum of around 2 million. The number of captives in Russian hands remains high in the following years. The French figure, like the Soviet, falls off only slowly, although from a much lower initial level. The British pattern differs considerably: the number of captives explodes in the second quarter of 1945, yet already by the fourth quarter of 1945 the number of releases has reduced the overall total of captives far more drastically than for any other country—although this fast process of release does not continue and extend to all the captives. The American numbers again develop differently. From the first to the second quarter of 1945, the number of captives multiplies eightfold, from 300,000 to over 2.5 million—and this despite the fact that transfers of prisoners to other Allies were already taking place. On the other hand, the United States is the first country to effect a complete release of its prisoners.

I now turn to the fate of prisoners according to the country in whose custody they were held. The analyses are based on the findings of the Maschke Commission, and are limited to those countries of concern to Bacque.

THE UNITED STATES

Against a background of considerable diversity of documentary sources derived from so many different countries, the best documentation of the story of the German prisoners of war concerns those held in American custody. Besides published and unpublished American reports, the following documents are available:

- reports by repatriated prisoners (diaries, tape recordings, and so on) and published literature;
- the three-volume report of the ICRC of June, 1948, concerning its activities during the Second World War and its aftermath (September 1, 1939–June 30, 1947);
- the memorandum of the Friedensbüro Stuttgart on the fate of German POWs in American custody;
- the four-volume examination of the history of the POWs by the German Red Cross.[32]

On the European continent, sizable numbers of German POWs did not begin to fall into American custody until around the beginning of 1945, and a considerable growth in their numbers really began only with the occupation of the Rhineland (250,000 prisoners) and the taking of the Ruhr pocket in April, 1945 (325,000 prisoners). From the beginning of April to the end of May (that is, less than 2 months) 1.8 million soldiers surrendered. Immediately after the capitulation, many hundreds of thousands more were taken into custody, but these now received the status of "disarmed enemy forces."[33] No exact figures for the number of DEFs are available, but according to an announcement by the Allies, on June 22, 1945, a total of 7,614,794 persons—POWs and DEF/SEPs—were held in American and British camps, of whom 4,209,000 were soldiers captured before the capitulation and considered POWs. This leaves about 3.4 million DEFs and SEPs, who according to Allied agreements were supposed to be distributed fifty-fifty between Britain and the United States (but were

32. Böhme, *In amerikanischer Hand: Europa,* 1–5; Conférence Internationale de la Croix-Rouge, *Rapport du Comité International de la Croix-Rouge sur son activité pendant la seconde guerre mondiale, 1er septembre 1939–30 juin 1947* (3 vols.; Geneva, 1948); Deutsches Büro für Friedensfragen, ed., *Das Schicksal der deutschen Kriegsgefangenen des Zweiten Weltkrieges in Amerikanischer Gewahrsam* (Stuttgart, 1949); Deutsches Rotes Kreuz–Suchdienst, ed., *Zur Geschichte der Kriegsgefangenen im Westen* (Bonn, 1962), Vol. IV of DRK-Suchdienst, ed., *Zur Geschichte der Kriegsgefangenen,* 4 vols.

33. Böhme, *In amerikanischer Hand: Europa,* 9–11. "Disarmed enemy forces" (DEFs) were not recognized as prisoners of war. Thus, even though they remained under U.S. supervision, they were to be fed by German authorities. It was only on the basis of general humanitarian concern that the Allies felt obliged to feed these DEFs. The British designated this group "surrendered enemy personnel" (SEPs). For a critical view of these categorizations, see *ibid.,* 69–72.

not). However, apart from internal United States military statistics, there are no verifiable data that could support this estimate.

While the front line still lay west of the Rhine, prisoners were transported to France and Belgium. But after Allied Forces crossed the river the journey back became too long, and from April, 1945 (and, especially for DEFs, after the capitulation) transit camps had to be set up, which later became notorious as the Rheinwiesenlager. The most important and best-known of the altogether sixteen Rheinwiesenlager were Bad Kreuznach–Bretzenheim, Remagen-Sinzig, Rheinberg, Heidesheim, Wickrathberg, and Büderich (see map of American POW camps in Germany, pp. 14–15). Prisoners were starving in other camps, but in these particular six the conditions were quite indescribable.[34] Comprehensive accounts of the state of provision of food, clothing, and shelter, as well as of the health of the prisoners, can be found among the documentation of the Maschke Commission and in other publications. Protests against the state of these camps came not only from the Red Cross and other aid organizations; even the archbishop of Trier hurled public accusations from his pulpit.[35]

This situation lasted from the beginning of April into June and July of 1945. On June 12, the Americans surrendered control of three large camps—Rheinberg, Büderich, and Wickrathberg—to the British; on July 10, a further eight were given over to the French.[36] Subsequently, the United States was the first of the Allies to release all its POWs, so far as they had not been assigned to other custodial powers as labor forces.

The mortality rate in the Rheinwiesenlager between April and July, 1945, was high. The Maschke Commission cited contemporary eyewitness accounts in which the largest claim was that "32,000 fatalities had been heard of."[37] A comparison can be made between American figures for deaths, the figures known to the communities and parishes in which the camps were situated, and the accounts of former prisoners. The figures are as follows:

---

34. For a description of the deplorable conditions in other camps under American control, for example in Bavaria, see *ibid.*, 142–43.

35. *Ibid.*, 142–61. The DRK-Suchdienst dedicated a whole chapter to the conditions in these camps. See DRK-Suchdienst, ed., *Kriegsgefangene im Westen*, IV, 102–33. See also Deutsches Büro für Friedensfragen, *Das Schicksal*, 50–54, and Conférence Internationale de la Croix-Rouge, *Rapport*, I, 257–58. On the archbishop's protest, see Böhme, *In französischer Hand*, 29.

36. Wolff, *In britischer Hand: Uberblick*, 16.

37. Böhme, *In amerikanischer Hand: Europa*, 195.

Highest estimate in an eyewitness account	32,000 dead
Official American statistics	3,053 dead
Registered by parish authorities	5,311 dead
(4,537 from the six largest camps, 774 from all other camps)	

The 5,311 registered by parish authorities represents about 1 percent of the 557,000 who, according to the Maschke Commission, lived in these camps. The commission did not believe that this mortality figure was very accurate but considered it impossible that the actual number of deaths could have been more than double that cited.[38]

FRANCE

Among the numerous published and unpublished reports and materials, the following documents are particularly important:

• the three-volume report of the ICRC of June, 1948;
• the memorandum of the Friedensbüro Stuttgart on the fate of German POWs in French custody;
• the four-volume examination of the history of the POWs by the German Red Cross;
• General Buisson's *Historique du service des prisonniers de guerre de l'Axe, 1943–1948* (Paris, 1948); and
• *Notes Documentaires et Etudes*, No. 270 (March 26, 1946), and No. 659 (July 3, 1947), published by the information service of the French government.

In their essentials all these materials are in agreement with one another, despite the diversity of editors and publishers.[39]

Numerically, the situation during wartime and immediately postwar captivity is summed up in Table 7, and the fate of the French-held prisoners in Table 8. The figures in these tables agree with those of the United States. For the most part they are taken from the Buisson report. At this point it is necessary to say a few words about the registration methods. In 1945 the French forces' POW administration, led by Buisson, had begun to register all POWs, in accordance with international law. As is plainly set out in the Buisson report, at first the registration limped behind the

38. *Ibid.*, 204–205.
39. One can still agree with Bacque's critique of the Buisson Report, which oozes with self-praise. See *Der geplante Tod*, 150 (*Other Losses*, 127).

Table 7
Origin of French-held Prisoners of War

Origin	Original Figure	Corrected Figure
Captured in Europe by French forces		
Army	117,000	145,000
Interior French forces	20,000	20,000
Atlantic encirclement	72,000	72,000
Total	209,000	237,000
Captured in North Africa	63,000	63,000
Transferred from British		
from Feb. 22, 1945	15,000	15,000
from Dunkirk	4,000	4,000
from Fleury-sur-Orne	6,000	6,000
Total	25,000	25,000
Transferred from Americans		
Quota from Feb. 22, 1945	35,000	35,000
Quota of June/July, 1945	50,000	50,000
Quota of June/July, 1945	228,000	228,000
Quota of July/Sept., 1945	50,000	50,000
Quota of July, 1945	175,000	175,000
From Norway	50,000	50,000
From Norway	50,000	50,000
Returned to Americans	− 70,000	− 70,000
Immediately released	− 60,000	− 60,000
Quota of Feb./May, 1946	101,000	101,000
Total of all American quotas	740,000	740,000
Total of all prisoners of war	1,037,000	1,065,000

Source: General Buisson, *Historique du service des prisonniers de guerre de l'Axe, 1943–1948* (Paris, 1948), 37–38, 385–87.

actual numbers of prisoners. By mid-1947 only 900,000 cases had been registered, and not until the following year was the catalog complete. All the information was directed through the ICRC in Geneva to the German Red Cross Tracing Service; thus, the registry could be scrutinized in light of the knowledge of returning soldiers and their relations at home. The figures in the Buisson report represent the most reliable source of information available precisely because they are based on this catalog of individual cases that can be checked at any time. As already mentioned, all figures from the years 1945 to 1947 are of a provisional nature and considerably lower than the final figures, which explains how it is that the *Notes*

Table 8
Fate of French-held prisoners

	Total	Germans	Others
Released	750,965	613,148	137,817
			(109,817)
Returned to U.S.	70,000 ⎤	199,987	8,000
Contractual workers	137,987 ⎦		
Escaped	81,870	71,810	10,060
Died	24,178	21,810	2,292
Total (rounded)	1,065,000	907,000	158,000
			(140,000)

Source: Buisson, *Historique.* Buisson's uncorrected figures are given in parentheses.

of the French government's information service give significantly lower figures than Buisson, for instance, 734,632 prisoners for September, 1945, against the Buisson report's 870,000 for October, 1945. Even Buisson had to correct his figures: the numbers given in Table 7 as "original figures" were used in the main body of the Buisson report, but these required minor corrections (entered on the above table as "corrected figures"), which were set forth and justified in an appendix to the report.

The Buisson figures were by no means received uncritically and trustingly by the Germans. On the basis of reports on conditions and mortalities in the French camps, all the aforementioned sources came to the conclusion that Buisson's numbers for deaths were too low. The facts are, however, reconcilable with the Buisson figures, since it is highly probable that POWs who died before registration or while trying to escape were subsequently registered as "escaped" or not registered at all. Likewise (and especially in 1945 and 1946) there were further POWs who died in the camps or while being transported and were buried without registration. Accordingly, the DRK-Suchdienst survey records some 26,000 missing in France. Some of them may have been killed in action, others may have died in captivity or in flight from French POW camps. Considered together, all these various sources give reason to suppose that the actual number of Germans who died in French custody exceeds the official French figure of 21,000 by thousands—but not by hundreds of thousands, as Bacque wants us to believe.[40]

So what do we now know about the fate of German POWs held by

40. Böhme, *In amerikanischer Hand: Europa,* 88–94; Deutsches Büro für Friedensfragen, ed., *Das Schicksal,* 60–61.

France and the United States? On December 23, 1944, the French and the Americans reached an agreement whereby the latter would transfer German POWs to France as a labor force. The transfers began on February 22, 1945; the series of quotas can be seen in Table 7. In July, 1945, the American POW camps located in the French zone were handed over. The transfer involved some 182,400 prisoners in the camps Sinzig, Andernach, Siershahn, Bretzenheim, Dietersheim, Koblenz, Hechtsheim, and Diez. The French army prepared a report on the state of the camps and the prisoners they contained. Only a fourth of the captives had stable lodging in barracks or weatherproof tents. Women (about 500) and prisoners who were under eighteen, over fifty, badly injured, or unable to be transported (altogether over 62,000 people) were released immediately, the rest accommodated in other camps. But the French could not feed them any better than they had been fed before, and on August 21, 1945, the ICRC approached the Americans because the state of health of captives held in the French camps gave cause for concern. The ICRC warned that some 200,000 prisoners would die if not quickly given help. On October 6, 1945, Operation "A" was launched, whereby the Americans delivered enough provisions to raise the daily ration from 1,350 to about 2,000 calories and—according to the ICRC—the danger was removed. In the course of the winter the United States delivered additional clothing for the captives, and the French government carried out further aid measures known as Operation "F." [41]

On October 11, 1945, the French government responded to American reproaches that they were not properly treating their prisoners by claiming that the Americans had not transferred the agreed labor force, but instead a considerable number of sick. It was agreed to return to the Americans 70,000 peopled judged incapable of work, and to resume the transfers. When, at the beginning of 1946, the ICRC once again had to complain about conditions in the French camps, the Americans once again helped with provisions. In a similar vein, it was above all the United States that in 1947 and 1948 pressured the French government to release German POWs.

THE SOVIET UNION

The fate of German POWs in the Soviet Union does not appear to be of immediate significance for the present subject. What makes it important is Bacque's argument that about a million more soldiers fled from the eastern

41. Conférence Internationale de la Croix-Rouge, *Rapport,* I, 258, III, 125.

front to the West than was originally assumed. Thus it is necessary to recount briefly what is known about the number of prisoners in Soviet custody.

The first large quantity of prisoners was captured at the surrender of Stalingrad, December, 1942–January, 1943. Subsequently the number of captives rose continually (see Table 6). Major increases followed the collapse of the Central Army Group in July, 1944, with the loss of twenty-five divisions, and the encirclement battles in the Balkans. At Jassy alone, eighteen complete divisions and parts of three more were taken into captivity in August, 1944. A further large contribution to the figures was made by the Kurland Army, which after being encircled by the Soviets in January, 1945, nevertheless successfully defended themselves until the capitulation on May 18, 1945. Through these relatively early captures, the number of prisoners in Soviet custody (averaging over a million in the first quarter of 1945) had already reached 50 percent of its later maximum.[42] The explosion of numbers of captured shortly before or after the capitulation, so obvious among the Western Allies, did not take place with the Soviets. This difference largely reflects the efforts of all Wehrmachtangehörigen to end up in American or British, rather than Soviet, captivity. As already mentioned, the surrendering troops' evasive movements westward were partially successful; but what is most important for the present discussion is that the course of events be known.

The question is what we know of the numbers of prisoners of the Soviet Union. As the Soviet Union had not ratified the Geneva Convention, during the war she was not obliged to notify the ICRC of the names of captured Germans, nor did she indeed do this. The Wehrmacht for its part did not publish any figures for losses throughout the entire war. Thus expectations about survivors after the end of the war were high. At the Allied foreign ministers' conference of 1947 in Moscow, the Soviet foreign minister, Molotov, stated that there were still 890,532 German POWs in the Soviet Union, whereas 1,000,974 had already been released.[43] However, according to the expectations then held, there should still have been around 2 million in Soviet camps. Thus, if Molotov's statement was correct, a million more soldiers had lost their lives in the Soviet Union than had been assumed. The disbelief of relatives gave rise to claims that whole divisions were held in secret camps; this is where the questions began about the

---

42. A very detailed breakdown can be found in Böhme, *In sowjetischer Hand,* 10–50.
43. Deutsches Büro für Friedensfragen, ed., *Das Schicksal,* 10.

"Missing Million."[44] To support arguments against the Soviet figures, the registration of 1947 was carried out. In subsequent years repeated efforts were made, as already described, to obtain the most exact information possible as to the fate of soldiers deployed on the eastern front.

The Maschke Commission undertook further inquiries, and its calculations fill a volume of almost five hundred pages.[45] First, a set of figures for Wehrmacht losses was drawn up from the records I have already cited. To this were appended the Soviet figures for captives, regularly published by *Pravda* with the exception of those prior to 1943. The figures after Stalingrad were shown to be reliable by the Maschke Commission; *Pravda* no longer had reason to exaggerate, as the numbers were so large anyway that to have enlarged them further would have made them less credible. A third set of figures was calculated on the basis of the statements of 150,000 returning soldiers regarding where, when, and with how many others they had been held captive. These three sets of figures differ in absolute value, but their relative developments over time move in a parallel fashion. They give the result that the total number of POWs came to about 3.1 to 3.5 million, a result that tallies with the registrations.[46] On the basis of the known information about the number of repatriates, the commission came to the conclusion that of the probable 3.1 million POWs, about 1,111,000 had died and 1,959,000 had been repatriated. It should be noted that the number of dead is based on the lower limit for total number of POWs, and that if the top limit is taken, the number of dead rises to perhaps 1.6 million.[47]

Where did people at the time suppose that their relatives were to be found? Looking at the periodicals and relevant publications, one finds numerous interesting articles with titles such as "Where Are the Vanished Divisions?"[48] When the Maschke Commission publicly put forward its conclusion that in addition to the millions killed in action on the eastern front, a further million German soldiers had died in the Soviet Union, and that no further repatriations were to be expected, there was a storm of indignation. The commission was accused of writing off the "Missing Million," who were to be found in secret Soviet camps and were not to be forgotten. The controversy finally came to the courts. How widespread this

44. Böhme, *In sowjetischer Hand*, 151–57.
45. *Ibid.*
46. *Ibid.*, 49.
47. *Ibid.*, 151.
48. "Es gibt keine verschwundenen Divisionen," *Der Heimkehrer*, No. 2 (1954), 5.

view was is witnessed by the hundreds of newspaper articles provoked by the publication of the Maschke documentation.

Losses Among the Prisoners of War

The reader has now been given a brief overview of the fate of the prisoners of war. A concluding breakdown of the pertinent figures, according to the countries in whose custody the prisoners were to be found, appears in Table 9. The apparent precision of some of the figures might be interpreted as meaning that the losses are indeed known to the last digit, but this is not the case. The figures are intended, rather, to give the scale of mortalities. It is quite possible that the number of deaths in any one country or altogether may exceed the stated numbers by several tens of thousands, without in any way casting suspicion on the calculative methods used by the Maschke Commission.

Interesting—and hardly surfacing at all in public discussion today—are the percentages. Percentagewise, the mortality rate in eastern and southeastern Europe was almost as high as that in the Soviet Union; this high rate results mainly from some 80,000 deaths in Yugoslavia. Likewise of significance is the difference between Britain and the United States. Although the number of prisoners in the custody of each of these countries was similar, the losses in American custody were almost four times higher than in British custody. This difference was a result of deaths in the Rheinwiesenlager, which the British were able to avoid.

Table 9
Losses Among the Prisoners of War

Country	POWs	Losses Absolute	Losses %	Returned Absolute	Returned %
France	937,000	24,178	2.6	912,822	97.4
USSR	3,060,000	1,094,250	35.8	1,965,750	64.2
E. and S.E. Europe	289,000	93,028	32.2	195,972	67.8
Britain	3,635,000	1,254	—	3,633,746	100.0
USA	3,097,000	4,537	0.1	3,092,463	99.9
Other	76,000	675	0.9	75,325	99.1
Totals	11,094,000	1,217,922	11.0	9,876,078	89.0

Source: Ratza, "Anzahl und Arbeitsleistungen," in Maschke, *Zusammenfassung*, 208, 224–29.

Postwar West German Statistics

Up to this point, the presentation has for the most part been based on the findings of the Maschke Commission. Naturally, there is the question of how reliable this information is. I will attempt to answer this question in the following by comparing the Maschke findings with those of other investigations—the accumulations of statistics and the registrations. One definitional problem should be kept in mind: the Maschke figures are based on "country of custody," whereas other figures about POWs often refer to "countries of residence" and registrations of missing refer to "countries of last contact." In some cases, such as the Soviet Union, these terms tend to coincide; in other cases, such as the United States, they differ to a high degree and change over time.

The first basis of comparison is the population and occupation census of October 29, 1946, which was carried out in all four zones of occupation, including Berlin. The census distinguished between the population at large and those interned in POW camps and civilian detention camps. It showed that there were 96,517 male internees in camps within the American zone of occupation. If this count is compared with the Maschke Commission figures (Table 6), which for the fourth quarter of 1946 give an average total of 72,000 prisoners, a total that is steadily declining, the two figures are relatively reconcilable.[49]

Chronologically, the next data come from the registration of 1947–1948, which was carried out in only three zones, thus giving only partial results. One could object to the employment of these figures on the grounds that they are not representative and that no conclusions that apply to the whole of Germany can be validly drawn from them. In response to this it can be said that conscription into the army bore no relation to geographical origin, and that army units were not deployed according to any criteria of geographical origin. It is thus impossible that, for example, Rhinelanders would generally have been deployed in the West. Therefore, statistics gathered from particular regions may be legitimately used for estimates extending to the entire country.[50]

Extension of the registration results to all four zones shows that

49. Ausschuss der deutschen Statistiker für die Volks- und Berufszählung, ed., *Volks- und Berufszählung vom 29. Oktober 1946 in den vier Besatzungszonen und Gross-Berlin* (Berlin, n.d.), Appendices, 2. Although the first figures are based on countries of residence and the Maschke figures are based on countries of custody, they can be compared because at that time the United States only held POWs in camps in its zone of occupation.

50. Smith, *Heimkehr,* 70.

1,685,000 male Wehrmachtangehörige were missing and 1,142,000 were held in captivity.[51] In only a few states are the results broken down according to the country in which the missing had last been heard of. The state of Hessen is one such case; the breakdown is as follows: USSR, 48 percent; eastern and southeastern Europe, 23 percent; Germany, 22 percent; France, 4 percent; all other countries, 3 percent.[52]

One of the few cases in which data are categorized not only by country of last contact, but also by the date of that contact, is summarized in Table 10. Although they are based on countries of last contact, whereas the Maschke statistics relate to countries of custody, the figures in the table clearly confirm the findings of the Maschke Commission—that the overwhelming majority of missing persons disappeared in the East, and for the most part before the end of 1944.

The results concerning the distribution of POWs are likewise quite clear. The figures for three individual states appear in Table 11. The absolute values are less interesting than the proportions. Not only were the majority of missing persons taken to be in the USSR and eastern and southeastern Europe, but also the majority of POWs whose whereabouts was known were in these same places. Again, and importantly, the figures are in proportional agreement with those of the Maschke Commission.

No general breakdown for the data of the 1947 registration was made, but the case was different in the 1950 registration. Carried out from March 1 to March 11, 1950, in West Germany (including West Berlin), this registration produced 1,407,000 names, among which were 69,000 detainees (POWs, criminals, and people detained for investigation), 1,148,000 missing from the Wehrmacht, and 190,000 missing civilians.[53] Over the

51. "Vorläufiges Ergebnis der Kriegsgefangenen-, Wehrmachtvermissten-, und Zivilvermisstenerhebung im Lande Nordrhein-Westfalen im Oktober 1947," in *Statistischer Kurzbericht Nordrhein-Westfalen,* ed. Statistisches Landesamt Düsseldorf, No. 1 (December 12, 1947), 3.

52. These data relate to Hesse. See "Kriegsgefangene und Wehrmachtvermisste aus Hessen: Endgültige Ergebnisse der amtlichen Registrierung vom 20.–30. Juni 1947," *Staat und Wirtschaft in Hessen: Statistische Mitteilungen,* ed. Hessisches Statistisches Landesamt, No. 1 (February, 1948), 20–28 (here 27). All figures have been rounded. The data were continuously updated until the end of October, 1948. Similar results were reported from Niedersachsen (Lower Saxony). See "Die Kriegsgefangenen-, Wehrmachtvermissten-, und Zivilerhebung in Niedersachsen," *Statistische Monatshefte Niedersachsen,* No. 1 (1948), 2–4. For data from the British zone (albeit without distinguishing between the various custodial countries), see "Kriegsgefangene und Wehrmachtvermisste nach Altersgruppen, 1947 (vorläufige Zahlen)," *Statistische Monatszahlen,* No. 2 (September, 1948), 4.

53. Böhme, *Gesucht wird,* 108–10.

Rüdiger Overmans

Table 10
Missing Wehrmachtangehörige for the State of Württemberg-Baden

| Country of last contact | Number | | Date of Last Contact (%) | | |
	Absolute	%	Up to 1944	1945	No Data
Germany	12,724	14.9	2.1	12.8	—
West Europe, USA, and Canada	7,195	8.4	5.2	3.2	—
USSR	45,693	53.6	42.5	11.0	0.1
E. and S.E. Europe	16,260	19.1	9.8	9.3	—
Other	3,371	4.0	1.7	1.8	0.4
Total	85,243	100.0	61.3	38.1	0.5

Source: [?] Fiedler, "Die zurückerwarteten Kriegsgefangenen und Vermissten der Wehrmacht des Landes Württemberg-Baden nach dem Stande von Mitte 1947," *Statistische Monatshefte Württemberg-Baden,* No. 2 (February, 1948), 36.

Table 11
Prisoners of War by Custodial Power

| | Hessen | | Württemberg-Baden | | Niedersachsen | | Masch* |
	Absolute	%	Absolute	%	Absolute	%	%
USSR	44,338	47.4	38,683	46.1	12,479	56.4	52.7
E. and S.E. Europe	5,981	6.5	5,342	6.4	1,680	7.6	9.4
France	25,792	27.6	25,834	30.8	4,418	20.0	22.4
Britain	11,393	12.2	9,228	11.0	3,138	14.2	11.5
USA	—		247	0.3	49	0.2	—
Other	6,004	6.3	4,543	5.4	379	1.7	4.0
Totals	93,508	100.0	83,877	100.0	22,143	100.1	100.0

*Figures of the Maschke Commission for the fourth quarter, 1947; see Table 6.
Sources: Fiedler, "Die zurückerwarteten Kriegsgefangenen," 34; Hessiches Statistiches Landesamt, e "Kriegsgefangene und Wehrmachtvermisste aus Hessen," 21; "Die Kriegsgefangenen, Wehrmac vermissten, und Zivilvermisstenerhebung in Niedersachsen," *Statistische Monatshefte Niedersachs* No. 1 (1948), 3; Ratza, "Anzahl und Arbeitsleistungen," in Maschke, *Zusammenfassung,* 196–97. percentage figures are rounded.

years there were a further 300,000 reports from the GDR or from immigrants from the Soviet Union, so that there was a total of 1.7 million reports of people missing; for the reasons already advanced, the eastern origin of these additional 300,000 missing has no significance for their distribution according to year and region of last contact.

In 1953 the DRK-Suchdienst made a quantitative analysis of the details produced by the 1950 registration as they concerned 1,388,680 missing members of the Wehrmacht (see Table 12). In its essentials this analysis confirms the results of the 1947–1948 registration. There were almost no missing persons in the West, with the exception of the territory of the Deutsches Reich. Three-quarters of the disappeared were registered in the USSR or eastern and southeastern Europe. The development over the years corresponds to the events on the fronts in question: the first significant losses on the eastern front in 1942, then rising figures in 1943 and 1944 during the retreat. In 1944 the eastern front reached the eastern European countries, and correspondingly the figures for eastern Europe rise in 1944 and 1945. The eastern front crossed into German territory in the winter of 1945, and this explains the relatively large proportion of cases last contacted in Germany in 1945. This last point is amplified by figures from the state of Rheinland-Pfalz (see Table 13), which, with their distinction between the zones of occupation and the territories east of the Oder–Neisse border, clearly show that even within the area of the former Deutsches Reich the majority of registered missing occurred while defending against the Red Army in the East at the end of 1944 and beginning of 1945.

Table 12
1950 Registration

Country of last contact	Year of Last Contact (%)				
	1942	1943	1944	1945	Total
Germany	0.1	0.2	1.7	20.6	22.6
USSR	8.4	15.8	19.9	3.1	47.2
E. and S.E. Europe	0.2	0.6	13.9	13.2	27.9
Other (Finland, Italy, Austria)	—	—	0.2	0.9	1.1
Total	8.7	16.6	35.7	37.8	98.8

Source: Böhme, *Gesucht wird,* 111, 116. Excluded from the table are 1.2 percent of reports for which no year was given. The data for 1942 also cover the years 1939–1941.

Table 13
Wehrmacht Missing for the State Rheinland-Pfalz

Country of last contact	Number		Last Contact	
	Absolute	%	Up to 1944	1945
Four occupation zones	4,665	7.9	1.7	6.1
*Oder-Neisse Terr.	6,203	10.5	1.2	9.2
USSR	29,903	50.4	46.9	3.3
E. and S.E. Europe	12,683	21.4	11.6	9.6
Other	5,926	10.0	6.9	2.7
Total	59,380	100.2	68.3	30.9

*Former German territory east of the Oder and Neisse rivers.
Source: Statistisches Landesamt Rheinland-Pfalz, ed., *Die Kriegsgefangenen und Vermissten in Rheinland-Pfalz: Ergebnisse der Registrierung in der Zeit vom 1.–11. März 1950*, Kleine Schriftenreihe des Statistischen Landesamtes Rheinland-Pfalz, XII (Bad Ems, 1950), 7. All percentages are rounded. The figures for Baden are similar to those for Rheinland-Pfalz. See Hermann Schubnell, "Die Kriegsgefangenen in Baden," *Statistik in Baden: Zeitschrift für Statistik und Landeskunde*, No. 4 (1950), 19–31.

Because the 1950 registration unfortunately categorizes only according to the region of last contact, and not according to custodial power, it cannot be directly compared with the results of the Maschke Commission. Nevertheless, one thing becomes quite clear: by 1950 there were very few missing persons in the West; the POWs had either returned home or were registered as dead.

Let us now turn to mortality statistics, where figures exist for both West and East Germany. In Table 14 the year 1938 is used as a basis for comparison. For the years 1939 to 1945, there are no figures with which a division of the Deutsches Reich into the later West and East Germany can be made. For 1945, the West German figure is an estimate derived from the records of smaller areas.[54] For reasons already given, deaths caused by wartime hostilities in the former West German area are divided into civilian and military deaths and categorized according to the year of death, whereas in the former East German area the figures are undivided and

54. For statements concerning single states of West Germany, see Andreas Würthner, "Die natürliche Bevölkerungsbewegung in Württemberg-Hohenzollern, 1938–1946," *Württemberg-Hohenzollern in Zahlen: Zeitschrift für Statistik und Landeskunde*, No. 2/3 (1948), 25–41 (here 37); *Die Bevölkerungsentwicklung zwischen beiden Weltkriegen*, Statistisches Landesamt Baden-Württemberg, ed., *Jahrbücher für Statistik und Landeskunde von Baden-Württemberg*, 1954–55, pp. 168–73 (here 169).

Table 14
Mortality, 1938–1950

Year	West Germany Civilian Dead Absolute	West Germany Civilian Dead per 1,000	Military Dead	East Germany Absolute	East Germany per 1,000
1938	443,166	11.4	—	197,171	11.9
1939	—	—	9,516	—	—
1940	—	—	37,248	—	—
1941	—	—	155,925	—	—
1942	—	—	228,883	—	—
1943	—	—	273,199	—	—
1944	—	—	412,181	—	—
1945	—	(16.4)	610,082	—	—
1946	535,091	12.3	25,665	413,505	22.9
1947	525,889	11.6	11,613	358,948	19.0
1948	479,373	10.3	7,152*	289,803	15.2
1949	479,931	10.2	—	253,153	13.4
1950	493,416	10.3	—	215,140	11.7
Total		1,771,464			

*Includes military dead and judicial declarations of death in the following years.
Sources: Hermann Schubnell, *Der Trend der Bevölkerungsentwicklung in Deutschland,* Deutsche Akademie für Bevölkerungswissenschaft, Akademie-Veröffentlichung, Series A, No. 7, (Hamburg, 1964), 3; Statistisches Bundesamt, ed., *Bevölkerung und Wirtschaft: Langfristige Reihen 1871 bis 1957 für das Deutsche Reich und die Bundesrepublik Deutschland,* Statistik der Bundesrepublik Deutschland, CIC (Stuttgart, 1958), 17; Statistisches Bundesamt, ed., *Standesamtlich beurkundete Kriegssterbefälle und gerichtliche Todeserklärungen von Personen mit letztem Wohnsitz im Bundesgebiet,* Bevölkerung und Erwerbstätigkeit, Special Ser. 1, Ser. 2: *Bevölkerungsbewegung* (Stuttgart, 1981), 77–79. In the case of the GDR, the statistical yearbook does not record the absolute number of deaths, but only the death rate per 1,000 population. The absolute figures have therefore been arrived at by calculating back. *See* Staatliche Zentralverwaltung für Statistik, ed., *Statistisches Jahrbuch der Deutschen Demokratischen Republik 1955* (Berlin, 1956), 8, 34.
Note: The first column shows civilian dead, including war dead and judicial declarations of the death of civilians; the third column shows military dead and judicial declarations of the death of Wehrmachtsangehörige. Excluded are a total of 7,116 deaths comprising people of unknown status, cases of death not clearly identified as having occurred in a particular year, foreigners, stateless persons, and persons of uncertain nationality. The figure in parentheses for the West German total in 1945 is an extrapolation.

categorized according to the year in which the deaths were reported. This explains the relatively constant death rate in West Germany on the one hand, and the rise of 1945–1946 in East Germany on the other hand. As it is possible to distinguish civilian from military deaths for West Germany, these figures are the more meaningful. The approximately 1.7 million military cases of death they show are interesting not so much on account of the absolute number, but rather on account of the distribution over the years: the deaths peak heavily in 1944–1945 and fall drastically thereafter. The civilian statistics show a comparable development. These findings will be important for the discussion of the Bacque theses.

One last set of statistics needs examination here: the census of 1961. The figures counterposed in Table 15 show differences but the general trend is the same. It should be remembered that the census shows only those who were still living in West Germany in 1961, and that the Maschke Commission classified POWs according to the last power holding them, whereas the 1961 census asked for the country that had held them the longest. Further, POWs were generally released into the zone occupied by the custodial power; for example, prisoners from the USSR were generally released in the Soviet zone, which is excluded from the above figures. Another point is that in the 1961 census the British Commonwealth was subsumed under the "Other" heading, "Britain" being understood *stricto sensu*, whereas the Maschke Commission included Commonwealth figures

Table 15
1961 Census

Custodial Power	1961 Census		Returned POWs	
	Absolute	%	Absolute	%
France	530,000	10.0	912,822	9.2
USSR	1,178,000	22.2	1,965,750	19.9
E. and S.E. Europe	217,000	4.1	195,972	2.0
Britain	1,151,000	21.7	3,633,746	36.8
USA	1,857,000	35.0	3,092,463	31.3
Other	369,000	7.0	75,325	0.8

Sources: Eberhard Gawatz, "Heimgekehrte Kriegsgefangene, Zivilinternierte, und Zivilverschleppte: Ergebnis der Volkszählung 1961," *Statistische Monatshefte Baden-Württemberg,* No. 4 (1964), 104–105 (here 105); "Ehemalige Kriegsgefangene, Zivilinternierte, und Zivilverschleppte: Ergebnis der Volkszählung am 6. Juni 1961," *Wirtschaft und Statistik* (1964), 20–22 and Appendix 6. For the number of returned POWs, see Table 9 in this essay.

in the British ones. Nevertheless, the proportional comparison of France, the United States, and the Soviet Union is important. The proportions of ex-POWs living in West Germany in 1961 correspond to the proportions of returning soldiers calculated by the Maschke Commission. A point that merits noting here (although it is not here evidenced) is that the figures for dates of repatriation given by the census and by Maschke also agree.[55]

So what can we say by way of summary? All postwar sources agree in their essentials with the findings of the Maschke Commission. It therefore seems justifiable to regard these findings as reliable. As has already been emphasized, this evaluation does not mean that the commission's figures are exact to the last digit; even the commission did not make any such claim. It is quite possible that the actual number of POWs, deaths, and returning soldiers varied by some tens of thousands from the cited figures, and yet these relatively small variations (small when calculated as a percentage of the total of 11 million POWs) would not call into question the meaningfulness of the Maschke figures.

Bacque and German Historiography

What do all these observations say for the theses of James Bacque and the fate of the POWs? What do we know about the number of DEFs and dead? In the following it will not be possible to check Bacque's arguments in all details. The discussion will be limited to a comparison of Bacque's construction of the figures and his presentation of the conditions in the Rheinwiesenlager with the sources available in Germany.

Let us proceed chronologically. One of Bacque's central claims is that at the end of May, 1945, the number of German prisoners in American hands was not—as officially claimed—about 2.9 million in all, but rather consisted of about 2.9 million POWs and about 1 million DEFs and some other groups not important in this context—altogether 3.9 million persons.[56] Contrary to Bacque's opinion, this information is nothing new, because in Volume X, Part 2, of the Maschke Commission report, published in 1973, it was already stated that on May 20, 1945, 2,884,762 Wehrmachtangehörige, excluding DEFs, were to be found in U.S. custody. It

55. Eberhard Gawatz, "Heimgekehrte Kriegsgefangene, Zivilinternierte und Zivilverschleppte: Ergebnisse der Volkszählung, 1961," *Statistische Monatschefte Baden-Württemberg*, No. 4 (1964), Appendix 6.

56. Bacque, *Der geplante Tod*, 67, 286 (*Other Losses*, 54–55).

was well known that the number of the registered POWs/DEFs was lower than the real figure. If the Bacque findings on prisoners in American custody in Europe as of June 2, 1945—about 3.9 million persons—are compared with the Maschke figures of 3.8 million for the same time, the similarity is obvious.[57]

In the same way, Bacque's descriptions of the conditions in the Rheinwiesenlager hardly qualify as fresh news. As has already been said many times, the criticism of the conditions for the period April to July, 1945, is on the whole justified. But Bacque's allegation that there were no reports is wrong. Not only German authors in numerous publications—some of them are cited in this essay—but also the French (Buisson report) have indulged in tossing accusations at the Americans.[58] Moreover, when Bacque tries—for example—to describe the overcrowding of those camps by taking the situation in Continental Central Prisoner of War Enclosure No. 18 as typical, it should be said that this was a permanent camp in Namur, Belgium, whereas the Rheinwiesenlager were transient camps in Germany.[59]

The background to the situation in the Rheinwiesenlager has been examined by other contributors to this volume and there remains only one question: Why does Bacque conceal one of the essential factors mentioned in all the reports, namely, mismanagement by the German camp administrators? Böhme cites a report from one camp to which Bacque also frequently refers: "In Thorée-les-Pins the camp administrators would organize boxing and football matches in the evenings. The participants could hardly walk, they were so excessively healthy. After these matches our emaciated bodies would smell the aroma drifting from the kitchens (roast meat), from which the participants would strengthen themselves." The Americans are said to have involved themselves so little with the internal affairs of the camps that in the Rheinwiesenlager of Dietersheim one German doctor managed to set up, unnoticed, a twelve-strong harem.[60]

In June and July, 1945, these camps were handed over to the French

57. Böhme, *In amerikanischer Hand: Europa,* 11; Bacque, *Der geplante Tod,* 67, 286 (*Other Losses,* 54–55).

58. Bacque, *Der geplante Tod,* 177 (*Other Losses,* 150). For a few examples of Germans who have written thus, see note 22 to this essay.

59. Bacque, *Der geplante Tod,* 50–51 (*Other Losses,* 34–35); Böhme, *In amerikanischer Hand: Europa,* 32–33.

60. Böhme, *In amerikanischer Hand: Europa,* 43–44, 155; Buisson, *Historique du service des prisonniers de guerre de l'Axe, 1943–1948* (Paris, 1948), 360.

and British. Bacque critically remarks that no reports of this handover are to be found in French archives. Yet even in the Buisson report, so heavily criticized by Bacque, there is a detailed account of the conditions in the camps and the measures the French took.[61]

An important aspect of the losses in French custody are the events of winter, 1945–1946. According to Bacque, from September, 1945, the ICRC had been complaining about conditions in the French camps, these complaints culminating in the warning that as many as 200,000 prisoners would die if not helped very soon.[62] In Bacque's construction of things, the Americans never afforded any help, so the prisoners eventually died.[63] But that is not so.

The report of the ICRC quite clearly states that on September 21, 1945, the ICRC turned to the Americans because the state of health of the inmates of the French camps gave cause for concern, and among other things, it was stated that some 200,000 prisoners would die if not soon helped. Thus far Bacque is correct. Nevertheless he "forgets" to inform the reader of the subsequent well-documented course of events. On October 6, 1945, Operation "A" began, whereby the Americans delivered sufficient food to raise the daily ration from 1,350 to approximately 2,000 calories, and—according to the ICRC—the danger was removed. In the course of the winter the Americans delivered additional clothing for the prisoners. The French government undertook further aid measures, known as Operation "F." When at the beginning of 1946 the ICRC again had to draw attention to the conditions of the French camps, the United States once again helped out with food. So, contrary to Bacque's claims, those of the 200,000 who were not returned to the Americans did not die. The ICRC report expressly states that thanks to American help, these people survived the winter.[64]

61. Bacque, *Der geplante Tod*, 105 (*Other Losses*, 88); Buisson, *Historique*, 107–10, 359–61.

62. Bacque, *Der geplante Tod*, 153, 104–12 (*Other Losses*, 129, 87–95).

63. *Ibid.*, 153, 118, 121–31, 148–49 (129, 100, 102–11, 125–26).

64. "Ces démarches eurent pour résultat une importante action de secours, qui fut appelée plus tard 'action A' (américaine). Elle débuta le 6 octobre; lorsq'elle prit fin, une vingtaine de jours après, l'état physique et moral des prisonniers s'était sérieusement amélioré, et la promesse du Gouvernement français de porter leur ration journalière à 2.000 calories permettait de les considérer comme hors de danger." See Conférence Internationale de la Croix-Rouge, *Rapport*, III, 115. "Grace a leur [the French and American governments'] aide rapide, la valeur des rations passe de 1.400 à 2.000 calories et la catastrophe fut évitée." *Ibid.*, I, 258. For a similar assessment, see Buisson, *Historique*, 43.

Bacque would have it that the 167,000 cited in French statistics as *per-dus pour des raisons divers* ("other losses") are in fact those who died in the French camps in the winter of 1945–1946. Ignoring for a moment the fact that the above points have already proved this impossible, it can also be pointed out that in 1949 the Friedensbüro Stuttgart stated that the 167,000 figure concerned children and old men from the Volkssturm, women, and the sick from the Rheinwiesenlager, who were all informally released from detention by the French.[65]

But what can be said about Bacque's central thesis that about 800,000 to 1,000,000 prisoners died in American custody? Supposedly these were soldiers who fled from the eastern front to save themselves by falling into the hands of the Western Allies. To begin with, as has already been mentioned, although such movements did indeed take place, their size is sufficiently well established that we can exclude the idea of an extra million hiding somewhere in the figures. Let us continue the train of thought. This million are supposed to have been interned together with other millions in the camps—probably the Rheinwiesenlager. But as these were transient camps, the alleged million would have had plenty of contact with other prisoners. In view of the then-prevailing situation in Germany, it is quite inconceivable that those who died later would have been unable to contact other prisoners or their families before, and it is also quite inconceivable that these prisoners would not have been reported as missing by their relatives. Considering the importance of certification of death for the relatives, the latter would have been compelled to ascertain the fates of the missing.

From all this it is obvious that the vast majority of any extra "million" missing in the West would definitely have been recorded in the registrations of 1947–1948 and 1950. But the registrations show nothing of the kind. The 1947–1948 registration, which unfortunately was not centrally evaluated, shows a proportion of only around 20–25 percent supposed missing in western Europe, including all parts of Germany. Against a total of 1.6 million missing persons overall, this amounts to only 300,000 to 400,000, by no means all of whom would have been in the American camps. Even clearer is the result of the registration of 1950. In this registration, of about 1.4 million still regarded as missing, only 1.1 percent—about 15,000 persons—were presumed disappeared in the entire world excluding Germany,

65. Bacque, *Der geplante Tod*, 146–49, 153 (*Other Losses*, 124–26, 129); Deutsches Büro für Friedensfragen, ed., *Das Schicksal*, 74–75.

the USSR, and eastern and southeastern Europe. Only 22.6 percent were presumed disappeared on German soil, of whom two-thirds had disappeared before 1945 and/or in the eastern parts of the Deutsches Reich. Thus, altogether, a mere 120,000 missing persons come into question for the entire world, including the four zones of occupation in Germany.

The results of the registrations clearly do not confirm Bacque's theses; however, let us continue with the argument. Even if the relatives had not known the approximate whereabouts of the missing, they would at least have needed a judicial declaration of death. So let us check the relevant statistics. Of the approximately 4.3 million war deaths and judicial declarations of death registered by the Deutsche Dienststelle, only about 1,771,000 are shown in West German statistics.[66] Of these only about 610,000 relate to 1945 (see Table 14). If we project this proportion onto the 4.3 million total, we come to about 1.47 million deaths during hostilities or captivity in 1945. Of these, some 600,000 to 700,000 occurred in the Soviet Union, and a further 680,000 took place in battles on the territory of the Deutsches Reich from January to May of 1945.[67] This leaves about 200,000 dead, which would include, among others, those who died in American camps. The Maschke Commission established that about 120,000 deaths occurred in camps outside the Soviet Union, of which the majority were in eastern and southeastern Europe in 1945 and 1946. Consequently, the maximum possible number of casualties in Western Allied hands is in the ten thousands—but not 800,000 or a million. Furthermore, large-scale military deaths could not have been hidden in civilian mortality figures because the numbers in the civilian statistics for 1945–1946 are only slightly higher than in normal years (Table 14). To repeat, it is certainly possible that some additional tens of thousands of deaths occurred, but a further 800,000 to 1,000,000 are not reconcilable with the facts. A minor sidelight here is Bacque's claim that the Germans in reality assumed their soldiers to be missing in the West. As evidence, he cites a political statement by Chancellor Adenauer during a parliamentary meeting on May 5, 1950.[68] If one reads the minutes of the *Deutscher Bundestag*

66. Deutsche Dienststelle [WASt], ed., *Arbeitsbericht 1986/87/88* (Berlin, 1989), 13–14.

67. Minimum exploitations on the basis of Böhme, *In sowjetischer Hand,* 149, and Wehrmacht figures, based on the following calculation: army dead (250,000) plus navy and air force dead amounts to *ca.* 300,000; army missing (1,000,000) plus navy and air force missing amounts to *ca.* 1,150,000, of whom at least one-third are assumed to be dead; total: 300,000 plus 380,000 amounts to 680,000. See Tables 1 and 3.

68. Bacque, *Der geplante Tod,* 181 (*Other Losses,* 153–54).

(Parliament), one finds that this statement related to a TASS report concerning the POWs in the Soviet Union.[69] So much for Bacque's careful use of sources.

Nevertheless, let us continue with Bacque's arguments. If indeed 726,000 soldiers had died in the American camps (Bacque's number excluding those who supposedly died in French custody or after discharge), what became of the bodies? As Arthur Smith has pointed out, the camps constituted a 200-kilometer strip along the Rhine in one of the most densely populated areas of Germany, a country which is densely populated anyway. Bacque's 726,000 dead would mean roughly 3,600 dead per kilometer, or 5,800 per mile—better than one corpse per foot. Yet despite the widespread construction work carried out after the war, not a single one of these legions of dead was found.[70] Once again, it becomes apparent that Bacque's theses are untenable.

Despite everything, let us follow Bacque's argument still further. According to his construction of events, about 1 million fewer soldiers were taken into Soviet captivity than has been assumed up to now. For reasons already given, we are unusually well informed about the state of affairs there. If the established 3.1 million soldiers captured by the Soviets were in fact to amount to only 2.1 million, then after deduction of the approximately 2 million returned soldiers, there would remain a mere 100,000 or so who died in Soviet captivity, which is obviously an absurd result. Of the soldiers captured at Stalingrad alone, we know that more than 100,000 lost their lives. So in this respect as well, the theses of Bacque cannot be reconciled with the results of research. One could nevertheless try to "find" the further million by claiming that the total of all captives was not 11 but 12 million, but as was said earlier, the maximum of 11 million is well established.

A final piece of evidence is the number of returning soldiers. The 1961 census shows that of the 3.1 million POWs released by the Americans and not transferred to other custodial powers, about 1.9 million were still living in West Germany in 1961 (see Table 15). According to Bacque, of these 3.1 million some 800,000 (minimum) would have died and only about 2.3 million been released. Thus, in the sixteen years between the end of the

69. *Verhandlungen des Deutschen Bundestages*, 1. Wahlperiode 1949, *Stenographische Berichte*, III (Bonn, 1950), 2253, 2281.

70. Bacque, *Der geplante Tod*, Appendix 1, 258 (*Other Losses*, 186); Arthur L. Smith, "Der geplante Tod?" in *Deutschland zwischen Krieg und Frieden: Beiträge zur Politik und Kultur im 20. Jahrhundert*, ed. Karl Dietrich Bracher, Manfred Funke, and Hans-Peter Schwarz (Bonn, 1990), 108–16 (here 114–15).

war and the census, only 400,000 of the released prisoners would have died or emigrated outside West Germany (East Germany, Austria). When one considers that of 910,000 prisoners released from French custody, only some 530,000 (a little over half) were still alive in 1961, then it again becomes apparent that the hypothesis is absurd. Here again Bacque's theses fail to accommodate the facts.

Against all these German soruces, Bacque might argue that his figures are from primary sources, whereas the German sources are secondary. First of all, most of the German sources cited in this article are primary sources themselves. Second, primary sources are often more valuable than secondary ones, but this is not necessarily the case. Sometimes figures compiled later, with distance and care, are more exact than hastily pulled-together primary statistics, and it is like that here. Third, if many figures match and only one does not, it is only rational to question the rogue figure.

How can this rogue figure be explained? Where is the central mistake in Bacque's argument? Essentially, he assumes that the conditions that admittedly prevailed in 16 of the 200 camps for a certain period (April to June or July, 1945, according to camp) in fact extended to all 200 American camps for the whole period 1945–1946, a basis of procedure that can be proved false.

Nothing in what I have said here is meant to deny that there were considerable cruelties against the POWs. The French figures in particular tend toward the lower casualty limit, rather than the realistic number. Likewise, the number of deaths in the American camps may well have exceeded the roughly 4,500 established by the Maschke Commission. Had Bacque claimed that, instead of approaching 5,000, some 50,000 prisoners had died, the available material would hardly have sufficed to disprove his claim. However, a group of people as large as the 800,000 to 1,000,000 he postulates would have to be traceable somewhere in the various German statistics. From the fact that this is not the case, it can justifiably be concluded that the theses of James Bacque are false.

Some Reflections on the Maschke Commission

Rolf Steininger

A T THE END of World War II many civilians and soldiers knew what had happened to Russian prisoners of war in German hands: they had suffered an overall loss rate of 60 percent. They had died of starvation and disease or had been deliberately executed or liquidated on orders peculiar to Operation Barbarossa. Out of 5.7 million Red Army prisoners, only 2.4 million had survived.

Now it was tit for tat: long before the collapse of German resistance on both the eastern and western fronts, it was known what fate would befall German troops captured by the Red Army. Those who survived the seemingly endless marches and rides in freight trains would face eternal frost and suffering in Siberia's wasteland. The expectation of subhuman conditions in Soviet POW camps caused German units to operate in a manner that would make their capture by American or British forces at least a possibility. Anything was better than falling into Russian hands.

Many succeeded. In the end the Western Allies had on hand 7,614,794 POWs—a figure officially released in June, 1945. The Allies were not in any way prepared to accommodate properly this tremendous number of POWs. We all know the result, or at least we thought we knew it. The handling of the prisoners in American hands was disorganized, to put it mildly. Hundreds of thousands of the captives were put in open fields surrounded by barbed wire; these were called "Prisoner of War Temporary [or Transient] Enclosures" (PWTE). The worst of them were the big "Rhine meadow camps"; living conditions were appalling, but relatively few prisoners died—between 3,000 and 4,000 according to official American and German sources. That was lamentable in itself, but absolutely nothing compared with what happened in the East; out of 3,155,000 German POWs in Russian hands, more than a million died. Hundreds of thousands did not even reach the camps, where conditions were utterly horrible. And whereas the Western Allies had discharged their prisoners by 1948, the Russians kept theirs. Only during the Moscow visit of Chancellor Adenauer of West Germany in September, 1955, did the Soviets agree to release those remaining in Soviet camps in return for reopening diplomatic relations between the Federal Republic and the Soviet Union, and an exchange of ambassadors. In 1956 the last German POW returned home—eleven years after the end of hostilities.

One year later, the West German government set up an official commission to write the history of the German POWs. It took the "Scientific Commission for the History of German Prisoners of War" nearly sixteen years to do the job with a series of twenty-two books (See Appendix B for a complete bibliography). This exhaustive study covered subjects such as the following:

1. German soldiers in Yugoslavian captivity, including their treatment by partisans.

2. German soldiers accused of misdeeds by the Yugoslav authorities—trials, sentencing, and execution, as well as a record of those who perished while in captivity.

3. German prisoners of war in the USSR (three volumes), their camp life psychology, ranks, structure of inmates, similarities and differences in facing their status, religious life, efforts at maintaining solidarity, and political education.

4. The major issue of hunger for German soldiers in Soviet captivity, the rationing of food, hunger strikes, theft of food, denunciation, types of dystrophy, complaints about and control of available foodstuffs, dysentery, and starvation.

5. Forced labor as a major issue for German POWs in the USSR, prisoners' working to atone for the damage done to Russia by the German army, "socialist competition," areas of labor camps (the central, eastern, and Volga regions, the Urals, western Siberia, south-central Asia, and Kasakhstan), and compensation for work performed.

6. German soldiers and civilians in Soviet penal camps, their selection for sentencing to those camps, the structure of the camps, including their supervision by the Soviet organ for state security, and location of camps within the Soviet Union, including the special camps

of Vladimir, Verchneuralsk, Aleksandrovsk, and Novocerkassk, and the clinical camp, Kazan.

7. Cultural and antifascist education within the camps.

8. German prisoner deaths and repatriation from Soviet control.

9. German prisoners in Polish and Czechoslovakian control, their living conditions, mortality rate, mail privileges, medical care, and work assignments.

10. German POWs in American custody in the United States, their living conditions, health, assistance from religious organizations, attempts at reeducation, and work schedule.

11. German POWs in American custody in Europe, effects of unconditional surrender on German units, forced return of German prisoners to East European powers, aspects of capture, subsequent care, religious life, mortality and illness rates, and discharge of prisoners.

12. German POWs in British custody, their treatment in different parts of Europe, reeducation efforts, living conditions, and work assignments in camps in Europe and overseas.

13. German POWs under Dutch, French, and Belgian control.

14. Spirit and life-style of German troops captured by their Western adversaries; adult education programs, camp newspapers, public performances, and creativity.

15. History of German war prisoners, their statistical administration, visits to camps by International Red Cross representatives, and the fate of female prisoners.

16. Recollections and personal diaries of individual prisoners of war.

The Maschke volumes have a long and complicated publication history. When the German Parliament passed the legislation that financed the Maschke volumes, it also stipulated that the Foreign Office had to review each and every volume before publication in order not to "provoke" foreign countries. During a debate in the German Bundestag in 1969, Foreign Minister Willy Brandt explained the rationale for placing the Maschke volumes only in research libraries as a source collection with an archival character, instead of making them available to the general reading public: a massive publication of the material might lead people abroad to think that the Germans had a "political agenda" and wanted to "unleash" a broad discussion of the POW issue at home and abroad. This might "open old wounds among many of those who were part of it and would not have served the foreign policy of reconciliation [of] the Federal Republic well." [1]

This debate about preserving the record of the German POWs also dealt with the sensitive issue of German *Vergangenheitsbewältigung* ("mastering the past"). Brandt was asked by the conservative representative Dr. Czaja whether he agreed that an "objective record" of the "crimes against humanity" committed against Germans would help to "clear the atmosphere" and whether evidence of such crimes needed to be carefully collected. Brandt agreed in principle but reminded the German Parliament that Germans must "resist the temptation to dismiss all those things for which Germans are rightly blamed by pointing the finger towards the misdeeds of others." Brandt added that the decision had been made some time ago to decide about opening up the Maschke documentation to the public once the project had been completed. [2] Bacque characteristically dwells on the idea of not "provoking a public discussion," but never mentions Brandt's sensitivity about engaging in recrimination by finger pointing. Just as characteristically, he buries in an oblique reference in an endnote the fact that the complete set of twenty-two Maschke volumes had been publicly available for some *seventeen years* at the time of his writing *Other Losses*. [3]

The Maschke Commission officially completed its work at the end of 1972 and opened the twenty-two volumes without any restrictions to the general public. Wolfgang Benz is correct in criticizing the "secrecy" (*Geheimniskrämerei*) around the work of the commission, which "hurt the reception of the research results of the POW Commission." As a result of the "unfortunate politics with the publication," the general public never became widely cognizant of the fact that "historians dealt early and thoroughly with the history of the POWs." Benz concludes that even though recent archival discoveries have been made on the history of German

1. *Verhandlungen des Deutschen Bundestages,* 5. Wahlperiode, 1969, *Stenographische Berichte,* LXIX (Bonn, 1969), 12630; also quoted in the introduction by Wolfgang Benz in Wolfgang Benz and Angelika Schardt, eds., *Kriegsgefangenschaft: Berichte über das Leben in Gefangenenlagern der Alliierten von Otto Engelbert, Kurt Glaser, Hans Jonitz, und Heinz Pust* (Munich, 1991), 10–11. The author and the editors are grateful to Rüdiger Overmans for providing them with these valuable sources. James Bacque also cites this passage, translated slightly differently, in *Other Losses: An Investigation into the Mass Deaths of German Prisoners of War at the Hands of the French and Americans After World War II* (Toronto, 1989), 154–55.

2. *Stenographische Berichte,* 12630–31.

3. Bacque, *Other Losses,* 225 n 29, see also 154–55.

POWs, they were never substantial enough to correct the basic results, or even most of the details, of the Maschke Commission's essential findings. Benz also bemoans the fact that the massive Maschke documentation was for a time restricted to research libraries, with two unfortunate results: first, it opened the door wide for conspiracy theorists like Bacque to discredit the work of the scientific commission; second, from the very beginning it provided vast opportunities for mythmaking.[4]

Bacque himself is one of the mythmakers when he perverts the sensitivities of the German Foreign Office by charging that the "Maschke series was not allowed to inflame the public." He construes a "cover-up" arising out of the West German "fear of criticizing the USA and France." He goes a step farther in his American-edition Epilogue when he denounces the historians of the Maschke Commission as "client-academics" who "tamely published a series that reproduced lies by the French and Americans, omitting vast tracts of history, statistics and experience that millions of ex-prisoners and their families knew were crucially important."[5] Here, of course, he oversteps the boundaries of mythmaking and enters the territory of libel with his attacks against the professional integrity of the first-rate and thorough historical investigations of the Maschke Commission in particular and the entire German historical profession in general.

German historians have largely ignored Bacque's book as the work of an amateur not worthy of their attention. Or, they come to such devastating conclusions as Wolfgang Benz's: "It is a book full of negligence—written with the steamy zealousness of one looking for revelations—in which individuals, writers and officials are attacked as being unobjective or devious, which operates with across-the-board conspiracy theories, and which relentlessly mistakes repetition for being the proof of the pudding."[6]

To make the point absolutely clear: After the horrendous crimes of the Nazis, the foreign policy of the Federal Republic during the postwar period was indeed directed toward reconciliation with neighbors and old enemies. While Chancellor Konrad Adenauer directed his attention to the West (France and the United States), Willy Brandt concentrated on making amends with the Eastern European neighbors of Germany. Brandt was rightly very sensitive to the possible political repercussions of warming up mutual German and Soviet recriminations about ugly treatment of POWs

4. Benz and Schardt, eds., *Kriegsgefangenschaft,* 11.
5. Bacque, *Other Losses,* 150, 155–56; Bacque, *Other Losses* (Los Angeles, 1991), 177.
6. See the Benz introduction in Benz and Schardt, eds., *Kriegsgefangenschaft,* 11.

during World War II, especially during the active phase of his *Ostpolitik,* from the late 1960s to the early 1970s, when normalizing relations with Poland and the Soviet Union would not have been helped by trumpeting out the "crimes" of Soviet treatment of German POWs.[7] Brandt may have erred on the side of timidity, but there was certainly no "whitewash" intended here.

One American historian does not have it completely right when he concludes from the publication history of the Maschke volumes that "perhaps the social-democratic (SPD) government of Helmut Schmidt did not want to remind the German people of the suffering of millions of their sons, and thus reopen old wounds and possibly upset former enemies, whereas the Christian Democrats appeared less troubled by such concerns." Nevertheless, one has to agree with him when he adds that "no effort was spared to delve as deeply and accurately as possible into the conditions that befell several million members of the German armed forces."[8]

Yet concerning the POWs in American hands, Bacque now calls the massive work of the Maschke Commission "a soothing series," a kind of Cold War cover-up operation.[9] The Americans "supplied the Small Number" (of deaths); the Germans accepted it "because they felt guilt about their camps, or about the war, or because the Small Number reduced the evidence of their humiliation. . . . Within a few years to doubt the Small Number had become an implied treachery, for any good German who doubted Americans was *ipso facto* an enemy of both states. So the Americans were in effect forgiven without even being accused."[10]

But this was definitely not the way the commission worked. How then did it work? Its chairman, Erich Maschke, stressed the point of international cooperation. The commission made use of the records of the capturing powers (*Akten den Gewahrsamsmächte*). But that did not mean very much with regard to American records. In 1961 the commission addressed

7. Gerhard Weinberg comes to similar conclusions about the relationship of the Maschke volumes' publication history with Brandt's *Ostpolitik* in his review of Bacque's American edition in the *Washington Post Book World,* July 7, 1991. Bacque (with the help of Colonel Ernest Fisher) responds to Weinberg's critical review by trying to refute Weinberg's "errors" by the crude device of simply repeating once again old Bacque charges against the U.S. Army; as is typical of him, Bacque does not deal in his letter with Weinberg's valid point about Brandt's *Ostpolitik.* See Washington *Post,* August 25, 1991.

8. Martin Sorge, *The Other Price of Hitler's War: German Military and Civilian Losses Resulting from World War II* (New York, 1986), 81–82.

9. Bacque, *Other Losses,* 157.

10. *Ibid.,* 143.

the United States Army, which then sent printed material, photocopies of written orders, camp manuals, regulations on how to treat POWs, and so forth. It was enough material with regard to the camps, *enough* to paint a complete picture, as the commission says (*"Unterlagen . . . von seltener Vollständigkeit"*).[11]

Bacque's main accusation is that the United States Army and the French army casually annihilated about one million men, most of them in American camps. According to Bacque, several hundred thousands died in the notorious Rhine meadow camps. What does the commission say about the conditions and the death rate in these camps? The commission printed testimony from dozens of ex-prisoners (an early example of what is now called "oral history"). These reports confirm that, indeed, the camps were harsh, even brutal. The commission came to the conclusion that the American policy of punishment was spread to the POWs, that there was cruel indifference, but that there was an explanation: "It was the time when the Allies for the first time saw with their own eyes the horrors of the concentration camps, it was the time of collective guilt of the German people." However, according to Kurt W. Böhme, the historian of the German POWs in American hands in Europe, "this lasted only a few weeks and was followed by a time when they realized that they were on a crusade to put an end to nazism, not to kill people who were victims of this ideology."[12]

How many POWs died? Were there mass deaths or not? The Maschke Commission figures for the six worst camps (Bad Kreuznach–Bretzenheim, Remagen-Sinzig, Rheinberg, Heidesheim, Wickrathberg, and Büderich, together holding a total of 557,000 POWs on May 8, 1945): 3,053 dead according to United States Army sources, or 4,537 dead according to local authorities. If one accepts these figures the death rate was *ca.* 1 percent, compared with a mortality rate of 20–25 percent in Russian camps. The commission's conclusion: "There were no mass deaths in the west." Reports from other German local authorities confirm this.[13]

At one point the commission had doubts with regard to these figures. Reports and diaries of ex-prisoners differed, figures from local authorities differed, there was no complete picture of all the camps; but still, "even if

11. Erich Maschke *et al.*, *Die deutschen Kriegsgefangenen des Zweiten Weltkrieges: Eine Zusammenfassung*, Zur Geschichte der deutschen Kriegsgefangenen im Zweiten Weltkrieg, Vol. XV (Munich, 1974), 50.

12. Kurt W. Böhme, *Die deutschen Kriegsgefangenen in amerikanischer Hand: Europa* (Munich, 1973), 139, 176, Vol. X, Pt. 2 of Maschke Commission.

13. *Ibid.*, 203.

we accepted a death rate double as high, *i.e.*, 9,000, it would still be much lower than in the East and would not justify speaking of mass deaths." [14]

Was the commission's report a whitewash with only a modest publication to avoid provoking a public discussion which would open old wounds and would not serve the reconciliation efforts of the Federal Republic's foreign policy, as Bacque charges? [15] My answer is no.

The commission collected a huge amount of useful material; it did a good job. There is excellent material in the twenty-two volumes and part-volumes; the series is still regarded as the authoritative study of the German POWs and probably will be for a long time to come. But still, with Bacque's publication a few questions call for answers. The fact remains that members of the Maschke Commission never went to the archives in Washington to see for themselves; they relied on the material they got from the United States Army. When, in 1980, Paul Carell and Günter Böddeker published their book on POWs in Germany, they were convinced that POWs in the Rhine meadow camps had "died like flies." [16] There was no public outcry over such a statement then, even though "died like flies" was an expression the commission had used only in connection with German prisoners in Russian hands, who had indeed died that way, many before even reaching the camps.

Carell and Böddeker did not provide any new evidence, but relied mainly on the Maschke volumes. Therefore I felt quite satisfied with the commission's work and summarized it in 1981 in a book, coauthored with Heribert Schwan, on Germany in 1945. [17] In that book we devoted an entire chapter to the Rhine meadow camps. Also, for the first time, this human tragedy was illustrated with color photos, taken by soldiers of the U.S. Army Signal Corps in 1945. [18] I had discovered this previously classified American film material in 1978. Here were pictures of all the POWs cramped in the camps, but no evidence of mass deaths or mass graves. Our documentary with that material was shown on German television in 1979; after the publication of Bacque's book it was screened again in Germany

14. *Ibid.*, 205.

15. Bacque, *Other Losses*, 159.

16. Paul Carell and Günter Böddeker, *Die Gefangenen: Leben und Überleben deutscher Soldaten hinter Stacheldraht* (Berlin, 1980), 160. Although the authors seem to have had some doubts on the matter of mass deaths, they end up saying there were none (p. 149).

17. Heribert Schwan and Rolf Steininger, *Als der Krieg zu Ende ging* (Frankfurt am Main, 1981).

18. *Ibid.*, 104–109.

in 1989. Then and now, ex-prisoners confirmed all the stories about the camps, but gave no evidence of mass deaths.

Still, some questions remain.

To begin with, there is the "disarmed enemy forces" (DEF) business on the American side (about 1.6 million prisoners). For Bacque, the reclassification of German POWs as DEFs was a precondition for the alleged mass killings. The British did not use the classification DEF for prisoners whom they knew they could not treat according to the letter of the Geneva Convention; instead, they invented the category "surrendered enemy personnel" (SEPs—about 2.4 million) to distinguish their postsurrender POWs from the ones previously taken. The commission knew of the categories DEF and SEP. The commission explained, "With millions of prisoners the Allies were not able to treat these people according to the Geneva Convention." The result was "extreme conditions" in the camps, and "the death rate was commensurate." But the commission added, "Whoever says this was done on purpose does not take into account the difficult situation of suddenly having millions of POWs on hand in a country which was destroyed." [19]

Was this a whitewash? In Volume XIII of the series, one can read that the International Committee of the Red Cross (ICRC) insisted on treating the POWs according to the Geneva Convention and did succeed. "And indeed, the Western Allies energetically tried to treat prisoners according to the Geneva Convention." ("Und in der Tat haben sich die westlichen Siegerstaaten mit Nachdruck um die Einhaltung der Bestimmungen der Genfer Konvention bemüht.")

Further, the commission confirms that there was a serious food shortage in the Western world; the Western Allied armies lacked supplies. Bacque says there was no such thing—except for Germany. Bacque is wrong: there was a food shortage. Dozens of reports written at the time confirm this. But according to Bacque, many strange things happened. He describes requests for supplies for the German prisoners being denied, he relates stories about help being kept away from the camps.

For example, there is the story of the YMCA, which, like the Red Cross, visited camps for prisoners, helping them irrespective of their nationality, race, or creed. Bacque says that when the YMCA wrote to the State Department in July, 1945, proposing to pay for all goods received from the United States Army so that it could feed German POWs in American

19. Maschke *et al.*, *Zusammenfassung*, 238, 246.

camps in France, the army refused permission. According to Bacque, the documents to prove this are missing. I think we should not accept Bacque's charges, but rather should look into the records of the YMCA. There is nothing on this matter in the commission's series, despite the fact that it used YMCA material. So here is one of the questions that remains open.

Even more to be questioned is the story surrounding the work of the International Committee of the Red Cross (ICRC). For instance, the United States War Department banned all mail to or from all German POWs in American hands on May 4, 1945. When the Red Cross suggested a plan for restoring mail to the prisoners in July, it was rejected. I would like to know the reason for that. There is nothing on this in the commission's series. The British reopened mail communications during the course of July and August, 1945. There was no Red Cross in the American zone; in the British and even French zones the ICRC and the local German Red Cross were operating. Perhaps the reason for all this appears in the files of the Red Cross. Where are those files?

In the same vein, Bacque charges that the United States government refused to allow the ICRC inside the camps to visit the prisoners, in direct defiance of American obligations under the Geneva Convention. When the German government began to disintegrate toward the end of the war, the United States authorized the Swiss government to take over from the Germans the role of protecting power. This step was apparently meant to ensure that the ICRC would continue to visit the camps and report to the Swiss government after the war. With May 8, V-E Day, and no German government, the State Department—according to Bacque—no longer accepted the Swiss government as protecting power and informed the ICRC that there was no point in continued visits, as there was no protecting power to report to, adding at the same time that the United States would continue to treat the prisoners "in accordance with the provisions of the Geneva Convention." [20]

If hundreds of thousands of POWs were dying in those camps—and I am absolutely convinced that this was *not* the case—there must be evidence of it in the Red Cross reports. The reports are vital to our problem. So again the question is, Where are the files of the Red Cross?

According to Bacque, the ICRC was still refusing in 1988 to release the prison-camp reports to private researchers. But after intervention by the German Foreign Office, the Maschke Commission was allowed to use these reports, altogether numbering about 5,000 and including 2,500 re-

20. Bacque, *Other Losses*, 70.

ports on French camps for the period 1944–1948, 570 on American camps for 1944–1945, and 310 on British camps for 1943–1948 (there are no reports on Russian camps, since the Soviet Union had not signed the Geneva Convention). The commission says that these reports were of "great importance" (*erhöhte Bedeutung*) to its work.

It strikes me that in the reports from March and April, 1945, there apparently was no word of alleged mass dying of German POWs. If prisoners really were "dying like flies," I would like to know where those reports are, if they ever existed. Perhaps in the archive of the ICRC in Geneva? (I have asked the Red Cross in Geneva for access to their archives, with no answer as of this writing.) The same applies to the fact that the commission did not find reports dated after May 8.

In summary, there is excellent material in the twenty-two volumes published by the Maschke Commission—although Bacque makes very few references to it. Based on some 45,000 diaries and personal testimonies by prisoners, most of them written years after the event, the commission's findings cover a wide range of POW history. There is one basic message: even though the conditions in some American and French camps at the end of the war were appalling, most of the missing men were the responsibility of the Russians. The commission found no evidence to believe of mass killings in Western camps. I, too, see no evidence of mass killings of German POWs/DEFs in American hands in Europe, let alone Bacque's million. There is enough evidence to show that Bacque is absolutely wrong. Nevertheless, with the publication of his sensationalist account, a few new questions have been raised and wait to be answered by historians. We should try to answer them—and in the process rewrite the entire history of the prisoners of war during and after World War II, not just the story of the German POWs.

III

Conspiratorial History

A British Variety of Pseudohistory

Thomas M. Barker

J AMES BACQUE, a novelist by trade, has clearly succeeded in roiling professional historiographical waters in North America with his sensational, headline-catching, albeit inexcusably tendentious *Other Losses*. An analogous, virtually contemporaneous case in the United Kingdom deserves to be brought to the attention of the reading public in the Anglophone New World, the press of which has largely ignored it. To be sure, Nikolai Dimitrievich Tolstoy-Miloslavsky, whose aptitude for writing history is as dubious as that of his Canadian counterpart, has experienced consequences of a kind that Bacque will never have to face. Unlike Dwight D. Eisenhower, one of the three Britons falsely accused by Tolstoy of having committed a war crime after the May, 1945, armistice is still alive and can speak in his own defense. Determined to restore his personal honor, and resorting to his nation's formidably strict libel laws, Brigadier A. R. W. "Toby" Low, now Lord Aldington, has sought and obtained unprecedented redress in court—although his victory is most likely to prove Pyrrhic in a financial sense. The parallels with the North American controversy are not only intriguing per se, but one may draw from them certain broader conclusions regarding the craft of historian.

Tolstoy's personal background is highly germane to the publicity storm he has raised in his native land. Born in 1935 in Maidstone, the son of a White Russian refugee who became a distinguished barrister, and the grandson of a Cossack officer who fought the Reds, he is three-quarters English by blood, through his mother and paternal grandmother. Yet, having frequented émigré salons in London as a youth, he has identified strongly with the former noble dynasty represented by his patronym.[1] He

---

1. See Nikolai Tolstoy, *Tolstoys: Twenty-Four Generations* (New York, 1983).

is only remotely related to Russia's literary titan, and the comital title by which the popular press regularly refers to him has no legal basis at all—as his most persistent historian-critic, Professor Robert Knight of Loughborough University, has been at pains to emphasize. Tolstoy received his public school education at Wellington, a military-preparatory brand of establishment college. He also served briefly in the British army in conjunction with a spell at Sandhurst (an institution as exigent as West Point) but was "invalided out" after one term. His subsequent military experience has been limited to historical reenactments. He received an honors M.A. degree in politics from Trinity College in Dublin (1954) and taught for a few years on the secondary level.

Although Britain's *Who's Who* has so far failed to list him despite his unquestionable visibility as a writer, Tolstoy responded in 1979 to an invitation from the United States publication *Contemporary Authors,* and filled out a questionnaire. One of his answers to the editors' queries provides a clue of sorts to his motivations:

> My prime interest has always been in history of all periods and in the widest sense, including the subdivision now known as sociology. My aim is to amuse and, I hope, to enlighten. When writing *The Secret Betrayal,* I was spurred on through many difficult years by a determination to honor and vindicate the memory of so many of my unfortunate compatriots who suffered appalling barbarities and indignities, whilst "radical chic" progressive writers in the West praised their persecution and exulted over the sufferings of their fellow humans. My family has lived a privileged existence for many centuries; I suppose it is time to repay the debt.[2]

Tolstoy's "revisionist" account of Churchill's and Roosevelt's dealings with Stalin, which appeared in Great Britain under the title *Victims of Yalta* and was succeeded by *Stalin's Secret War,* was enthusiastically received in émigré and other right-wing circles. Conversely, the scholarly response to these demonstrations of noblesse oblige was a resounding silence.[3] Although this fact was hardly an advertisement for someone whom some

---

2. *Contemporary Authors,* Vols. 81–84, ed. Frances Carol Locher (Detroit, 1979), 566.
3. *The Secret Betrayal* was published in New York by Scribner's and *The Victims of Yalta* in London by Hodder and Stoughton. *Stalin's Secret War* appeared in London in 1981 under a Johnathan Cape imprint. Among various extreme statements found in the latter book is the assertion that homosexuality and treason are "symbiotically" related; see pp. 334–36. If the *Book Review Index* is correct, not one of Tolstoy's historiographical forays has ever been reviewed in a major scholarly journal with but a single exception (see note 5). However, he has attracted regular notice in the more serious popular British periodicals such as the *Economist,* the *Observer,* the *Spectator,* and the *Times* (London) *Literary Supplement.*

British journalists still label a "historian," it was proof for Tolstoy—
Bacque's attitude is similar—of the clannishness of the professionals.
However, an article published in the voguish intellectual organ *Encounter*
enabled him to flesh out his charge of a "Klagenfurt Conspiracy." [4]

In 1986, Century Hutchinson of London published a full-blown version
of Tolstoy's theory, a volume entitled *The Minister and the Massacres.* [5]
Tolstoy's chief point was that the late Harold Macmillan (Lord Stockton),
in 1945 resident minister at Allied Forces Headquarters (AFHQ) in Caserta
(Naples), a close friend and political adviser of Field Marshal Harold
Alexander's, plotted with General Sir Charles Keightley, commander of
the British Fifth Corps (which had just occupied Austria's southern prov-
ince of Carinthia), to return some 26,000 escaped Yugoslav quislings—
Slovene White Guards, Serbian Chetniks, and Croatian Ustashi—plus
43,000 Nazi-employed "Cossacks" to their Yugoslav and Soviet home-
lands. [6] This was done, Tolstoy maintained, in deliberate defiance of government policy and of orders from Alexander as well as from his subordinate, General Richard McCreery, commander of the British Eighth Army
(Allied Fifteenth Army Group). Both officers were also said to have been
systematically deceived about what was happening.

Macmillan and Keightley purportedly knew for certain that the surrendered enemy personnel they planned to pack off—the only Germans involved were some officer and noncommissioned-officer cadres—would be
killed by Tito and Stalin, as indeed a large proportion of them later were.
Among the victims of the intrigue, according to Tolstoy, were several
thousand legally exempt "White Russians." The scheme was supposedly
hatched in a brief, tête-à-tête meeting at the Klagenfurt airport on May 13,
1945. Aldington, the battle-tested, highly decorated Fifth Corps chief of
staff, was depicted as an accomplice in the commission of a hideous crime

4. *Encounter,* LX (May, 1983), 24–37.

5. The book appeared only in Great Britain. The *English Historical Review,* which had
previously (1980) critiqued but one of Tolstoy's books—the meticulously annotated, albeit
entirely anecdotal *Half Mad Minister: Thomas Pitt, 2nd Baron Camelford* (New York,
1979)—did take note of *The Minister and the Massacres.* Reviewer Stephen K. Pavlowitch
characterized Tolstoy as being "obsessed" and his work as unconvincing. See *English Historical Review,* CIV (1989), 274–76. The general reluctance in the U.K. to consider Tolstoy's
earlier "scholarly" ventures may well have been due to legal as well as to quality considerations. However, the attack upon the aged Macmillan was apparently hard to ignore.

6. The use of quotes around the word *Cossacks* indicates that such persons were by no
means entirely Cossack in the strict ethnic-sociocultural sense. Other examples of murky
usage in Tolstoy's writings are "White Russians" and "Caucasians" (in reality a mélange of
ethnic groups from the high terrain of the Caucasus).

instigated by Macmillan because the latter was being blackmailed by the NKVD. A further allegation was that after the war official British records were deliberately expurgated to remove proof of what had occurred.

Aldington, in 1945 a thirty-one-year-old law graduate whose much-reputed officer father fought in the First World War and died at sea in the Second, left Carinthia and military service nine days after Macmillan's visit—which did in fact take place—and began an illustrious career in Parliament and business. He served at one point as deputy chairman of the Conservative party and was granted his peerage during Macmillan's prime ministership. By the 1980s he was, among other things, chairman of the Sun Alliance Assurance Company and warden or chief trustee of his alma mater, Winchester College. In the former capacity he put his signature to the rejection of an appeal for payment of a £50,000 accidental-death-benefit claim made by a policy beneficiary, a widow with a dying son. This act was of a routine, technical character, a purely formal approval of investigators' judgment that Sun Alliance was not obliged to settle since the insured person, who died (1975) by slipping in his bathroom, had failed to report to the company the fact that he had become an alcoholic.

Nevertheless, the widow's indignant brother, Nigel Watts, son of a diplomat, Harrow graduate, and Kent property renovator, blamed Aldington and began a long vendetta replete with personal harassment. Advertising in the *Times* (London) for a researcher possessing data on "Toby Low" and the 1945 repatriations from Carinthia that he knew, by chance, had involved Aldington, Watts received a reply from Tolstoy. The result was a pamphlet, "War Crimes and the Wardenship of Winchester College," in effect anticipating *The Minister and the Massacres* and contending that as a war criminal, Aldington was unfit to serve Winchester. In the spring of 1987, Watts distributed Tolstoy's unsigned text in an edition of 10,000 copies to the staff, parents of students, "old boys" (alumni), and other people associated with the college, to the villagers of Aldington's titular domain, to the press (traditionally hostile to "Mac the Knife" Macmillan), and to members of both houses of Parliament.

Lonely, confused, nonagenarian Macmillan refused public comment before he passed away (December 29, 1986), but according to his biographer, Alistair Horne, suffered greatly over charges that he could not refute due to poor health and a puzzling failure to gain access to official records.[7] However, after considerable hesitation, the younger (if also el-

7. *Spectator,* October 8, 1988, p. 88. Since Macmillan's death, Horne has fully succeeded in clarifying the matter and in demonstrating, as do Anthony Cowgill and his research

derly) Aldington undertook his libel action against Watts, Tolstoy, and his publisher. For its part, Century Hutchinson quickly deemed it juridically and financially prudent to resolve the matter in private—£30,000 changed hands—and to withdraw Tolstoy's opus from the market.

A Rumpole-style, nine-week jury trial in the High Court ensued. Conducted by heavy-duty, immensely costly Queen's Counsels and presided over by colorful, occasionally outspoken Judge Michael Davies, it was marked by a multinational parade of aging ex-quislings, angry outbursts, tears, much travail for Aldington, and in the view of most observers, a witness-box demeanor on Tolstoy's part that did little to advance his cause. As time passed, the jurors, directed by the technically fastidious Davies, seemed to acquire the self-confidence required to render a clear decision in a case of enormous—indeed, almost unique—complexity.

On November 29, 1989, the citizen's panel found in Aldington's favor. Despite the judge's advice to exercise a degree of moderation, it set damages—the verdict was based upon the pamphlet only—at £1,500,000 and obliged Watts and Tolstoy to pay another £550,000 in costs (their own expenses are thought to have been almost as high). It was a staggering sum, roughly treble the largest previous award in British legal history.[8] The earlier settlement with Century Hutchinson, which conceded libel and hence bore upon the trial, also imposes what from a North American perspective seems to be an especially stringent rule: the book itself is banned. If libraries allow it to circulate, they do so at the risk of civil suit; as with obscene works, copies must remain under lock and key, and are available only upon special application.

The decision, based upon a monumental accumulation of unpublished source material and the testimony of surviving British protagonists, was upheld by the Court of Appeal on July 19, 1990.[9] Thus Tolstoy, who at the end had to act as his own counsel, has been forced into bankruptcy. (Providentially, the still-outspoken, unchastised Watts has assets only in his

---

team (discussed later), that the resident minister's brief visit to Klagenfurt (for which there is virtually no direct documentation) was anything but the occasion of a malevolent conspiracy. See Alistair Horne, *Macmillan, 1894–1956* (2 vols.; London, 1989), I, 252–78. See also *n* 16 of this essay.

8. London *Times*, December 1, 1989, pp. 1 (24), 2, 3; Manchester *Guardian*, December 1, 1989, pp. 1 (24), 2, 23; and London *Sunday Times*, December 3, 1989, pp. B1, B7. The inordinate size of the award and the concomitant expenses of the court spectacle have intensified a debate in the U.K. over reform of libel law.

9. *Independent* (London), July 20, 1990, pp. 3, 18.

wife's name.) A fund effort endorsed by a uniquely cosmopolitan assort-
ment of "patrons"—a group made up of morally incensed fellow Britons
including an earl, two White Russian celebrities, a retired Croatian American academic of Yugoslav royalist orientation, the late ruling prince of
Liechtenstein, the son of the Soviet-executed commandant of the infamous
Fifteenth Waffen SS (Cossack) Cavalry Corps, and several members of
Austria's legally extinct aulic nobility—did bring in a substantial amount
of money from East European émigré or émigré-descended sympathizers
around the world. Cash was also raised in the United States with the help
of Senators Strom Thurmond and Jesse Helms, who were prevailed upon
to grant an audience to Tolstoy and his forlorn hope.[10] However, all of
this—and it was not enough—vanished into the gullets of the defense lawyers and their many adjutants in the course of the original proceedings.

Tolstoy's judicial drubbing has not weaned him from his habit of making
extravagant press declarations (promises of "new evidence") or stopped
him from exploiting the sympathy and esteem that he still enjoys among
leading figures of Britain's literary set. The probable explanation, apart
from the éclat of his most recent work, which is of a (totally) fictional
character, is the influence of one of his indigenous fund-raisers, Nigel
Nicolson.[11] Son of the late Harold Nicolson and Victoria Sackville-West,
Nicolson is an accomplished author in his own right; however, the chief
reason for his having lent his prestigious surname to Tolstoy is evidently
his own role and that of others, including two fellow English "patrons" of
Tolstoy, as dissenting, low-level military witnesses to the indisputably very
ugly events of 1945 in Carinthia. This facet of the story is in fact sui
generis and will be examined further on.

Fortunately, the historiographical consequence of the affair overshad-

---

10. *Forced Repatriation Defence Fund* (a flier distributed by Tolstoy in early 1989).
£500,000 was collected. (One "patron," Dr. Ariprand Thurn-Valsassina of Bleiburg, Carinthia, has since changed his mind about things; Thurn-Valsassina to Anthony Cowgill, December 15, 1990, in possession of author.) Tolstoy's own assets were quite modest. After his
court defeat and in view of his inevitable bankruptcy, a second fund, allegedly to support his
wife and four children, was set up by another of the original "patrons," Sir Bernard Braine,
M.P. (see also *n* 28), and television personality Ludovic Kennedy, noted for his unrelenting,
biased interview of an obviously senile Macmillan (December 21, 1984). *Independent*, January 11, 1990, p. 1. Putting words in the mouth of a debilitated old man (U.S. Army Colonel
Philip S. Lauben) is apparently also a hallmark of Bacque's method of investigating the past.

11. Tolstoy's recent writings include *The Quest for Merlin* (Boston, 1985) and *The Coming of the King: The First Book of Merlin* (New York, 1989). The latter, a deftly written,
630-page tome that draws upon Welsh mythology, shows once again that Tolstoy is very much
at home in the world of fantasy.

ows its piquant features and more than compensates for its sordid or pathetic aspects. Among the persons troubled by Tolstoy's initially plausible arguments, which after all touched upon the honor of both the army and a former national leader, was Brigadier Anthony Cowgill, a retired regular soldier who had served under Montgomery in western Europe. Together with the journalist Christopher Booker, who also took Tolstoy seriously at the start, Lord Thomas Brimelow, a onetime Foreign Office man responsible for implementing the Yalta repatriation policy, and Brigadier Teddy Tryon-Wilson, the Fifth Corps's former chief administrative officer, Cowgill formed a private, self-financed historical investigating team.

Four years of scholarly labor in probing rich deposits of papers in London's Public Record Office and Yugoslav archives resulted in the publication in October of 1990 of a two-volume study, *The Repatriations from Austria in 1945*.[12] The evidence, some of which was provided to the trial lawyers and all of which is reproduced in Volume II, has led to solidly based conclusions. In the mind of this writer and other military historians such as John Keegan, the rank distortions and a priori reasoning of Tolstoy's research have now been fully exposed.[13] The sole virtue of his work has been, as in Bacque's case, to compel broad, public discussion of what is after all a major historical issue. Although never deliberately swept under the rug, the story was unknown to most readers of English until the 1974 publication of Nicholas Bethell's study *The Last Secret*, which related at least the Yugoslav half of the tale.[14]

The most important points documentarily substantiated by Cowgill and his coinvestigators may be summarized as follows:

1. The repatriations must be seen in the context of the immediate postwar Trieste crisis, which also involved Yugoslavia's claim upon

---

12. Anthony Cowgill, Christopher Booker, and Thomas Brimelow, eds., *The Repatriations from Austria in 1945: The Report of an Inquiry* (2 vols.; London, 1990). The first scholarly review of the book was in the *Army Quarterly Defense Journal*, CXX (October, 1990), 90. The conclusion is that Cowgill and his colleagues have successfully exonerated both the military and political personages linked to the Carinthian imbroglio.

13. See Keegan's review in the London *Daily Telegraph*, October 19, 1990.

14. Nicholas Bethell, *The Last Secret: The Delivery to Stalin of Over Two Million Russians by Britain and the United States* (New York, 1974). Lord Bethell condemned Tolstoy's work, if quite gently, in a letter to the *Daily Telegraph* on December 26, 1988, p. 18. For the extent of knowledge in official British circles just after the war, see Cowgill, Booker, and Brimelow, eds., *Repatriations from Austria*, 161–74; on p. 166 it is revealed that as early as August 30, 1945, J. M. Addis, the Foreign Office man responsible for the region, conceded privately that a "ghastly mistake" had been committed.

partly Slovene-inhabited southern Carinthia, Tito's troops having arrived in the Klagenfurt basin at the same time as the British.[15] Alexander had resolved upon military action to expel the Yugoslavs from both regions, which were crucial to the West's sharing the occupation of Austria with the USSR as well as to future power political relationships. The Fifth Corps was overextended and had only a tenuous line of communications back to the Po Valley. It was necessary, in Alexander's own phrase, to "clear the decks" and be rid of the impossible logistical burden posed by the presence of the "Cossacks" and their collaborationist Yugoslav confreres. The situation was made all the worse by Keightley's other tasks: disposing of 150,000 Wehrmacht soldiers, as well as the remnants of Hungary's army, other military oddments, and a horde of displaced persons—probably half a million people altogether—plus caring for Carinthia's civilian population.

2. The "Cossacks"—consisting of both the Fifteenth Waffen SS Cavalry Corps, which had served as part of Army Group Southeast in Yugoslavia, and another heterogeneous collection of predominantly Soviet citizens, including "Caucasians" who had carried out an important counterinsurgency (anti-partisan) mission for Reichsführer SS Heinrich Himmler in Italy's northeastern region of Friulia—were handed over in keeping with the Yalta Repatriation Agreement approved by Britain's cabinet in full cognizance of the mortal danger to the persons in question. Concern for Western POWs liberated by the USSR was a major consideration.

The few Wehrmacht and German SS soldiers (perhaps 800 men) and Russian émigrés caught up in the transfer suffered their harsh fate because Keightley's pragmatic decision was to proceed on the basis of the putative national character of individual units. The Waffen SS division "Galicia," made up partly of poorly disciplined Ukrainians (Ruthenes) who had been Polish citizens in 1939 and partly of a detachment of indubitably White Russian collaborationists from the Nazi puppet state of Serbia, were excluded. Some 2,000 "Cossacks" and "Caucasians" were also spared on an individual basis. This occurred despite the fact that the Fifth Corps's orders specifically discouraged screening and made no mention of émigrés—the exact opposite of Tolstoy's claim.

3. The Yugoslav quislings were sent back at Alexander's express command in violation of the declared policy of the British and United

15. See Thomas M. Barker, *Social Revolutionaries and Secret Agents: The Carinthian Slovene Partisans and Britain's Special Operations Executive* (New York, 1990), 55–79.

States governments and notwithstanding the protest of the diplomatic representative at AFHQ, Alexander Kirk. (Other Slavic liegemen of Hitler, who managed to slip out of Istria, cross the Isonzo-Soča River into Venetia, and surrender to the British Thirteenth Corps, were exempted; they were not as much of a logistical hindrance to the projected attack on Tito.) Large numbers of the White Guards, then known officially as *domobranci,* were immolated, especially in the horrifying "Pits of Kočevje [Gottschee]," located at the hub of what had been the Slovene partisans' home turf, shortly after the Fifth Corps tricked the Guards into entering trains destined not for Italy but for their native land. The Ustashi and Chetniks hardly fared better, although none of the former died on Carinthian soil at Bleiburg [Pliberk] as Tolstoy asserted.

In this writer's view, the field marshal's decision represents an especially interesting case in the history of civil-military relations, inasmuch as he later sought to justify his action on grounds of grave operational necessity. "Alex" was never reproved for his decision. Perhaps he should have been, perhaps not. The case can be argued either way. He found himself in what was perhaps a gray legal area: never formally ordered to stop the repatriations, he was a kind of a Roman proconsul endowed with wide, although in the last analysis politically circumscribed, authority in *both* the civil and military realms.

4. Not a shred of evidence exists for positing a "Klagenfurt Conspiracy"—as Knight, another connoisseur of the sources, stressed in a vitriolic press debate with Tolstoy in 1986.[16] It is equally impossible to sustain the charge of a deliberate, "nefarious" destruction of records, even if vetting and the strange disappearance of official materials are not unheard-of phenomena in Great Britain. Cowgill and his team in fact discovered far more than they expected to, and a great deal that was totally unknown to Tolstoy. Although they demonstrated the existence of a universal reluctance right after the war to delve into the affair, they failed to discover anything like a concerted cover-up.

---

16. See the summer, 1986, issues of the *Times* (London) *Literary Supplement.* See also Robert Knight, "Harold Macmillan and the Cossacks: Was There a Klagenfurt Conspiracy?" *Intelligence and National Security,* I (1986), 234–54. See also *n*7. Tolstoy, an apparent homophobe (see *n*3), despises Knight to the point of having mailed him photos of female underwear! Manchester *Guardian,* December 1, 1989, p. 23. A rabid anti-Communist, Tolstoy has also attempted to smear the very independent-minded Knight as a Marxist. This is a fate most people (including this writer) who dare to disagree with the approved émigré line must accept.

5. General McCreery was fully aware of what was transpiring in Carinthia. He took major initiatives and carried out his duties according to the customary, rigid principles of a military chain of command. In no sense was the Fifth Corps operating autonomously, arbitrarily, or deceptively. Aldington, however important his on-the-spot role at a moment of great urgency, was but one cog in a professional leadership mechanism that, admittedly, sputtered and coughed perceptibly during the confused crisis.

6. Macmillan's involvement in the series of events that led to the return of the Nazis' Soviet auxiliaries was relatively marginal. He simply advised Keightley and his staff that the Yalta Repatriation Agreement be observed; he was not even asked about the émigrés because the problem had not yet been recognized at the time of his visit. The purpose of his trip was simply to brief the Fifth Corps's demonstrably perturbed top officers about the overall crisis in relations with Tito. The future prime minister had nothing at all to do with the decision to ship back the Yugoslav quislings.

A further point may be stressed by this writer, who has independently studied the problem. There seems every reason to believe that Keightley and Low did not know of the awful destiny that awaited the Yugoslav collaborationists, even if a handful of British intelligence officers, especially at AFHQ, and Fitzroy Maclean (who had meanwhile returned to the U.K.) strongly suspected that they would be massacred. Belgrade's chief spokesman in Carinthia, Major (now Dr.) France Hočevar, assured the Fifth Corps staff that the captives would be treated fairly and has since orally confirmed to the writer that he was personally convinced of the truth of what he was telling his interlocutors. Since Tito issued a general army order regarding the matter on May 13, Hočevar's witness can hardly be questioned. Among the various written records is a Thirteenth Corps intelligence report which states, *inter alia,* that "the dissident Jugoslavs have been handed over to Marshal TITO's forces under a guarantee of humane treatment and orderly trial for war criminals." (The Thirteenth Corps had its guns trained on the Communist-led Yugoslav troops in Istria and Trieste.)[17]

Why the dreadful hecatomb then took place is another question that is only now beginning to be examined in Slovenia and Croatia. The best

17. Barker, *Social Revolutionaries and Secret Agents,* 69, 73, 75, 219, 222; 13 Corps Periodical Intelligence Summary No. 1, (May 28, 1945) in Public Record Office, Foreign Office 371/48828, R 10003/24/92.

guess at this stage as to why Tito revoked his May 13 order on May 26 is that he and his confidants concluded that the quislings would constitute a kind of fifth column to be used by the West in the case of war over Trieste. There are also grounds for positing an involvement of Allied counterintelligence agencies. If this is true, the collaborationists were in the last analysis victims of an international power-political gambit. It now also appears that far fewer of them died than the 11,000 persons whom émigré Slovenes long asserted were slaughtered and that the Communist regime systematically chose individuals whom it considered especially suspect.[18]

If Tolstoy's attempt to write history has now been shown to be hopelessly flawed, the question remains why he was able to win the backing of so perceptive and analytic an author as Nigel Nicolson. Known for his elegantly composed, carefully researched, albeit—in contrast to Tolstoy's work—unannotated biography of Field Marshal Alexander, Nicolson has credentials such that his view of the matter cannot be lightly dismissed[19] (although he has not had formal training as a historian either). His indisputably powerful feelings of humanity and his long exposure as a young Guards Brigade intelligence officer to the bestialities of the North African and Italian campaigns almost certainly have much to do with the public stance he has recently taken and indeed took at the time the collaborationists were about to be freighted off to their horrendous fate.

Nicolson was in fact reprimanded by his divisional commander for warning in one of his regular, singularly chatty intelligence bulletins, or "sitreps," that the returnees were likely to be butchered. He rapidly changed his tune, much to his "shame," as he is now at pains to admit. One may thus fairly ask why, in his chef d'oeuvre, *Alex,* he made short shrift of the Carinthian episode yet simultaneously emphasized the fact that the field marshal was under very heavy pressure from Churchill to fend off the Yugoslavs. It seems strange not only that he neglected to express his qualms of conscience in 1973—although he refers in his book to many other occurrences that he personally witnessed—but also that in light of

18. Professor Tone Ferenc of the University of Ljubljana is head of a group entrusted by the government of the Republic of Slovenia with carrying out a historical investigation of the matter insofar as it appertains to his own country, and he has access to the records of the formerly Communist-controlled Interior Ministry.

19. See Nigel Nicolson, *Alex: The Life of Field Marshal Alexander of Tunis* (New York, 1973). Nicolson has also distinguished himself as the editor of the letters of his mother and Virginia Woolf. Deselected for Parliament at the time of the Suez crisis (1956), he is perhaps best described as a "liberal" Conservative. His statements at Tolstoy's trial struck some observers as equivocal.

his military expertise, he could not discern the relationship between events on the brigade level as he experienced them and the responsibilities of his division, his corps, the Eighth Army, the Fifteenth Army Group, and SACMED. A strikingly similar case is that of Colonel Ernest Fisher, the retired military historian who wrote the Foreword to *Other Losses* and the only scholar supporting Bacque, even though he himself apparently voiced not the slightest suspicion of any "mass deaths" for over four decades.[20]

In all events, both combat and its immediate aftermath tend to be agonizing experiences. A particular case relating to Bacque's work may be cited. A former United States Army guard stood up during a special panel at the annual meeting of the American Historical Association (December 28, 1990) devoted to the subject. Although rejecting Bacque's analysis, the World War II veteran expressed intense personal remorse over the brutal treatment meted out to Wehrmacht prisoners in the camp at Remagen where he had served. The emotional reaction of the British troops who had to effect the coercive repatriation of the "Cossacks" and the (mainly covinous) transfer of Hitler's Yugoslav auxiliaries was the same. Although less eloquent than Nicolson's tardy protest, many recent statements—precipitated by the Tolstoy-Aldington legal donnybrook—by some of the men involved in the business confirm this feeling. Nor has Aldington himself, like many historically famous generals (including "Alex" and Ike), failed to express publicly his repugnance for the malignity of war.

If these instances are symptomatic of the severe anguish that is often the soldier's lot, there is likewise, with respect to Nicolson's enduring intellectual malaise, a profound irony. It was his own hero, the personally gentle, high-minded, and beloved Alexander, who, implicitly recognizing the grave risk to which he was subjecting the collaborationists—he granted that it might turn out to be "fatal to their health"—ratified the order that led to what was, for Nicolson, "a major betrayal" of humane principles.[21] When all is said and done, war itself is that.

It is all well and good to criticize Allied commanders for employing the German generals' (and, indeed, every military man's) excuse of "only following orders" and for having neglected a moral imperative. Chivalry, understood as indulgent treatment of the vanquished foe, is a random

20. "Tito's Victims, the Allies' Shame," *Independent Magazine* (London), April 22, 1989, pp. 22–27; Nicolson, *Alex,* 278–79; and Barker, *Social Revolutionaries and Secret Agents, passim.*

21. "Tito's Victims."

thing, historically speaking. Even in the case of armies organized by democratic polities, warfare may blur the boundaries of what is ethically admissible and what is not. Another question is whether "Alex," Churchill's protégé, was deliberately induced to take the rap for his benefactor and the cabinet. The answer is probably not, for taken as a whole the situation at the time is perhaps best described—so Brigadier Cowgill to this writer—as a "cock-up" (foul-up). On the various staff levels at any rate, the decisions—in Robert Knight's incisive phraseology—were those of "men in a hurry." [22] Of course, they were likewise consciously gambling, at least at AFHQ, with human lives, although this too is an intrinsic feature of war.

This writer, an academic historian himself, by no means wishes to imply that he and his fellow practitioners should have a monopoly of the effort to understand the past. The shining example of Brigadier Cowgill and his associates—there are of course many other instances—demonstrates that it is not imperative to have been subjected to the rigors of graduate study in the field in order to produce work of high caliber. What is required above all else is the right mind-set. One cannot determine in advance the correct line to take, as, for example, the editors of British periodicals partial to Tolstoy (including the *Independent,* the *Spectator,* and most recently the *Sunday Times*) have done. Over the longer haul the risk of embarrassment, indeed even of legal liability (particularly in the litigious U.K.), is rather high. [23] Nor, for that matter, do the directors of television documentaries always succeed in avoiding this kind of mistake. [24]

22. *Times* (London) *Literary Supplement,* October 19–25, 1990, p. 1126.

23. The London *Sunday Times,* which printed Robert Harris' review of Cowgill's work in the "Sunday Comment" section of the October 21, 1990, issue ("Here's a Way Out for Every War Criminal"), had to agree to pay a total of £1700 in damages and solicitors' costs for having impugned the personal integrity of Cowgill's group—which was accused of *conspiring* to produce a "whitewash"—and to print an objective article on the subject by the well-known professional historian Professor Norman Stone ("Judgment Best Left to History," December 30, 1990, "News Review 11"). Stone rates the Cowgill volumes highly. The idea of a "Cowgill Conspiracy," aided and abetted by the British government, was suggested to Tolstoy by Chapman Pincher, a not-always-credible writer who has specialized in exposing intelligence agency misdeeds. See Christopher Booker in the London *Sunday Telegraph,* November 4, 1990, p. 3. Although Cowgill and his colleagues certainly profited in their work from good personal relations with the Defence Ministry, any suggestion of a high-level plot is preposterous, albeit characteristic of the genre of writing in question.

24. The BBC, which of late seems to delight in attempting to embarrass Conservative governments, past and present, produced a film, "British Betrayal," with Tolstoy as its main advisor, and ran it on the second channel, January 11, 1991. Predictably and cleverly slanted

Thomas M. Barker

Finally, a critique of Tolstoy's (and by extension Bacque's) approach to historical research is in order. The subject may be considered first from the broader vantage of the general public's perennial receptivity to charges of conspiracy, the basic ingredient of a common recipe for writing best sellers. Naturally, the focus must be upon a major historical figure. Tolstoy and Bacque necessarily claim that their respective protagonists, Macmillan and Eisenhower, were war criminals. It is always a purported occult involvement—high-level connivance—that titillates the gullible layman reader and places the writer in the favorable light of having uncovered a distasteful truth that the professionals were incapable of, fearful of, or constrained from revealing to the world at large.

In cases such as Macmillan's and Eisenhower's, the books are snapped up because obloquy is heaped upon former national leaders—although their actual role in the events described was at best peripheral—and, at least with regard to the Macmillan model, because of mysterious, sinister, SMERSH-style forces beyond the ken of the everyday apparatus of government. Thereby, the amateur author fails utterly to grasp the overall historical context: Tolstoy cannot fathom the nature of the immediate postwar power political struggle in the northwestern Yugoslav–northeastern Italian– southern Austrian theater, and Bacque is unable to perceive the administrative chaos and grave nutritional crisis that characterized conditions in central Europe during the late spring and early summer of 1945. Moreover, neither man shows much grasp of fundamental military realities, in particular the functioning of highly crucial command and control networks that, although well articulated in all modern armed forces, tend to be subject in practice to what Carl von Clausewitz aptly called "friction."

Tolstoy's work is of course marked by yet other elementary flaws. It constitutes a particularly egregious example of the fallacy of conclusions deriving from "romanticism," as certain British observers have opined, or in this writer's less charitable view, from maudlin sentimentalism.[25] It likewise seems obvious that preconceived notions of reality, political-ideological prejudice, and a proclivity for conjecture enter into the picture.

---

as well as drawing upon oral evidence that can no longer be corroborated, it seeks to avoid making actionable statements, yet may not prove to be immune from Aldington's solicitors (who if they won would surely be able to collect much more money than in Tolstoy's case!). See *Radio Times,* program for January 11, 1990.

25. It is particularly well revealed in his filiopietistic account of his family origins (see note 1 to this essay).

In any event, Tolstoy, or as the case may be, Bacque, simply cannot go about picking the evidence to fit propositions and write valid history. To claim that the establishment has ganged up on you will not do. The documents, once they are all *punctiliously* collated by teams such as Cowgill's (or Ambrose's), have the last word.

Any attempt to delve into the intricacies of Tolstoy's psyche would naturally be—as in Bacque's case—quite futile. All that can be said with certainty about the man is that his conviction of being correct regardless of the crushing weight of the evidence against him well exceeds normal parameters of obduracy: an announced forthcoming appeal to the European Court of Justice against the judicial rebuff in his native land provides further proof, were it needed, of his almost unique pertinacity.[26]

Although, in a sense, Tolstoy has always hovered at the edges of the establishment and the squabble with Aldington might well be considered an internal affair of British society's essentially diffuse ruling stratum, his self-portrayal as its victim has evidently garnered him the sympathy of left-wingers who otherwise might be put off by his reactionary attitudes.[27] At least until most recently he has continued to enjoy solid support from a wide range of less easily classifiable luminaries. Among public figures, one may single out the "Father of the House of Commons," Sir Bernard Braine (whose epithet means only that he is the Commons' longest-serving member), and the lately ennobled Hugh Thomas, famed for his encyclopedic narrative history of the Spanish civil war.[28] Overly facile journalistic commentators include John Jolliffe and Auberon Waugh. (The latter, son of the late Evelyn, is editor of the *Literary Review* and a diarist, essayist, and novelist. He once ran for Parliament on a dog-lovers' ticket and is the *Independent*'s principal reviewer. His visceral scorn for the now-dead Macmillan, preciously vented in a *Daily Telegraph* article, appears to be the reason for the line taken by the *Independent,* not to mention his own

26. Tolstoy has been barred from appealing to the House of Lords. For his charge of a "fix" by Cowgill *et al.,* see note 23 in this essay and, in a legally prophylatic form—*i.e.,* by the art of insinuation, of which he is a past master—his review of Cowgill's work in the *Spectator,* December, 1990, pp. 45–46.

27. See *Le Monde,* December 6, 1989, p. 3.

28. Braine (see *n* 10), is a maverick Conservative backbencher with a record of supporting a wide variety of right-wing policies and causes. Lord Thomas has recently distanced himself a bit from Tolstoy. Among Tolstoy's other auxiliaries are Sir Nicolas Cheetham, a retired diplomat, and Colonel Professor Gerald Draper, a former German war-crimes trial prosecutor, international-law expert, and champion of the Palestinian Arabs.

magazine, which continues to print Tolstoy's diatribes on the same subject.) Tolstoy's literary connections have also led to an opportunity to argue his case to the North American public.[29]

As for Aldington, who himself proposed reducing the damage award, it seems almost certain that he will be unable to collect much money from the reckless yet nimble Tolstoy and will have to pay almost all his legal bills himself. Tolstoy, meanwhile, had at last report become close to playboy Greek shipping millionaire "Taki" Theodoracopoulos and was consorting with the likes of Claus von Bülow and Joan Collins—for example, at a lavish, Taki-funded bask at the Savoy held to celebrate the demise of communism. Taki was apparently also aiding Tolstoy covertly, as he had promised publicly that he would do. And Watts, having refused to keep quiet, was in danger of being jailed for contempt of court.[30]

29. For Jolliffe, see the *Spectator,* October 20, 1990, pp. 17–18, and for Waugh, the London *Daily Telegraph,* October 20, 1990, p. 21. Jolliffe is treasurer of the latest Tolstoy fund-drive (see note 10 to this essay). For an example of Tolstoy's writings for North American publications, see Nikolai Tolstoy, "Bare Bones: The Massacres at Kočevje," *New Republic,* December 24, 1990, pp. 16–18. This pure vintage piece contains so many readily demonstrable inaccuracies, distortions, omissions, and untruths that the present space will not suffice even to list them.

30. Christine Booker, "The Victims of Tolstoy," London *Sunday Telegram,* October 21, 1990. As of February, 1991, it appeared that Aldington would recover only £100,000 from Tolstoy's impounded assets and would still owe his lawyers £300,000. For Tolstoy's newfound friends among the jet set, see Taki, "Getting Off Lightly," *Spectator,* December 9, 1989, p. 49, and London *Daily Mail,* October 29, 1990, p. 19. On Watts, see *Independent on Sunday,* January 20, 1991, p. 1.

Bacque and Historical Evidence

Günter Bischof

The methodology used in [Bacque's] book is speculation, based on crown witnesses and bits and pieces from the archival record, culminating in a numbers game whose projections cannot be proven.
—Wolfgang Benz, in Wolfgang Benz and Angelika Schardt, eds.,
Kriegsgefangenschaft

THE PREVIOUS ESSAYS in this collection have refuted James Bacque's charges point by point. In conclusion, Bacque's (ab)use of historical evidence must be reiterated and reemphasized. The professional historians' controversy with Bacque is fourfold. First, although Bacque has done a considerable amount of research, much of it is superficial or highly selective. As is demonstrated in the Introduction to this volume, he ignores a vast body of scholarly literature on the subject matter; moreover, he has only skimmed the vast body of primary sources. Second, he commits egregious errors in (mis)interpreting the historical evidence that he does use (a careful checking of his endnotes reveals so many mistakes that it is hard to take him seriously). Third, as has been shown again and again in these essays, his ignorance about the larger historical context of the POW/DEF story leads him to make up fables. Fourth, his carelessness and selectivity in using oral-history evidence is methodologically unacceptable.

In this essay, these shortcomings of Bacque's, outlined in earlier chapters, are further substantiated. But it is necessary to go beyond the refutation of methodology so poor that it constitutes an insult to the historical profession. For Bacque's treatment of a serious historical issue may ultimately have the more devious outcome of relativizing the unique German responsibility for the destruction of the Jews by way of constructing a nonexistent American holocaust.

On a different level, the prospect of amateur historians writing conspiratorial history raises troubling questions. For one, the careful, professional historian's inquiry is directed by the message of his sources and not by an obsession to prove a hypothesis that flies in the face of the sources. Yet professional historians ("flightless swans" in Bacque's diction) will always find it difficult to refute convoluted conspiracy theories that are appealing to a lay audience. Bacque's principal conspiracy, of course, is that of Eisenhower and the United States Army designing the categories "DEFs" and "Other Losses" to put the German POWs beyond the pale and hide a devious policy of secretly starving them to death. Lately, in order to answer his critics, Bacque has let his imagination carry him on toward inventing new conspiracies. For example, in the case of the 663,576 Volkssturm troops listed in a 1945 military governor's report as "other losses" (see the photocopy on page 24 of this volume), Bacque's odd historical methodology becomes revealing. Since most of Eisenhower's reports are lies, Bacque finds it easy to "discredit" this monthly report by Eisenhower as a fake. With a further fantastic twist in his convoluted cycle of conspiracy theories, he claims that Eisenhower and the army "camouflaged" dead POWs/DEFs by listing them as "discharged Volkssturm."[1] If perfectly reliable documents such as the monthly reports by the military governor, which were written by subordinates and not by Eisenhower himself, undermine Bacque's case of "other losses" being deaths, the documents must have been "doctored," in Bacque's reading. Eisenhower had documents changed to hide his heinous crimes from gullible historians and posterity!

Perhaps the best (or worst) example of the desperate lengths to which Bacque will go in this regard is his reaction when faced with a document bearing a perfectly reasonable definition of *other losses* as "all losses other discharge or transfer to custody of another nation; i.e. normal attritions, desertion, release without discharge of Volkssturm personnel and civilians" (clearly, the word *than* should follow *other* in this passage). The definition, along with ones for *gains* and *transferred,* two other categories in the document, are typed directly onto a carbon copy. Anyone familiar with army paperwork can readily conceive of a dozen commonplace reasons why this might have been done. But not Bacque. Since for him "other

---

1. See the new Appendix 11 in Bacque's American edition, James Bacque, *Other Losses: The Shocking Truth Behind the Mass Deaths of Disarmed German Soldiers and Civilians Under General Eisenhower's Command* (Los Angeles, 1991), esp. 230–38; hereinafter cited as *Other Losses* (Los Angeles, 1991).

losses" must mean deaths and only deaths, Eisenhower or someone closely in conspiracy with him must have called in a typist and had the false (of course) definition added to the document.[2] (Why the definition was added only to the few documents in this same set, when countless others must have been available, is a mystery Bacque fails to address.) The whole thing would be almost humorous were it not chillingly reminiscent of the "doctored evidence" of the McCarthyite witch hunts of the 1950s.

Indeed, the whole example of Bacque raises troubling questions that cannot be answered here. Why do the conspiracy theorists—usually amateur historians—get such vast audiences? Do they merely want to produce best sellers? Do they want to titillate readerships with a short attention span by sensationalizing stories even if they defy common sense? Or, worse, do they have a political agenda? The conspiracy theorists of history always center their tales around well-known and highly respected historical figures such as Prime Minister Macmillan (see Thomas M. Barker's essay) or President Kennedy, whose assassination to this day attracts hordes of conspiracy theorists.

In the case of Bacque's attack on Eisenhower, the use of common sense still provides one of the best ways to refute the fantastical charges.[3] How could a single man order one million men killed without being caught in the heinous act? How could the bodies disappear without one soldier's coming forward in nearly fifty years to relieve his conscience? How could the Americans (almost one-third of whom are by ethnic background German) conspire for so long to cover up such a vast crime? (My Lai should give ample instruction as to how skillful investigative journalists quickly catch up with most war crimes.) If a historian suspends disbelief too willingly, fiction will be the result. Yet in spite of the inherent incredibility of Bacque's conspiracy theories, the professional historian still has to test the man's hypothesis, study the documents he used, and check his endnotes. Let us do so here.

There is a vast body of archival collections and historiography on the subject of German POWs during and after World War II. In 1957, thirty years before James Bacque became interested in the fate of German

2. *Ibid.*, 234–36. "Rewriting History," *Fifth Estate* (CBC), 1991 (Copy of transcript at the Eisenhower Center, University of New Orleans), hereinafter cited as "Rewriting History," touches on this matter through the testimony of a typewriter expert.

3. See also Stephen E. Ambrose, "Ike and the Disappearing Atrocities," *New York Times Book Review,* February 24, 1991, pp. 1, 35–37.

POWs, the West German government initiated the *Wissenschaftliche Kommission für deutsche Kriegsgefangenengeschichte* (Scientific Commission for the History of German POWs), which eventually became known as the Maschke Commission, named after its chairman, Erich Maschke.[4] In keeping with the grand and thorough traditions of German historical scholarship, Maschke and his experienced professional historians documented over the course of sixteen years of research the fate of an estimated 11 million World War II German POWs in minute detail. Some 45,709 autobiographical reports, diaries, oral histories, and related materials were collected by the commission in its massive historical enterprise.[5] The twenty-two volumes and part-volumes of the Maschke Commission are full of the tragedy that befell the German soldiers in captivity all over the world, including in the American camps in Germany.[6] Anyone who has taken even a cursory look at the Maschke volumes knows that it is a malignant accusation of Bacque's to sanctimoniously charge that the survivors of the camps "are still being tortured spiritually by those who deny that they have suffered at all." No historian is trying to "cover up" the suffering of the prisoners; no one is trying to forget those who died in the camps.[7]

4. See also the Steininger and Overmans essays in this volume.

5. For the 45,709 reports, see Erich Maschke, "Quellen und Methoden," in Maschke *et al., Die deutschen Kriegsgefangenen des Zweiten Weltkrieges: Eine Zusammenfassung* (Munich, 1974), 45–47, Vol. XV of Maschke Commission.

6. The first volume dealt with the German POWs in Yugoslav hands and appeared in 1962. See esp. Maschke's Introduction, "Das Schicksal der deutschen Kriegsgefangenen des Zweiten Weltkrieges als Aufgabe zeitgeschichtlicher Forschung," in Kurt W. Böhme, *Die deutschen Kriegsgefangenen in Jugoslawien, 1941–1949* (Munich, 1962), vii–xx. For a history of the Maschke Commission and summaries of its results, see Maschke *et al., Zusammenfassung.* For a popularized condensation of this exhaustive collection of material, see Paul Carell and Günter Böddeker, *Die Gefangenen: Leben und Überleben deutscher Soldaten hinter Stacheldraht* (Berlin, 1980).

7. See Bacque, *Other Losses* (Los Angeles, 1991), 174. In this connection, it is a great mystery in the historical community and among his colleagues why Colonel Ernest F. Fisher, who in a long career with the Historical Division of the U.S. Army appears never to have breathed a word about Eisenhower's alleged "death camps," after his retirement associated himself with Bacque's sensationalistic charges. It is indeed an enigma why a professional historian in the employ of the U.S. Army had to wait for an amateur historian to come along and uncover the "long night of lies" perpetrated by that same U.S. Army and its professional historians. See Ernest F. Fisher, Foreword, *ibid.*, xix–xxi; and *ibid.*, 4. It is quite transparent that Fisher's collaboration with Bacque is meant to give the treatise an aura of scholarly depth that it does not merit. In the CBC documentary "Rewriting History," Fisher indicated that he was somewhat troubled by Bacque's contacts with Holocaust revisionists and neo-Nazis, and suggested that he himself would be prepared to fudge the issue of "casual annihilation of a million" German POWs.

It is outrageous to dismiss this vast and impressive body of scholarship as being designed to produce "soothing conclusions" for the German public, as Bacque puts it. Ultimately the German historical profession will have to salvage its honor and answer Bacque's attack against its members on the Maschke Commission: did Maschke's "client-academics" (whatever that means), as Bacque alleges, "tamely [publish] a series that *reproduced lies by the French and Americans,* omitting vast tracts of history, statistics and experience that millions of ex-prisoners and their families knew were crucially important"?[8] There is a precedent for best-seller-writing amateur historians' turning historical facts on their head: when Nikolai Tolstoy-Miloslavsky defamed the reputation of well-known British individuals by constructing vast but unfounded conspiracies, a court of law made him pay the price for his personal libel.[9]

Gerhard L. Weinberg, the distinguished historian of Nazi Germany, has recently deflated another of Bacque's conspiracy theories. Weinberg has shown that the West German government of Willy Brandt did not try to "suppress evidence" to please its American allies in the late 1960s, as Bacque has charged. On the contrary, in his pursuit of Ostpolitik, Brandt thought it wise to limit the distribution of the Maschke volumes to libraries and research institutions "to avoid exacerbating relations with the *Soviet Union.*"[10] Having experienced the raw POW existence in Russian and American hands themselves, Erich Maschke and Kurt Böhme had firsthand knowledge of what they wrote about. They had absolutely no reason to produce politically correct history as Bacque charges.

Maschke and his historians built their careful study on every bit of evidence that they could lay their hands on in the 1960s and 1970s. Like most historians, they were keenly aware of the clear hierarchy in the value and reliability of source materials. Primary sources such as direct correspondence between historical actors, cabinet records, notes on meetings, and contemporary letters and diaries are always more reliable sources than the reminiscences of the human memory.[11]

8. Bacque, *Other Losses* (Los Angeles, 1991), 155–57, 176–77 (emphasis added).

9. See the Barker essay in this volume.

10. See Gerhard L. Weinberg's critical review of the American edition of *Other Losses* in *Washington Post Book World,* July 7, 1991 (the emphasis in the quotation is Weinberg's). Bacque, *Other Losses* (Los Angeles, 1991), 157, complains of the Maschke series that "only 431 copies were sold, mainly to universities and research libraries." He seems to think that expensive documentary collections routinely end up on the bookshelves of people's homes.

11. On the "evidentiary value" of oral history, see William Moss, "An Appreciation," in *Oral History: An Interdisciplinary Anthology,* ed. David K. Dunaway and Willa K. Baum

Günter Bischof

As regards such written POW records, we have today access to far more American, British, and French sources than had the Maschke Commission in the 1960s. Since the completion of the commission's work, new records have been opened in the National Archives, the Eisenhower Library, the Public Record Office in London, and the French Military Archives in Vincennes, many of which Bacque has not consulted. There are also numerous edited source collections that Bacque failed to use, as well as the voluminous raw files of the Maschke Commission open to researchers (see the Overmans essay). All these records are more reliable historical sources than personal recollections—but only if adequately reported by the historian who uses them. As other essays in this volume demonstrate, the trouble with Bacque is that he frequently succeeds in misinterpreting the very limited body of sources that he did look at.[12]

Most scholarly reviewers of Bacque's book have pointed out that Bacque fails to establish the proper historical context for his historical narrative. He ignores the chaotic situation in central Europe at the end of the most destructive war in history. A continent in turmoil, torn apart and disrupted by six years of aggressive and murderous German warfare, constitutes the real backdrop for Allied POW/DEF policy, not a vindictive Eisenhower or vengeful American policies as Bacque suggests. Worse, the historical records that Bacque did use are amateurishly misrepresented and often misleading and wrong. Once Bacque's endnotes are checked, frequent misreadings of documents are easily discernible.[13]

A careful reading of the published wartime *Eisenhower Papers,* for

---

(N.p. [American Association for State and Local History in cooperation with the Oral History Association], 1984), 87–101.

12. See esp. the Villa and Cowdrey essays.

13. See F. H. Hinsley, "Various Reasons," *London Review of Books,* August 30, 1990; Michael Howard, "A Million Lost Germans," *Times* (London) *Literary Supplement,* September 14–20, 1990; Rüdiger Overmans, "War Eisenhower ein Mörder?" *Das Parlament,* July 6, 1990; Henry Rousso, "L'Invention d'un génocide," *Le Monde,* April 27, 1990; Sélim Nassib with Henry Rousso, "En Quête des champs de la mort pour soldats du Reich," *Libération,* December 4, 1989; Rolf Steininger, "Kriegsverbrecher oder Fehlkalkulation," *Frankfurter Allgemeine Zeitung,* December 21, 1989; David Stafford in *Canadian Historical Review* (1990), 408 f; Günter Bischof, "'Der Tod war geplant,'" *Die Furche,* February 22, 1990; John Keegan to London *Sunday Telegraph,* November 12, 1989; Michael Schnieber, "Fragwürdige Hochrechnungen des Schreckens," *Schwäbische Zeitung,* May 22, 1991; and the transcripts of CBC's "Rewriting History." All of the foregoing are heavily critical of Bacque, and "Rewriting History" in particular raises serious questions about Bacque's faulty endnotes.

example, shows that Bacque sometimes misrepresents the meaning of entire documents. Claiming that Eisenhower was "responsible" for a death
rate of "30 percent or worse" among German POWs, Bacque concludes
by citing the *Eisenhower Papers* that "the initials DE on the SHAEF Cable
Logs prove that he knew from the beginning of the DEF policy and probably drafted it." The cable that he refers to in the *Eisenhower Papers* is
indeed one from Eisenhower to George C. Marshall, October 4, 1944.
However, it does not deal at all with any "DEF policy" as Bacque asserts.
Rather, it concerns the obscure matter of a trial run for the "adjusted rating
card system" for redeployment of American troops after the war. In this
cable Eisenhower pleads with Marshall not to bother the troops with such
administrative details, as the two U.S. armies under his command are brac-
ing for "one more major, desperate battle to break the German defenses in
the west." [14]

At other times Bacque is so selective in reporting individual documents
that he does not present their principal thrust. His primary evidence is often
circumstantial—of the sort that since German POWs were treated badly,
Eisenhower personally must have given the order. The reasoning goes
as follows: Demonstrating that the U.S. Army "deliberately" deprived
German POWs of food and shelter, Bacque assumes that it is "highly unlikely" that such "a major decision" would have been taken or implemented "without the knowledge of the Supreme Commander." Eisenhower had a reputation of being a very efficient commander who took care
of minute details under his command. Bacque makes the reader believe
that many of the details Eisenhower dealt with were trivial. For example,
he claims that Eisenhower watched over "the sponsorship of dances for
enlisted men and what make of car should be driven by what rank of officer
in which area." If a commander had time to worry about dances and cars,
Bacque deduces, he surely must also have been aware of the welfare of
German POWs. Eisenhower certainly was aware of the welfare of the German POWs—but not based on the evidence that Bacque cites. The cable
under discussion does not deal with trivial matters as Bacque suggests. On
the contrary, it was late February, 1944, and Eisenhower was preparing his
troops for the D-day invasion. In order to prime them for optimum team-
work in the upcoming campaign, he wanted to make sure that all units

14. Bacque, *Other Losses* (Los Angeles, 1991), 165, 273n11; Alfred D. Chandler, Jr.,
Stephen E. Ambrose, *et al.*, eds., *The Papers of Dwight David Eisenhower: The War Years*
(5 vols., Baltimore, 1970), IV, 2208; these five volumes and Vol. VI, *The Papers of Dwight
David Eisenhower: Occupation, 1945*, ed. Chandler and Louis D. Galambos (Baltimore,
1978), are hereinafter cited by volume as *Eisenhower Papers*.

shared their "work opportunities and recreational facilities." In the case of sponsoring "dances and similar entertainment," Eisenhower wanted to make sure that all unit organizations made the same arrangements and were prepared for overcrowding. The purpose of this order thus was to make sure that "equal opportunities of service and recreation" be guaranteed to every American soldier "regardless of branch, race, color, or creed." In other words, Eisenhower had the welfare of his troops in mind, as every commander of armies should. He wanted to make sure that morale among his men did not suffer during the long months of training and waiting for D day. If one reads the cable in the proper context, "the sponsorship of dances for enlisted men" is hardly the trivial matter Bacque tries to make of it.[15]

In a new Epilogue and Appendix 11 (also new) to the American edition, Bacque tries to answer his critics—Eisenhower and army "apologists," as he calls them.[16] Bacque makes much ado about General Mark Clark, the American high commissioner in Austria, and prisoner transfers from Germany to Austria. Since the numbers of transferees sent and received do not match up in Bacque's superficial reading of the extensive Clark papers at The Citadel Archives-Museum in Charleston, South Carolina, the bulk of the prisoners must have died during their transfer![17]

---

15. Bacque, *Other Losses* (Los Angeles, 1991), 163, 273n4, 273n5; Eisenhower to Lee, February 26, 1944, in *Eisenhower Papers,* III, 1749–50. In the other instance raised by Bacque, Eisenhower was upset over the fact that Winston Churchill had made a "tour of the battlefields" driven in only a Chevrolet by the army commander, whereas in the rear brigadier generals were driving "very fine looking Packards." With his order Eisenhower simply wanted to make sure that army and corps commanders drove vehicles that were in "excellent operating conditions," presumably in part to be better prepared for driving around high-level visitors. See Eisenhower to Lee, March 14, 1945, *Eisenhower Papers,* IV, 2529. On Bacque's misrepresentation of documents, see also the Villa essay in this volume and "Rewriting History."

16. Bacque, *Other Losses* (Los Angeles, 1991), 174–95, 230–44, 274–76, 280–82.

17. *Ibid.,* 182. For his Canadian edition, Bacque ordered a few copies from the Clark papers (the General Mark W. Clark Collection, The Citadel Archives-Museum, Charleston, S.C., hereinafter cited as Clark Collection). For his American edition, he spent one day of research in the Clark papers. It took this author two trips to The Citadel Archives-Museum and two weeks of research—with more than a thousand pages of copies made for a further careful analysis of the most important documents at home—to sift through the ten boxes of the Clark Collection that relate to Austria, as well as Clark's extensive diary. The results are presented in Günter Bischof, "Between Responsibility and Rehabilitation: Austria in International Politics, 1940–1950" (2 vols.; Ph.D. dissertation, Harvard University, 1989), and Bischof, "Mark W. Clark und die Aprilkrise, 1946," *Zeitgeschichte,* XIII (April, 1986), 229–52. Brian Loring Villa will deal with the transfer of 132,374 "other losses" to U.S.

This astonishing assumption sets the stage for Bacque's next conspiracy theory. According to Bacque, a horrified Clark "discovered" in August, 1945, upon assuming duties as military commander in Austria, "deplorable conditions" in the Ebensee camp in Upper Austria.[18] Bacque speculates that Clark tried to "exculpate himself before history" when he wrote a "memo 'for files.'" Bacque asserts that Clark overstepped his authority—insinuating that he was circumventing Eisenhower's sinister orders—when he directed that overcrowding at Ebensee be relieved at once and that food rations of "approximately 2,800 calories" be handed out to the inmates. From this episode Bacque concludes that Clark provisioned camps "on the sly" and adds: "He [Clark] mentions no problem about finding the necessary extra space, shelter or food. All of this could have been done months before, both in this camp and 200 others in Germany."[19]

What is the real context of Clark's extra rations for the Ebensee camp? Clark's policy was not a conspiracy against his good friend Eisenhower.[20] It makes perfect sense if one knows that Ebensee was not a POW/DEF camp, as Bacque makes his readers believe by comparing it to "200 others" in Germany, but principally *a camp for displaced persons.*[21] During the war Ebensee had been a subcamp of the heinous Mauthausen concentration camp system. In 1943 the SS relocated part of Hitler's rocket production program from Peenemünde to underground caverns in the sheltered

---

Forces, Austria, in his forthcoming book, tentatively entitled *Writing History, Writing Fiction: The James Bacque Charges and Controversy.* On the same topic, see also Axel Frohn, "Das Schicksal deutscher Kriegsgefangener in amerikanischen Lagern nach dem Zweiten Weltkrieg: Eine Auseinandersetzung mit den Thesen von James Bacque," *Historisches Jahrbuch,* CXI (1991), 149, 156 (Table IV).

18. Bacque, *Other Losses* (Los Angeles, 1991), 183, maintains that Clark assumed his duties on August 12. In fact, Clark assumed his duties on August 6, arriving in Salzburg from Verona, Italy. See Clark Diary, in Clark Collection.

19. See "Memo dictated by General Clark for files," August 30, 1945, in Folder 4, Box 40, Clark Collection; Bacque, *Other Losses* (Los Angeles, 1991), 183–84, 275–76n13.

20. Had Bacque studied the Clark Collection more carefully, he would have discovered that relations between Clark and his superior Eisenhower were excellent at this time. Not even a hint of circumvention of orders can be found in the Clark papers, let alone in the extensive correspondence between the two men. See Boxes 5 and 6, Clark Collection. Their close friendship went back to the 1930s, when Clark was Eisenhower's personal mentor; they remained lifelong friends. See Daniel D. Holt's excellent essay "An Unlikely Partnership and Service: Dwight D. Eisenhower, Mark Clark, and the Philippines," *Kansas History,* XIII (Autumn, 1990), 149–65.

21. See the map of Allied DP camps in eastern Austria in Thomas Albrich, *Exodus durch Österreich: Die jüdischen Flüchtlinge, 1945–1948* (Innsbruck, 1987), between pp. 32 and 33.

"Ostmark" mountains of Ebensee to produce his "miracle weapons" with forced labor. Of the approximately 8,200 inmates who were worked to death by the Nazis in Ebensee, 38 percent were Jews. On May 6, the U.S. Army liberated Ebensee with 16,000 starving inmates remaining, along with 1,200 bodies stacked at the crematorium. The inmates' average body weight at the time of liberation was seventy-five pounds. As a result of months of daily rations between 500 and 1,000 calories, 735 of the inmates died after liberation from physical exhaustion. Some of the inmates, particularly the Polish Jews, were not repatriated after the war and became charges of the U.S. Army.[22] It was some 2,000 leftover Polish Jews in the Ebensee DP camp whose rations Clark wanted to see drastically improved, not German POWs/DEFs as Bacque implies. In raising the calorie levels in late August, Clark responded to the famous Harrison Report of August 1, 1945, which was extremely critical of U.S. Army's treatment of Jewish DPs in its German and Austrian camps.[23]

Both Clark and Eisenhower were piqued about Harrison's accusations, since they were already giving Jewish DPs preferred food rations of 2,000 calories. With 2,800 daily calories, Clark simply responded to the Harrison Report more quickly than did Eisenhower, who raised his ration levels for Jewish DPs to 2,500 daily calories in October.[24] How could Clark have justified 2,800 daily calories for German POWs/DEFs when the Austrian civilian population did not even get 1,000 calories? Had Bacque followed the DP-camp story in Austria, he would have found that in mid-September, two weeks after the memo "for files," Clark made an inspection tour of some of the larger DP camps in the American zone (not including Ebensee), noting in his diary that he "was exceptionally pleased with conditions of camps as to organization, supervision and operations."[25] Obviously,

22. For the statistics cited here, and on the liberation of Ebensee, see Florian Freund, *Arbeitslager Zement: Das Konzentrationslager Ebensee und die Raketenrüstung* (Vienna, 1989), 422–56. Thomas Albrich mentions that 2,000 Polish Jews lived in Ebensee in June; see *Exodus*, 21. On the horrors of Mauthausen and its horrific subcamps, see also Gordon J. Horwitz, *In the Shadow of Death: Living Outside the Gates of Mauthausen* (New York, 1990). I am grateful to Dr. Thomas Albrich of the University of Innsbruck, an authority on the post–World War II DP question in Austria, for confirming that Ebensee was primarily a DP and not a POW/DEF camp (some POWs may have been kept there, but only temporarily).

23. Albrich, *Exodus,* 27–36.

24. Dwight D. Eisenhower to Harry S Truman, October 8, 1945, in *Eisenhower Papers,* VI, 414–18. On the Harrison Report and DPs, see also Dwight D. Eisenhower to Henry L. Stimson, August 10, 1945, *ibid.,* 266–69.

25. Clark Diary, September 15, 1945. Eisenhower started his personal inspection tour of the DP camps at the same time and sent his report to President Truman three weeks later

conditions in the Austrian and German Jewish DP camps were rapidly improved after the controversial Harrison Report. It is absurd to argue that Clark was circumventing orders by his superior Eisenhower, who also happened to be an old friend.

It is also a gross misreading of history to assert that Clark in Austria (or Eisenhower in Germany) had plenty of food and shelter, as Bacque asserts. In fact, many Austrian cities were as badly destroyed as the German ones. Austria's housing shortage was as severe as Germany's. Eisenhower described the desperate lack of shelter to President Truman: "Added to this influx of population [*i.e.*, refugees and DPs], there is the loss of housing in bombed-out cities, averaging well over 50 percent; the necessity for billeting large numbers of our troops; and the accommodation required for prisoners of war." [26] In the summer of 1945 it was difficult to find shelter and food not only for the Austrian population, but also for more than two million DPs who were in Austria at the end of the war. Moreover, hundreds of thousands of POWs/DEFs poured into Austria in the final days of the war—the rest of the defeated German Wehrmacht flooding into the imaginary "Alpine redoubt" (*Alpenfestung*) from the Balkans, Italy, and Germany.

In mid-May, Clark was in the center of the food crisis developing in southern Austria as a result of the surrender of entire German armies. As the commander of Fifth Army, he complained that the "food and guard situation" for the 300,000 "surrendered personnel" already taken (and 600,000 expected to be taken) was becoming "critical." He added that southern Austria was "becoming [the] clearing house for all stragglers[,] straggling formations[,] and refugees of all nationalities who require food and shelter." [27] At the same time, General Alexander, Clark's superior in the Mediterranean theater, explained to Eisenhower at SHAEF the problems that plagued him in southern Austria, where he had to deal with more than half a million prisoners and surrendered enemy personnel at the end of the war. Alexander complained that because of inadequate local resources in the area, he had to import food for the destitute Austrian population. He noted that he could not move the POWs/SEPs to Italy, since his

---

("efforts to improve their condition continue unabated"), see Dwight D. Eisenhower to Harry S. Truman, September 14, October 8, 1945, in *Eisenhower Papers,* VI, 353–54, 414–18.

26. Eisenhower to Truman, October 8, 1945, in *Eisenhower Papers,* VI, 414.

27. Mark Clark to Richard McCreery, May 14, 1945, in Folder 1, Box 44, Clark Collection.

resources in that country "were already severely strained" to feed the 425,000 POWs/SEPs in his charge there. Alexander's advice to Eisenhower was this: "As you know it has always been planned that Surrendered German Enemy Personnel should be fed by German administration from German resources." Eisenhower and SHAEF refused to take over the responsibility for some 500,000 POWs and refugees in Alexander's Fifth Corps area because of "the serious food situation in this Theater and the handling of three and a half million displaced persons in SHAEF area."[28] Contrary to what Bacque says about abundant food, the food crisis in central Europe was critical.

Between April 9 and May 20, 1945, Anglo-American commanders in Austria had taken 749,160 POWs/SEPs/DEFs and grappled desperately with the same problems that commanders faced in Germany—the masses of surrendered enemy forces created food problems that were irresolvable in the short term.[29] The desperate situation in southern Austria was further aggravated by "the possibility of hostilities" against the Yugoslavs, as Alexander had put it.[30] (Only a week after World War II had ended in Europe, war threatened to break out over the territorial demands of Tito Communist partisans in Trieste and Carinthia; see Thomas Barker's essay.)

This tremendous overcrowding of Austria at the end of the war—not to speak of the chaos prevailing due to the surrenders in Austria and Tito's expansionist desires—caused severe starvation conditions, as bad as anywhere in Europe. In June, 1945, the first Allied commission went into Vienna to explore conditions in the Soviet sector of Austria. It reported: "Food, or rather the lack of it, is today the principal concern of all civilians in Vienna." Soon after coming to Austria, Clark noted in his diary: "Acute hunger is general; the entire population is suffering privations of tragic

---

28. Harold Alexander to Dwight D. Eisenhower, May 16, 1945, in Folder 1, Box 44, Clark Collection; Eisenhower to Alexander, May 18, 1945, in *Eisenhower Papers,* VI, 62–65. Eisenhower added that an additional 2.5 million refugees and displaced persons had to be taken care of in Western Austria.

29. The British Eighth Army had to take care of 338,471 and the American Fifth Army had 410,689 prisoners. See "Memorandum for Staff" by [?] McMahon, May 22, 1945, in Folder 1, Box 5, Clark Collection.

30. Eisenhower reported to General Marshall on May 18: "Alexander has been almost desperate in the tone of his requests to me to take on the task of caring for and feeding several hundred thousand additional prisoners in the mountainous area, but our maintenance situation there is as bad as is his, except of course, that we do not have the threat of Tito's forces on our flank." Dwight D. Eisenhower to George C. Marshall, May 18, 1945, in *Eisenhower Papers,* VI, 65–67.

proportions." [31] Under the Soviets, the official food ration distributed to the Viennese population was at an average of 800 calories (1,600 calories for heavy workers). The official ration for all of Austria had not progressed beyond 1,200 calories by the spring of 1946 (after a brief interlude of 1,550-calorie rations in the fall of 1945). [32]

In fact, food supplies for a starved Austria caused growing East-West tensions over the divided nation, getting the Cold War under way there earlier than elsewhere. The Western powers demanded of the Soviets that they feed Vienna with food supplies from the Balkans, Austria's traditional breadbasket; the Soviets refused to comply. By September, 1945, Clark was gravely alarmed about the food situation in Austria, complaining about the Soviets' not sending in any supplies from Danubia. He added, "I am aware of the alarming proportions to which the US is becoming committed as the residual world supplier." Indeed, Clark ended up feeding both the American and the French zones until the United Nations Relief and Rehabilitation Administration (UNRRA) took over in the summer of 1946. [33] Bacque's understanding of the Austrian situation in the summer of 1945 is as fundamentally flawed as his analysis of Germany at the end of the war. Bacque sees American plenty in central Europe, when pitiful want and deprivation were the true state of affairs. [34]

Bacque is extremely selective and misleading not only with the written historical record and in missing the context; his use of oral-history evi-

31. Special Report of Vienna Mission (U.S. Contingent), June 15, 1945, in Folder 6, Box 44, Clark Collection; Clark Diary, August 14, 1945.

32. Report of Vienna Mission, June 15, 1945; Wilfried Mähr, "Von der UNRRA zum Marshallplan: Die amerikanische Finanz- und Wirtschaftshilfe in den Jahren, 1945–1950" (Doctoral dissertation, University of Vienna, 1985).

33. Clark Diary, September 18, 1945; Bischof, "Between Responsibility and Rehabilitation"; Klaus Eisterer, "Französische Besatzungspolitik in Tirol und Vorarlberg: Aspekte der sozialen, politischen, und ökonomischen Entwicklung, 1945/46" (Doctoral dissertation, University of Innsbruck, 1990); Donald R. Witnah and Edgar L. Erickson, *The American Occupation of Austria: Planning and Early Years* (Westport, Conn., 1985).

34. In his Epilogue to the American edition, Bacque refuses to address the overwhelming historical evidence that there was a great shortage of food in central Europe, beyond admitting that there was a food crisis in Germany in 1946. But again he turns the evidence on its head when he charges that "Allied policy [no longer does he heap the blame on the Americans alone, as in his Canadian edition] deliberately hampered the Germans in attempting to feed themselves." Bacque, *Other Losses* (Los Angeles, 1991), 195. The opposite is true. Had it not been for generous American-army GARIOA (Government Appropriations for Relief in Occupied Areas) aid, German and Austrian civilians would have had a much tougher time surviving the hunger months of 1945 and 1946.

dence also is similarly flawed. The problem with oral history is the perennial unease of scholars with its evidentiary value. How reliable as a historical source are the personal recollections and memoirs, decades after the events, of the actors and participants in history? People have selective and faulty memories—even more so as the events they try to remember turn dimmer, blurring into the fog of a distant past. This faultiness of the human memory is a crucial aspect to keep in mind in every oral-history project.[35] The mighty and the powerful can be misleading and dishonest about their contributions to history, as any reader of historical memoir literature well knows. Similarly, a World War II soldier may have a blinkered view of his past. He often remembers only the extremes of his experiences—tales of gallant heroism or unspeakable horror. The daily routine of soldiery often blurs in the mists of faulty memory. The careful researcher also realizes that the historical actor turned autobiographer can be reticent or—perhaps worse—overeager to tell his side of the story. This is true for both generals and privates. Every oral-history interviewer knows about such pitfalls. In other words, oral histories should never stand alone in reconstructing the historical record.

This is not to say that oral history is not a valuable tool. Practitioners of the new social history have come to rely increasingly on the oral-history interview to recover the experience of the common man—witness the recent popularity of "history from the bottom up." The history of everyday life on both the home front and the battle front during World War II can only be reconstructed from the survivors. Studs Terkel's work is a good example of oral history at its best, re-creating the mood and the "feel" of an era—the American home front during World War II. His model has been followed for World War II Germany.[36] Autobiographical recollections are also valuable in helping historians re-create the actual experience of the sound and fury of battle.[37] In his book *Wartime*, Paul Fussell relies

35. The Scientific Commission for the History of German POWs, which gathered most of its personal reports and oral histories in the 1960s, was very well aware of this methodological pitfall in doing oral histories. In its summary volume, the commission devoted a long essay to the phenomenon of the human memory's transforming events as they recede into the past. See Dieter Cartellieri, "Erinnerungsveränderungen und Zeitabstand: Ein Beitrag zum Problem der Erinnerungsleistungen in Abhängigkeit vom Behaltsintervall," in Maschke *et al.*, *Zusammenfassung*, XV, 103–93.

36. See Studs Terkel, *"The Good War": An Oral History of World War II* (New York, 1984) and Johannes Steinhoff, Peter Pechel, and Dennis Showalter, eds., *Deutsche im Zweiten Weltkrieg: Zeitzeugen sprechen* (Munich, 1989).

37. To date the Eisenhower Center has collected more than 700 oral histories of D-day

largely on diaries, poems, and autobiographical writings to convey the ennui, deprivation, and rawness of the private world of the World War II soldier.[38] On rare occasion, the collecting of oral histories may even recapture a historical moment that otherwise might have been lost to posterity.[39]

A case can be made that life within the POW/DEF camps and enclosures can only be reconstructed from oral-history evidence. Even so, Bacque abuses the process through his highly selective presentation of oral histories and memoir literature. Before looking more closely at Bacque's handling of personal POW remembrances, one should keep in mind the cautioning reminder of William Moss, a noted expert on the use and abuse of oral history: "Whatever other values oral history may have for journalists, novelists, dramatists, educators, and propagandists (and these values may be many), the historian must understand and respect the evidentiary limitations of recollections if he is to use them honestly in his attempts to master the past. He must understand that the evidence has been refracted several times before he confronts it in an oral history recording." Moss concludes that historians should never rely exclusively on oral history.[40]

Not only is the human memory selective, so are historians. Oral history sometimes can produce the results one wants to hear from one's witnesses. Bacque did not approach his oral-history interviews and his selection of personal-memoir literature with the necessary methodological rigor. In one of the two instances described in the following pages Bacque appears to have led his interviewee toward the answer Bacque wanted to hear; in the other, he may actually have fabricated an interviewee's testimony. In any case, Bacque obviously was looking only for confirmation of his hypothe-

veterans in its "D-Day Oral History Project." This collection constitutes a major historical resource on the collective memory of a crucial World War II battle.

38. Paul Fussell, *Wartime: Understanding and Behavior in the Second World War* (New York, 1989).

39. It is well known that for "security reasons" the American government relocated Japanese Americans in "concentration camps" in the interior United States during World War II. Up until recently it was hardly known at all that the government in the initial months of the war also planned to relocate Italian and German "enemy aliens" from the West Coast into the interior. Logistical problems with the vast numbers involved, as well as the anticipated domestic uproar, prevented the government from going ahead. Historian Stephen Fox has reconstructed this "white spot" in the American history books with oral history interviews in *The Unknown Internment: An Oral History of the Relocation of Italian Americans During World War II*, Twayne's Oral History Series, IV (Boston, 1990).

40. Moss, "An Appreciation," 91.

sis that the Americans (and French) committed atrocities on the scale of the Holocaust in "Eisenhower's death camps."

Bacque relies heavily on eyewitnesses to establish crucial links where gaps exist in his documentary chain of evidence. Philip Lauben and John Foster served—or were meant to serve—in the role of crown witnesses for Bacque's hypothesis of the "planned death" of German POWs. Bacque's manipulation of Colonel Lauben is central to his point.

Lauben was in the G-1 division of United States Forces, European Theater. He was involved in the release of all German POWs in the American zone of Germany. Bacque apparently pressed Lauben in his personal interview to say that the category "other losses" in the U.S. Army's reports meant "deaths and escapes." Given that there were relatively few escapees, Bacque took this statement as "unassailable evidence" that all "other losses" must inevitably mean deaths. The trouble is that Lauben is a ninety-one-year-old man who readily admits that his memory "has lapsed to a point where it is quite unreliable." [41] In his extensive interview with the BBC producer Neil Cameron, who did a documentary on the "other losses," Lauben noted that since his out-of-the-blue interview with Bacque he has taken the time to study the category "other losses" in U.S. Army reports on German POWs. After giving the matter some thought, Bacque's crown witness is convinced that "other losses" also includes "many, many thousands of transfers of prisoners of war, from one American command to another command." [42] Even a casual study of the written record readily confirms that "other losses" also included "normal attritions, desertion, release without discharge of Volkssturm personnel and civilians." Transfers, sometimes more than 100,000 in a single day from one U.S. Army group to another, as well as the massive discharge of Volkssturm troops, make up the vast majority of "other losses." [43]

Bacque's problematical use of oral history comes best to light in his interview with John Foster. Bacque thought he needed a missing link—a

41. Bacque, *Other Losses,* 2; Philip Lauben to David Hawkins (of CNN), March 6, 1990, copy in Eisenhower Center, University of New Orleans, hereinafter cited as EC. On Bacque's tendentious Lauben interview, see also "Rewriting History."

42. Neil Cameron interview with Philip Lauben. The Eisenhower Center is grateful to Mr. Cameron for providing a copy of the interview. It is quite in keeping with Bacque's conspiratorial approach to writing history that he now accuses the Pentagon of having "re-educated" Lauben. Thinking that the best defense is to be on the offensive, Bacque calls his critics Eisenhower "apologists," or in the case of Neil Cameron "naive." See *Other Losses* (1991), 180–82.

43. See the Cowdrey essay (esp. the Figures) in this volume, and the Volkssturm document (Fig. 1 in the Introduction).

"smoking gun," so to speak—to answer the question, "Where are the bodies?" of the Germans who supposedly died and vanished under the rubric "other losses." So he went in search of a witness to mass burials of starved German POWs/DEFs from the American camps. Bacque found Foster and apparently quoted him in the draft version of his Epilogue to the American edition as a camp guard "in charge of the work detail of fifty men, Germans and Americans, who did nothing all day but drag bodies out of the camp." The researchers of the CBC documentary, having read the draft Epilogue, tracked down Foster, who told them that "he never was a member of a burial detail, he never buried a body in his life[.] And he's unaware of any such activity in any of the camps." When confronted with Foster's spirited denial of ever having told Bacque that he was a member of a burial squad, Bacque told the CBC interviewer: "Well, he's wrong. He's just wrong."[44] This episode suggests that Bacque may have tried to manufacture some of the oral-history evidence that he needs to buttress his case. Yet he is circumspect enough not to print evidence produced out of thin air (Foster actually called the statements attributed to him "lies"); the troubled Foster interview does not appear in the published version of the Epilogue in the American edition.

To fully appreciate the blatant selectivity in Bacque's use of oral-history evidence, one must keep in mind the vast spectrum of personal experience of some 11 million German POWs during World War II.[45] This diversity also characterized the experience of German POWs in American hands. At one point, the Americans had charge of more than 5 million German POWs/DEFs in Europe and another 390,000 in the United States. Hundreds of thousands of the former POWs are still alive. There is no question that many have harrowing stories to tell about their ordeal in American hands, especially those who went through the Rhine camps. But there are also many who are not bitter about their experiences in American captivity. Naturally, these men are of little interest to Mr. Bacque.

The first big wave of German POWs were caught by the Allies in North Africa after the wholesale surrender of General Erwin Rommel's Afrika Korps. Even a cursory reading of the experience of the early German POWs reveals that they underwent a great variety of treatment. From POW diaries it is clear that the Allies already faced huge logistical problems in

44. "Rewriting History."
45. Maschke has called the history of German POWs "extraordinary," being characterized by the basic situation of captivity but also by a "boundless diversity" (*unendliche Mannigfaltigkeit*). See Maschke, "Einleitung," in Maschke, *et al., Zusammenfassung,* 3.

Günter Bischof

North Africa in their handling of German POWs. POWs were frequently transferred between Allied camps, they were harrassed by camp guards, they experienced inadequate shelter due to a lack of tents, and at times they also received insufficient food. A summary judgment was that German POWs were "treated well in British camps, badly in American camps, and criminally in French camps." [46]

Generally speaking, German POWs who were transferred to camps in the United States received good treatment and more-than-adequate rations. (Many of those captured in North Africa remained ardent Nazis, terrorizing their antifascist fellow inmates even when the war was over. Only after the end of the war did American reeducation programs counter such deeply ingrained ideological predispositions.)[47] Most of the German POWs in the United States worked as field hands on American farms and plantations, with regular workdays of eight to twelve hours. They received adequate medical treatment; they were allowed to organize their own entertainment, which included musical bands and stage plays. Some of them got college degrees by taking extension courses. In Camp McDermott, in Arkansas, German officers organized their own university, with regular college lectures, and built their own zoo in the swamps along the Mississippi.[48] In the first weeks after the end of the war—probably because the full tragedy of the concentration camps became widely known—there was a marked increase of harrassment by camp guards and a notable decline in the food rations; the rations improved again late in 1945. Dieter Braun recalls that at the end of the war the POWs in Canada were reduced from "excellent"

46. Excerpts from Hermann Schöppl von Sonnwalden Diary, copy of typescript in EC. See also the fascinating report "Reisebericht" in Kurt W. Böhme and Helmut Wolff, eds., *Aufzeichnungen über die Kriegsgefangenschaft im Westen* (Munich, 1973), 71–98, 2. Beiheft of the Maschke Commission. For the situation in the French *"dépots"* of North Africa, see Kurt W. Böhme, *Die deutschen Kriegsgefangenen in französischer Hand* (Munich, 1971), 11–14, 33–47, Vol. XIII of Maschke Commission.

47. Ronald H. Bailey, *Prisoners of War* (Alexandria, Va., 1981), 140–69; Arnold P. Krammer, *Nazi Prisoners of War in America* (New York, 1979); Hermann Jung, *Die deutschen Kriegsgefangenen in amerikanischer Hand: USA* (Munich, 1972), vol. X, Pt. 1 of Maschke Commission; O. W. Thiele Diary, copy of typescript in EC. "Usually the POWs from the Africa Korps were the unreconstructed Nazis," remembers Ernst Gies. See typescript at Eisenhower Center, UNO. See also "Reisebericht" in Böhme and Wolff, eds., *Aufzeichnungen,* 105 ff. On the struggle inside the camps between Nazis and antifascists, and on the American reeducation program in one American camp, see Bruce Blank, "Camp Plauché POWs: Germans Under the Huey P. Long Bridge, 1944–1946" (Master's thesis, University of New Orleans, 1991). See also Carell and Böddeker, *Die Gefangenen,* 131–36.

48. Thiele Diary; Hans Höller papers and oral history, in EC.

rations to "concentration camp rations." But any study at all of the German POW experience in the North American camps clearly shows that the overall experience was well within the Geneva Convention rules for POWs.[49]

In Europe, however, the Americans were totally unprepared to deal with the more than 5 million German POWs at the end of the war. As a result of chaos in Germany and a lack of food, somewhere between 4,000 and 56,000 German POWs perished—more than the 4,000 counted by the Maschke Commission and no more than the 56,000 given as an upper limit in the Cowdrey essay—but certainly far less than Bacque's million.[50]

Many German POWs/DEFs have survived to tell about their suffering in American camps and enclosures in Germany. That suffering, however, was not the result of American policy. It was rather the upshot of inadequate preparations to deal with the huge numbers of captured. Barely 2,400 men of the American 159th Regiment, for example, had to take care of and guard more than 300,000 German POWs/DEFs captured in the Ruhr pocket. They had to build the Remagen and Sinzig enclosures from scratch within a few weeks.[51] By April, 1945, entire German army groups were surrendering to the Allies. The numbers were too overwhelming for Allied shipping capacity; after March no further transfers were made to the relatively cozy camps in the United States. In the summer of 1945, the Americans needed all their available shipping to transport the European forces to the Pacific theater for the planned invasion of Japan. In spite of Bacque's contention that there was no transportation problem, the acute American lack of shipping also affected the available tonnage for moving food to Europe. The lack of shipping, next to the necessity of feeding more than 5 million German POWs and some 20 million DPs and refugees—not to mention the German civilian population under the tutelage of the U.S. Army—answers the question of one former German POW, who wondered

49. See secondary sources cited in notes 46–48; Schöppl von Sonnwalden Diary; and personal interviews with and written reports by Dieter Braun, Ernst Gies, O. W. Thiele, Karl Höller, Erich Luft, Josef Bischof, Josef Dietrich, Josef Emhofer, Franz Kornfeld, Johann Haslauer, Andreas Höppberger, tyepescripts and handwritten reports in EC.

50. See Overmans and Cowdrey essays in this volume (Overmans argues that the low count of the Maschke Commission may not be wrong). The CBC interviewers went back to the Swiss Red Cross official Jean-Pierre Pradervand, who told them that he found Bacque's high death count "idiotic" and "an immense exaggeration." He apparently had told Bacque in a 1988 interview that Bacque's numbers were wrong and that he should "drop a zero" from his overall totals. See "Rewriting History."

51. Dr. Shea Halle, Nicholas Gordon, and Dr. Albert Hammon oral histories and reports, in EC.

why there was such a deterioration in the food situation in the months following the end of the war.[52]

With regard to Bacque's use of oral history, it also needs to be pointed out that not all American camps in Germany were as bad as the notorious 16 transient enclosures on the Rhine. Bacque admits that there were more than 200 American POW camps in Germany (1,600 in France), many of them small ones (see the map on pp. 14–15 for the locations of the camps in Germany).[53] In most of these, people were treated as well as the chaos of May–June, 1945, permitted. At the end of the war, no one got a lot of food, simply because there was very little to go around.[54] In spite of the suffering of the DEFs in the Rhine meadow camps—resulting, to repeat, from the vast numbers, not from American policy—POWs were generally sheltered and treated as adequately as the situation permitted, especially after the first chaotic weeks in May and June.

No doubt human suffering became a daily routine for many POWs/DEFs in the first weeks after their capture. But contrary to what Bacque tries to make his readers believe, relatively few POWs/DEFs attribute their misery to a vindictive and murderous American policy. Harald Jesser, an officer in the 225th Infantry Division fighting in Courland at the end of the war, was captured on May 5 at Ratzeburg in eastern Germany. In his first

---

52. Bavaria in the U.S. zone, for example, had to cope with 1.7 million refugees. There were Bavarian villages that doubled their population in June, 1945; the city of Ingoldstadt quadrupled its population. Feeding these "aliens"—often through a quickly developing black market—and coping with the social dislocations resulting from such a massive influx virtually defines the social history of Bavarian villages after the war. See the outstanding essays by Juliane Wetzel and Paul Erker in *Von Stalingrad zur Währungsreform: Zur Sozialgeschichte des Umbruchs in Deutschland,* ed. Martin Broszat, Klaus-Dietmar Henke, and Hans Woller (Munich, 1989), 327–425. See also the Introduction to this volume. The former POW who wondered about the decline in the rations noted that they had been good until the end of the war and improved again "a few months following the end of the war." He added, "The same experience [of uneven food distribution over the course of 1945] has also been noted by German POWs in American camps both in France and the U.S." Personal report by Karl Becker, typescript in EC.

53. For a precise list of American camps in Germany, as well as complete maps, see Kurt W. Böhme, *Die deutschen Kriegsgefangenen in amerikanischer Hand: Europa* (Munich, 1973), 225–48 and following 330, Vol. X, Pt. 2 of Maschke Commission. For a precise list and complete map of French camps, see Böhme, *In französischer Hand,* 307–90 and following 392.

54. John E. Farquharson, *The Western Allies and the Politics of Food: Agrarian Management in Postwar Germany* (Leamington Spa, Eng., 1985). See also the Introduction and the Tent essay in this volume.

POW camp, in Behlendorf, he was sheltered in a German Wehrmacht tent; the provisions were minimal, but he has no difficulty accepting as an explanation the inadequate preparations of the Americans for "feeding masses of prisoners." In his experience, POWs were not harrassed and the camp guards were hardly noted. He fled, was recaptured, and went through four more camps; he received increasingly more food as the summer progressed. His discharge came on September 28, 1945. His assessment: "In general I had the impression that one cannot speak of a wholesale mistreatment of the POWs." He concludes: "The small rations, which were indeed life-threatening, were a result of the chaotic circumstances in Northern Germany in the first months after the end of the war." [55]

Anton Herr, a young Bavarian captain commanding tanks in the 21st Panzer Division, was captured outside Bad Tölz, on the Austrian border. Transferred to a camp in Ulm, he went through some bad weeks in May. He was hungry, but so was everybody else at the time. He did not witness any mass deaths. The Americans discharged him in June. They captured Rolf Franke-Prasse, another officer from the 21st Panzer, in Bavaria, kept him in a hospital train in beds with white linen, and discharged him after five weeks. The Americans captured Fritz Fellner, today a prominent Austrian historian, in northern Italy. He received adequate food rations. The fact that surrendered German prisoners were in open enclosures did not lead to desperate conditions under the sunny skies of Italy as it did under the rainy ones of the German Rhineland. [56]

Bacque's grisly Chapter 4, "The Cruelty of the Victor," relies almost exclusively on oral histories and personal reports. [57] This chapter, more than any other part of the book, sets the emotional tone for the allegedly murderous American treatment of German POWs. The most chilling document is the diary from one unidentified "Ph.D.," cited at length over four pages and taken from Kurt Böhme's *Die deutschen Kriegsgefangenen in amerikanischer Hand.* [58]

---

55. Harald Jesser, personal report to author, March 5, 1990, in EC.

56. Anton Herr and Rolf Franke-Prasse, personal interviews with author, transcripts in EC; Fritz Fellner, conversation with the author. Bacque does concede that Mark Clark provided enough food for the German POWs captured in Italy. Whether this was possible because of fewer logistical problems due to far lower numbers (291,000 German POWs), better weather conditions (making the lack of tents for sheltering prisoners a less pressing matter), or more food available in the Italian theater is not divulged. See Bacque, *Other Losses,* 164.

57. Bacque, *Other Losses,* 37–49.

58. *Ibid.,* 41–45. As a matter of principle, none of the persons who supplied the more

Günter Bischof

Bacque's highly selective use of this diary is a good example of his questionable methodology. The prisoner was of a philosophical and deeply religious bent and described his desolate state of bare survival from an existentialist point of view. Bacque carefully neglects to quote sections in which the language is very reminiscent of the Germany that had just collapsed.[59] Instead, he selects the most ghastly passages from the first few entries of the diary, when the prisoner was at the Rheinberg camp. Nor does Bacque tell his readers that after two miserable weeks at Rheinberg this prisoner, who had fallen ill, was transferred by the Americans to the medical camp (*Lazarett*) Lintfort at the end of May, where he was treated and operated on for an inflamed arm. At Lintfort the prisoner slept in a bed with blankets and received plenty of food. "It's like a dream," he noted on May 28. Transferred to Reydt, another *Lazarett*, on June 9, he was fed cheese and sausages and chicken. He commented: "The Americans are odd people. First they almost starve the prisoners to death. Before they [the POWs] bite the dust, however, they start caring for them with an attention that is touching (at least as far as the food is concerned)."[60] On June 16, said prisoner was transferred once again, to the American camp Wickrathberg—back to a miserable life under open skies, without tents and with minimal rations. Only when the British took over Wickrathberg on June 26 did the situation improve; the British immediately housed POWs in tents and fed them adequate rations. After another transfer to Rheinberg, the prisoner was discharged in Heilbronn on August 24.[61] In

---

than 45,000 personal reports and oral histories collected by the Maschke Commission is identified by name. Note that in the Canadian edition Bacque erroneously cites the diary as having been reprinted in Böhme's *Die deutschen Kriegsgefangenen in französischer Hand;* in fact, it is reprinted in Böhme's *In amerikanischer Hand: Europa,* 309–30. The error is corrected in the American edition (1991), 41.

59. For example, when the POWs get together to sing songs such as "Deutschland, heiliger Name," the prisoner wonders whether *Deutschland* is a "sacred word," and adds: "We lift up our spirit.—Germany is not lost yet!—There are some people with community spirit.—The people's spirit is expressed in the text and melody of the songs. Moral powers can be felt." ["'Deutschland, heiliger Name (*heiliges Wort?*).'—Wir erheben unseren Geist.—Noch ist Deutschland nicht verloren!—Es gibt noch Menschen mit Gemeinschaftsgefühl.—In Text u[nd] Melodie der Lieder spricht sich der Volksgeist aus. Sittliche Kräfte sind spürbar."] Entry of May 17, in Böhme, *In amerikanischer Hand: Europa,* 310 (translation by this writer).

60. "Der Amerikaner sind merkwürdige Leute. Zuerst lassen sie die Gefangenen fast verhungern. Wenn sie am Abschnappen sind, sorgen sie mit rührender Sorgfalt für sie (wenigstens was das Essen angeht)." Entries of June 9 and 11, *ibid.,* 321–22.

61. *Ibid.,* 324–30.

sum, Bacque extracted only the most harrowing mid-May passages from one diary to make the reader believe that conditions in Rheinberg, probably the worst among the American transient DEF camps, were the typical experience.

Bacque also fails to acknowledge the fact that the ghastly Prisoner of War Transient Enclosures—the "hunger camps" on the Rhine—had already been identified by Kurt Böhme almost twenty years before the publication of *Other Losses* as the worst of the American camps, with higher-than-average mortality rates.[62] When entire German army groups surrendered on the western front in the final days of the war—with the self-regulating cohesion of German military units inexplicably broken up by the U.S. Army—millions of German DEFs were rounded up in open-field, makeshift "cages," mostly on the western bank of the Rhine.[63] The sad condition in the enclosures was known to contemporaries and commented on in the press. For anyone who can read German, Böhme described the full horror of these "cages" on the basis of numerous eye-witness accounts in his volume on American POWs in Europe. It bears repeating that this outstanding scholar, who personally experienced the POW existence in a French camp, is maligned by Bacque as a "client-academic" who "reproduced lies by the French and Americans."

In May most of the Rhine transient enclosures held more than twice as many DEFs as they had been designed for. By the end of the summer of 1945, most DEFs in the Rhine camps had been discharged or transferred, and some of the camps had been handed over to the British or French. In the summer of 1945 conditions improved dramatically in the camps, as can readily be seen in the photographic record, because the Allies were finally organized and discharges were decreasing the number of prisoners. In spite of the months of bad conditions, Böhme insists that there were no mass deaths in the Rhine meadow camps.[64]

62. *Ibid.,* 194–205. Michael Schneider, who survived the "catastrophic conditions" of Sinzig and Andernach as a seventeen-year-old and personally witnessed the deaths of comrades, considers the careful work of the Maschke Commission more credible and conclusive than the "speculative percentage calculations masquerading as theses" in Bacque's "planned death." See *Schwäbische Zeitung,* May 22, 1991.

63. In the case of the American POWs taken at Wake Island in the Pacific theater, Gregory J. W. Urwin has shown that their survival rate in the dismal Japanese camps was relatively high because they managed to maintain unit cohesion. See Urwin, "The Defenders of Wake Island: Their Two Wars, 1941–1945" (Ph.D. dissertation, University of Notre Dame, 1984).

64. See Böhme, *In amerikanischer Hand: Europa,* 139. Although rejecting Bacque's no-

Bacque relies on six personal accounts for Chapter 4—three from the Rheinberg camp (by Thelen, Iff, and the "Ph.D." diarist), one from the Bad Kreuznach (by Heinz T.), one from Remagen (by von Luttichau), and one from an unnamed Rhine camp (by George Weiss). Böhme has singled out Rheinberg, Bad Kreuznach–Bretzenheim, Remagen-Sinzig, Heisdesheim, Wickrathberg, and Büderich as the DEF camps with the highest mortality rates in Germany.[65] To select out of 5 million German POWs in American hands six men who were held in three or four of the very worst camps is surely not the way to arrive at the most representative sample for making a persuasive case concerning the German POW experience in American hands.

This is not to deny that Bacque's six eyewitnesses fairly accurately reflect the appalling conditions in the Rhine meadow camps. The interviews in Neil Cameron's BBC documentary buttress this part of Bacque's oral-history evidence, as do countless other autobiographical reports and published memoirs.[66] There can be little doubt that conditions in the worst of the camps were horrific—in the first weeks of May, even inhuman. The small sample of diaries, reports, and oral histories I have gathered from Austrian and German POWs captured by the Americans at the end of the war and kept in the Rhine camps confirms Bacque's oral-history evidence of much human suffering. What cannot be confirmed from such personal memoirs is Bacque's high death rate. A few examples must suffice.

Hermann Greiner, a soldier in a tank battalion, was captured on April 8 in the *Ruhrkessel*. He ended up in an orchard in Remagen. He lived in a hole, without water, for days on end; the regular daily diet consisted of one

---

tion of 30-percent mortality rates, Axel Frohn is one German historian who nevertheless questions Böhme's low mortality rates. See Frohn, "Das Schicksal deutscher Kriegsgefangener."

65. Böhme, *In amerikanischer Hand: Europa,* 194–205.

66. "Accounts of a Forgotten Army," *Timewatch* (BBC), 1990, transcript in EC. See also Böhme, *In amerikanischer Hand: Europa,* 482–85, and Carell and Böddeker, *Die Gefangenen,* 147–59. The annotated bibliography by Paul Boytinck, "German Prisoners of War in American Camps: Personal Narratives," copy of typescript in EC, is useful, if one-sidedly pro-Bacque. The publication of a translation of Bacque's book in Germany (*Der geplante Tod* [Frankfurt am Main 1989]) produced a spate of newspaper reviews and reports, often followed by letters to the editor. Most of these letters reconfirmed the picture that Bacque painted of the Rhine camps. See, for example, Karl Heinz Janssen in *Die Zeit,* December 8, 1989, and letters under the title "Monatelang vegetiert," in *Die Zeit,* February 23, 1990; "Eine lange Nacht der Lügen," *Der Spiegel,* October 2, 1989, pp. 129–32, and letters *ibid.,* October 23, 1989, pp. 7–9; Torsten Harmsen's report in *Berliner Zeitung,* November 23, 1990. See also the personal reports cited in the following several footnotes.

cookie, one spoon of coffee, one spoon of egg powder, and dried red beets.[67] Karl Schranzhofer, a private first class in air force communications, was captured on the eastern front; he was happy to fall into American captivity, but his long report details his harrowing experiences in Rheinberg. He says he lost twenty-seven kilograms—nearly sixty pounds—of his body weight in two weeks (from sixty-five to thirty-eight kilos). Schranzhofer fully supports Bacque's charges but does not claim to have actually witnessed mass deaths.[68]

The wounded Sepp Kräftner was captured on the western front and frequently collapsed because of undernourishment and weakness in the Büderich camp. He saw people dying in Büderich and the French camp Rivesaltes, where the rations remained minimal in the fall of 1945. Despite his harrowing experiences, he does not believe Bacque's charges. Instead, he blames the suffering on the huge influx of German soldiers from the eastern front surrendering to the U.S. forces, which "totally surprised" the Americans.[69]

Josef Wimmer, a soldier from Cologne with an artillery company, was taken prisoner on April 8 on the western front. An American soldier with his left "arm full of wristwatches" took away everything Wimmer carried, including his war decorations, as trophies. In the night of April 8–9, Wimmer was herded with others into a Catholic church and not allowed to step out to relieve himself. He ended up in Andernach, another temporary enclosure on the Rhine; in the fall of 1945 he was transferred to a French camp in Sedan. During all this time he was never sufficiently fed. The sixteen-year-old Hans Hologschwantner was forced to join the Volkssturm in January, 1945. In training with other boys and women for antiaircraft deployment, he was captured by the American "Cactus Division" on April 28 in Upper Bavaria. First kept in a camp in Kaufbeuren without shelter in subzero weather, he received no food for two days. Transferred to Heilbronn, he lived in a hole in the ground for a few weeks, receiving C and K rations. His trials and tribulations continued in three different French camps; he was discharged in August, 1945.[70]

67. Hermann Greiner to Günter Bischof, April 16, 1990, in EC.

68. Mr. Schranzhofer has kindly advised me to stay out of "defending the machinations [*Machenschaften*] of Eisenhower's U.S. Army and his clique" since it only could destroy my "reputation as a historian." Karl Schranzhofer to Günter Bischof, March 12, June 16, 1990, in EC.

69. Josef Kräftner to Günter Bischof, February 24, 1990, in EC.

70. Josef Wimmer to Günter Bischof, September 19, 1990, and Hans Hologschwantner to Günter Bischof, February 24, 1990, both in EC. In the final months of the war, American

Dr. Otto Stur, a Viennese physician, was drafted into the Wehrmacht as a seventeen-year-old and was stationed in an antiaircraft battery on the western front. His personal diary tells of great deprivation. The U.S. Army captured him outside of Ulm in southern Germany on April 27. During his initial thirty hours in captivity he received no water. In the first days he received irregular but sufficient rations. Like Hologschwantner, he also ended up in the Heilbronn camp, in a cage with an open ditch serving as a latrine. The camp rations were minimal. He recorded in great detail how the starvation diet led to a quick deterioration of his health, an arrhythmic heartbeat (which stayed with him for the rest of his life), and frequent blackouts. On June 9 he managed to wash himself for the first time; on June 16 he received his first piece of soap. Only on June 19 was he finally given a tent, when transferred to another camp in the Heilbronn vicinity. He was transferred to a French camp in the Champagne on July 11, where he got somewhat better rations. He lost eleven kilos in body weight during his imprisonment (in spite of the improved French rations later in 1945). His estimate is that he and the other prisoners received 500 to 600 daily calories most of the time, and during a few weeks 800 to 900 calories. The prisoners frequently suffered from a lack of water; only once were they sprayed with DDT against lice. Stur's conclusion: "It's probable that POWs in worse physical condition than myself may have had a worse time surviving." [71]

The oral-history evidence of the German prisoners has to be balanced against the testimony of American camp guards. Bacque is characteristically selective in making the Andernach camp guard Martin Brech another of his crown witnesses. Brech, who has consorted with historical "revisionists" denying the Holocaust, has insisted on every possible occasion that starvation of POWs/DEFs was ordered as a matter of policy by "higher-ups" in the American army. [72] Dr. Shea Halle, Dr. Albert Hammon, and

---

units such as the 101st Airborne troops enclosed in Bastogne during the Battle of the Bulge fought for weeks on K-rations and without shelter. See Lawrence Kuenzi oral history, in EC, and the forthcoming (1992) book *Band of Brothers,* on E Company of the 101st Airborne, by Stephen E. Ambrose.

71. Dr. Otto Stur Diary and report, in EC.

72. Brech has repeatedly acted as Bacque's hit man, speaking of wholesale starvation conditions at Andernach, denial of water, and machine-gunning of DEFs. See his letter to the New York *Times,* quoted on the back dust jacket of *Other Losses* (1991); see also p. 189 of that edition. Brech has given the same evidence in Neil Cameron's BBC and Linden Mac-Intyre's CBC documentaries. The CBC documentary shows Brech lecturing before the "re-

Nicholas Gordon tell a different story from Remagen-Sinzig and Andernach. They do not deny the unspeakable chaos during the initial phase of these camps, as well as what Mark Clark called the "food and guard problem." They were part of the 2,400 men of 159th Infantry, with attached units, assigned to build and guard Remagen-Sinzig, Andernach, and Koblenz on the Rhine.

According to Dr. Hammon, three companies of approximately 200 men each "were to each receive, guard and care for 100,000 men each" at Remagen-Sinzig, Andernach, and Koblenz. Starting in mid-April, they built the enclosures from scratch with wooden poles and barbed wire, digging kilometers of slit trenches into plowed fields for prisoners to relieve themselves. Dr. Harmon describes the problem of numbers at Sinzig as follows:

> The 100,000 men arrived from the Ruhr in open trailers day and night. Perhaps 50 men to a truck. We turned them into an open field that had one strand of barbed wire three miles long, one mile wide, and the Rhine as one of the sides of the enclosure. Then it started raining. Day after day it rained. We were wet, the POWs were wet, and all were miserable. Fortunately it wasn't cold. At night we couldn't relieve the guards, since it was dark and raining. They would fire their machine guns at the slightest movement. (One strand of barbed wire offered little protection.) In the morning we would find dead cows, dogs, cats, etc.—no POWs, since they had no desire to leave. They could have easily crossed the Rhine, but few tried to escape. We would not have cared if they did escape, since the war was almost over and we had more than we could care for those first two-three weeks.
>
> We scrounged, stole, begged, and liberated all supplies we could at first, but by the end of the second week we had plenty of help and supplies.
>
> Yes, there were a few dead POWs at first. I don't know of any due to actions on the part of our troops. Most were SS men and killed by the German troops who shared the POW compound and hated and feared the SS.

According to Dr. Hammon, the burgomaster of Sinzig and the local population helped feed the prisoners the first few weeks until food supplies were organized.[73]

---

visionist" Topical Review Committee. Brech's lecture is introduced with the following words: "We are here tonight to hear an eyewitness report of an American war crime of such staggering magnitude and shocking barbarity as to provoke incredulity and disbelief." Brech has also written in notorious "revisionist" publications that deny the Holocaust. See "Rewriting History."

73. Written report by Dr. Albert R. Hammon, July 20, 1991, in EC.

Dr. Shea Halle remembers how the water problem was solved at Remagen-Sinzig:

> The next thing we were aware of was that there was no water. This, of course, was dreadful—the fact that there was no water for these people. I didn't know what the army was going to do. But about the third day or so—I imagine about the third day, this of course depends on memory, but it was several days without water—then the army engineers showed up and they put rowboats, they anchored rowboats into the Rhine River, and then they brought pipes from the rowboats. They had a chlorinator in the bottom of the boat. They brought the pipe out of the river and brought it right through, almost a half a mile long, right through the camp. Every fifty feet or so they put a spigot, and they had them at tremendous intervals—not big intervals. So there was no water problem. They solved the water problem in a very simple way with these chlorinators.
>
> No problem with water. Then it took a day or two more. The army unloaded rations—all kinds of American rations that the Germans were able to split up and break up. So about the fifth day they brought us loads of food.

There was still not enough food to go around, and prisoners did get diarrhea and blood in their urine due to malnourishment.[74]

These medical officers and the Remagen communications officer Nicholas Gordon insist that they did everything in their power to guarantee the best possible treatment of the POWs/DEFs in their charge. They are absolutely certain that they never received orders from "higher-ups" to withhold food and water from German prisoners. Given that they had little in terms of food and medical supplies to start with, they made the best of a desperate situation. These guards do remember deaths in the camp—not infrequently Germans killing Germans—which of course is not to say that no German POWs died from exhaustion and starvation.[75]

Starting on April 27, Lieutenant Colonel Jack McAllister built and commanded Camp Wickrathberg in northern Germany; on July 12, the

---

74. Dr. Shea Halle oral history, in EC.

75. Nicholas Gordon oral history, in EC; Halle oral history and Hammon report, *ibid.* Dr. Ted Grisell was the medical director of a camp in Laon, France. He reports that deaths were few. From his interpreter and assistant, von Ribbentrop—the son of the Nazi Foreign Minister—he heard, however, that "the animosity between the Wehrmacht, who were primarily the citizen soldiers of the German Army, and the SS troops caused the numerous altercations that resulted in several murders a week." Ted L. Grisell to *Indianapolis Star,* April 1, 1990, copy in EC. Nazis hounding anti-Nazis, sometimes ending in murder, was not an uncommon feature in the POW camps in the U.S. See Krammer, *Nazi Prisoners of War in America,* and Thiele Diary, in EC.

camp was turned over to the British. "My recollections are in violent opposition to the views expressed by Bacque," says McAllister and explains:

> Considering that at the time I arrived with a provisional Battalion from the Third Infantry Regiment at a piece of real estate upon which the Engineers were rapidly constructing a number of containment enclosures as well as installing a drinking water system to supply each compartment, we perforce had to draw upon (scrounge) the basic things to support the soon-to-arrive PWs. For example, large cooking kettles for each enclosure were "liberated" from industrial and other sources in the adjacent areas. Bread was made from flour which we furnished to some 16 local bakeries which were only too glad to be working. (Did you ever see a 6 × 6 truck loaded to the roof with long loaves?) I will concede that food initally, although adequate, was spartan until the supply chain became more effective. No one was starved!
>
> One enclosure was designated as a hospital area, equipped with tentage, etc., staffed with German medical personnel drawn from their own fellow PWs. As I remember, it had no unusual morbidity or mortality rate. During the time I was in command we had very few deaths. I remember a US Graves registration unit established a small location but had little activity. As to the adequacy of diet, I still remember the inspection I made with a British Brigadier who was to succeed me. When we came to the large farm barn structures where we had our supplies he asked, "And do you give these blighters all that jam?" Having enjoyed his hospitality at a mess at an adjacent British unit I suspected that his people would get a bit of a change for their bread.
>
> At its peak, the camp contained about 100,000 PWs. These arrived by the trainload from the East and were unloaded about 2 km from the enclosure and marched to the area. (In a citation I received it states, "received and processed 50,000 in one day.") We attempted to process and release PWs as soon as practicable, following General Patton's unofficial comment "Turn the B . . . s loose."[76]

These recollections speak for themselves. In this small but perhaps not unrepresentative sample of oral histories, only one man supports Bacque's charges, whereas the rest reject them—and even that man, despite having been in one of the very worst camps, does not say that he actually witnessed deaths on the scale claimed by Bacque. Privation, sometimes terrible, there certainly was, resulting in quite a few deaths—but not in mass deaths.

Conditions in the American camps were bad in the first chaotic weeks after the war ended. Those who died never had a chance to tell their story. Those

76. Jack McAllister to Stephen Ambrose, March 12, 1991, in EC.

who survived have spoken out long before Bacque's sensational book and provided sufficient detail to make the facts irrefutable.[77] To repeat the principal point: due to the chaotic conditions in the American enclosures during the first weeks of captivity, thousands of German POWs/DEFs died—but not a million or anything remotely approaching a million. Contrary to Bacque's sensationalist charges, the plight of these prisoners has been known in the towns along the Rhine since May, 1945. Moreover, the suffering was systematically recounted by the historians of the Maschke Commission in the 1960s and 1970s and popularized by Paul Carrell and Günter Böddeker, as well as by Rolf Steininger and Heribert Schwan in books published in the early 1980s. It is telling that these two popular books (with plenty of pictures) are never cited by Bacque, nor do they appear in his Bibliography.[78] Again, Bacque's unfamiliarity with the literature leads him to extravagant charges against the historical profession of suppression of evidence, "cover-up," "myth-making," and "whiting out" of evidence.[79]

Unquestionably, gruesome tales can be told from the Rhine camps. Yet the totality of German POW experience during and after World War II is a much more complicated story than Bacque's highly selective use of evidence makes readers believe.[80] He produces an emotional pitch of outrage in his Chapter 4, based on oral history and personal memoirs, so that a permanent image of gross and inhuman American (and French) behavior is created in the mind of the casual reader (this highly emotionalized pre-

77. Böhme, *In amerikanischer Hand: Europa,* 142–63.

78. Carell and Böddeker, *Die Gefangenen;* Heribert Schwan and Rolf Steininger, *Als der Krieg zu Ende ging* (Berlin, 1981). It is ironical that Ullstein, which published the Carell/Böddeker and Schwan/Steininger books, both clearly showing the plight of the German POWs, flooded the German market with a quickly translated German edition of Bacque's *Other Losses* that totally ignores those two books. Ullstein further sensationalized the charges by translating the cryptic title *Other Losses* as *Der geplante Tod* ("planned death"). In other words, the publisher made money from two German books that told the full tragedy of the German POWs, then made even heftier profits from publishing Bacque's false charge that German historians have failed to tackle the issue of German POWs! See also the Steininger essay in this volume.

79. See esp. Bacque's chapter "Myth, Lies and History," *Other Losses* (Los Angeles, 1991), 143–61.

80. A more careful scholarly approach can produce a representative sample of the global German POW experience, as is demonstrated in Johannes Steinhoff, Peter Pechel, and Dennis Showalter, eds., *Deutsche im Zweiten Weltkrieg: Zeitzeugen Sprechen* (Munich, 1989), 693–723. In this oral-history collection, nine POW stories are reported. Two are from American captivity—one positive experience from a camp in the United States, one negative experience from Sinzig. The rest are Russian captivity stories, including one positive one.

sentation of German POW suffering and the inherent anti-American drift of the thesis has lent the book best-seller status in Germany and Canada).[81] The lasting impression the reader draws from Bacque's book is an image of premeditated and willful American (and French) cruelty, resulting in a "million dead." The facts are different. In spite of some callous American treatment of German POWs, the vast majority of German POWs in American hands were treated as well as conditions allowed, and survived.

Bacque's technique leads to a more sinister conclusion that he never makes fully explicit. What emerges from the "million dead" is the notion that the American POW/DEF "death camps" are directly comparable to German concentration camps. Ernest Fisher sets the tone in his Foreword to *Other Losses:* "Not since the horrors of the Confederate-administered prison at Andersonville during the American Civil War had such cruelties taken place under American military control."[82] In the same vein, in his next-to-last chapter, Bacque at one point cites Robert Murphy, who visited a "camp" in which "our prisoners were almost as weak and emaciated as those I had observed in Nazi prison camps." The trouble with this citation is that Murphy wrote about an "*American internment camp . . .* of 'little Nazis' awaiting classification." Internment camps were the holding camps where the denazification process was administered; here the "little Nazis" on the local and provincial level were separated from the SS, the SA troopers (the *Sturmabteilung,* who made a name for themselves by intimidating and sometimes killing those who opposed the Nazis), and other potential German war criminals (the system admittedly was not perfect; Adolf Eichmann escaped the denazification process by putting on the uniform of an air force corporal).[83] Bacque, throwing POW camps and internment camps into the same hopper, much as he did with the Ebensee DP camp in Austria

81. Brian Villa is surely correct in observing that the success of the book in Canada and Europe has much to do with its "Yank bashing" quality. See Brian Loring Villa to the *Times* (London) *Literary Supplement,* January 4, 1991.

82. Fisher in Bacque, *Other Losses* (Los Angeles, 1991), xix.

83. Bacque, *Other Losses* (Los Angeles, 1991), 150–51; Robert Murphy, *Diplomat Among Warriors* (New York, 1964), 293–94 (emphasis added). In the American internment camps of Bavaria alone, around 100,000 Germans were held at the end of 1945 (90 percent of them Nazi party members) for investigation into possible criminal activity. The food situation in these camps also was very bad in the summer of 1945. In the case of the internment camp Nuremberg-Langwasser, German prisoners dug a secret tunnel under the fence to get to food supplies in a full American depot outside of the fence. See Christa Schick, "Die Internierungslager," in *Von Stalingrad zur Währungsreform,* ed. Broszat, Henke, and Woller, 301–25, esp. 306.

Günter Bischof

mentioned earlier, demonstrates his poor understanding of the historical context of Allied reeducation policy in Germany after the war. He fails to acknowledge that denazification constituted one of the centerpieces of American policy in postwar Germany.

Bacque closes his book by noting that with their "vengeful atrocities," American and French commanders were "sinking toward the evil which we had all supposed we were fighting." At this point Bacque probably has most of his readers convinced that the American "death camps" hardly differed from Nazi concentration camps.[84] The fact is that there were not a "million dead," nor were there any American "death camps." It seems to have slipped Bacque's attention that the Americans reluctantly came to the European continent to defeat the Nazis and not to copy their heinous crimes.

Following the emotionally charged controversy among German historians over the "comparability" of the Holocaust, Charles S. Maier has pointed out that the Holocaust is sui generis. Even "crimes against humanity" such as Stalin's wholesale starvation of kulaks and his ruthless purges of the opposition, the Turkish persecution of the Armenians, and Pol Pot's slaughter of Cambodians are of a different historical category. They were not racially motivated and industrially organized mass killings like the Nazi annihilation of the Jews. Because of the unique attempt by an advanced industrial nation to exterminate an entire group of people for racial reasons, the Holocaust cannot be compared to any other mass killing in history. Bacque's likening of the Rhine camps to Buchenwald and Dachau may be popular among "revisionists" of the Holocaust, America-haters, and some German survivors of the American camp experience.[85] But vis-à-vis the true victims of the Holocaust, such facile historical comparisons are not only utterly callous and insensitive to their unique suffering, but also factually grossly inaccurate. Relativizing these historical categories on the basis of misinterpreted evidence demonstrates both the superficiality of Bacque's historical judgment and the deviousness of his approach.

I repeat, the extent of human suffering by some German POWs in

84. Bacque, *Other Losses* (Los Angeles, 1991), 173. It should come as no surprise that Bacque's book has been of great solace to the supporters of David Irving and others denying the Holocaust. See "Rewriting History."

85. Charles S. Maier, *The Unmasterable Past: History, Holocaust, and German National Identity* (Cambridge, Mass., 1988). The CBC documentary "Rewriting History" shows contacts between Bacque and the Nazi sympathizers who deny the Holocaust.

American and French hands is not disputed here. Such harsh treatment has been readily explained from the available documentary evidence ever since Böhme's study. The harsh treatment of German POWs/DEFs after the war was due largely to immense logistical problems, and partly to the vindictiveness of the victors after the full tragedy of the German killing machine in the concentration camps had become known.[86] The real issue in Bacque's charges is not the treatment of POWs per se—the impressively thorough Maschke Commission had established those facts long before Bacque—but rather the numbers that allegedly perished: how many German POWs died as a result of careless treatment, exposure to the elements, and lack of adequate food rations? The issue is also whether the U.S. Army had enough food to give adequate rations to its German POWs—and if the Americans had the food, whether it was a "secret" policy and vast conspiracy to withhold it from the POWs. (The French had very little food for their own civilian population; in their German and Austrian occupation zones the French depended on U.S. Army food stocks to maintain the minimum nonstarvation calorie level for the civilian population agreed on by the Allies.) Finally, did the U.S. Army hide deaths of German POWs/DEFs in the documents in the categories "other losses" and "discharged Volkssturm"? These questions cannot be answered from oral-history accounts; they can only be dealt with in careful and objective investigations by analyzing the vast available documentation.[87]

Above all, Bacque fails to set the proper historical context. A casual reader might deduce from Bacque that the Americans came to Europe to abuse German POWs due to a deep-seated American hatred of the Germans. As John Dower has convincingly shown in his brilliant study *War Without Mercy,* the Americans hated the Japanese for racial reasons, not the Germans. Whereas Japanese atrocities and war crimes were blamed on "the Japanese" at large, Germany's crimes were blamed on the bad "Na-

86. See the Introduction to this volume.

87. Not only has Bacque used the materials in the National Archives extremely sloppily and selectively, but he also has failed to survey hundreds of boxes of material dealing with the German POWs. Among others, these include the Records of the Office of the Surgeon General (RG 112); the Reports of the 106th Infantry Division, responsible for the guarding of the German POWs, as well as the files of its superior Twenty-third Army Corps in the Records of the U.S. Army Commands (both in RG 338); and the Secretary General Staff Correspondence, the Surgeon Historical Files, the Surgeons Section Statistical Reports, and the Documents of the Judge Advocate General and the Inspector General, all in the Records of U.S. Theaters of War, World War II, European Theater of Operations (RG 332). See Frohn, "Schicksal deutscher Kriegsgefangener in amerikanischer Lagern," 150.

zis," not the good Germans. Dower wonders why the Japanese should be considered more treacherous and atrocious than the Germans, "who attacked neighboring countries without warning or provocation, engaged in systematic genocide against millions of Jews and other 'undesirables,' killed additional millions of prisoners, especially in the Soviet Union, mobilized slave labor from many countries with the explicit policy of working 'anti-social' persons to death, and executed tens of thousands of civilian and military 'hostages' in retaliation for the deaths of German officers, not hesitating to obliterate whole villages in such acts of reprisal (the destruction of Lidice and Ležaky in Czechoslovakia in 1942 being but the most famous of these)?"[88]

Bacque does not ask such questions. He also does not mention that Hitler's declaration of war brought reluctant Americans to Europe to defeat the destructive Nazi war machine, to stop his expansionist and racist ideology, to dislodge the Nazi totalitarian creed—which was considered a mortal threat to Anglo-American democracy—and to decapitate a murderous regime so cruel that it is without precedent in the history of mankind. Bacque neglects the basic rules of writing history—rules that apply to both professionals and amateurs re-creating the past—namely those of chronology and causation. Finally, Bacque begs common sense, as Stephen E. Ambrose has pointed out; if one million German POWs died in American camps, how could the bodies disappear without a trace?[89] We have learned from the long controversy over the Katyn massacre of 40,000 Polish officers by the Red Army that you can deny, but in the long run you cannot hide, the mass killing of so many people. Historical truth has its own way of emerging.

The Americans treated German POWs harshly. In some cases they did so because of the hatred of particular camp commanders vis-à-vis the Germans, especially after the full extent of the horrors of the German concentration camps became known. Others had become callous toward their enemy after many months of fighting the tough resistance of the Wehrmacht and the SS divisions, losing their comrades in the process. There was also the vindictiveness of German Americans who were guards in prison camps in the United States: "God protect you from storm and wind

88. John W. Dower, *War Without Mercy: Race and Power in the Pacific War* (New York, 1986), 33–34.

89. On the commonsense approach to Bacque's charges, see Stephen E. Ambrose, "Ike and the Disappearing Atrocities," *New York Times Book Review,* February 24, 1991, pp. 1, 35–37.

and from Germans who are in America," noted one adage among German camp prisoners.[90]

Conditions were appalling in the camps because there was not enough food to go around for everybody in Germany, not enough tents for millions of American soldiers, German civilians, eastern European refugees, and German POWs. Moreover, given that a considerable percentage of the housing in many German cities had been erased by Allied bombing, there was not enough shelter for the German civilian population and the refugees, let alone for 5 million POWs in May, 1945.

In other words, psychological and structural factors, which rarely show up in oral-history sources, caused the misery in the American POW camps in Germany, not the personal vindictiveness of Eisenhower—although certainly Eisenhower did despise the Nazis. But Bacque is not interested in such a complicated total picture of chaos and human deprivation at the end of a gigantic struggle unleashed by Nazi Germany; he is, rather, perfectly content to make his case by selecting finger-pointing oral-history sources, by frequently misinterpreting primary records, and worst of all, by inventing speculative conspiracy theories. On top of this, he ignores a vast body of secondary literature on the German POWs, above all the volumes of the Maschke Commission.

In the end we can only hope that all users of oral history will heed William Moss's sound advice:

> It is true that not only journalists and government report writers but also historians can and have misused analysis to serve subjective prejudices and ideologies. But, when they do, they are no longer masters of the past but rather creators of new mythologies in the present. Such efforts may have value in documenting present prejudices and interpretations, but they cannot properly be called good history that masters the past. Enhancing or suppressing particular bits of evidence not on the basis of relative evidentiary or insight value but rather in the service of a subjective purpose is inimical to mastering the past with the integrity that must be demanded by the discipline of history.

Moss also notes that "authoritative pretensions of historical analysis to mastering the past" may lead to conclusions that "when erroneous, may compound the illusion every time they are quoted or relied upon uncritically by subsequent scholars." [91] The careful scholarly analyses in this vol-

---

90. "Gott schütze dich vor Sturm und Wind und vor Deutschen die in Amerika sind." Heinrich Severloh to Günter Bischof, October 16, 1990, in EC.

91. Moss, "Oral History: An Appreciation," in *Oral History,* ed. Dunaway and Baum, 93.

ume aim at setting straight the record that has been so egregiously distorted by Mr. Bacque.

In the end, the citation for the commanding officers and men of the 159th Infantry probably comes close to the historical truth about the American dilemma with the millions of German prisoners on the Rhine:

1. On this date [July 10, 1945] the 159th Infantry is scheduled to complete an assignment lasting nearly three months, which is unparalleled in the history of the American Army. It has been difficult, arduous, and without precedent. It has demanded the exercise of the maximum in ingenuity, resourcefulness, and attention to duty on the part of all ranks.

2. On 16 April 1945 you started from Rennes, France, on a forced march to Germany to meet a desperate situation which was rapidly getting out of control of Communications Zone authorities. Arriving four days later your regiment was given the assignment of guarding German prisoners of war, who were then overcrowding by the tens of thousands, the meager facilities provided for their reception and safe guarding. Other tens of thousands were arriving daily. This initial mission was gradually expanded during the succeeding weeks until eventually your command was charged not only with guarding prisoners of war, but also with their screening, segregation, transfer, discharge, evacuation, and transportation by rail and motor to all parts of Germany and France.

. . . .

4. At the peak of your operations your four enclosures confined 298,708 prisoners of war. It is estimated that approximately 330,000 were processed through your control. More than 7,000 were discharged in a single day. The average daily rate of discharge exceeded 3,900 during the month of June when this activity reached its height. Each of these personnel had to be personally interrogated, documented, paid, and transported to his home kreis, or to an army reception center closest thereto.

5. You and your subordinates were constantly beset by an almost total lack of the most essential equipment, supplies, and medical facilities. Many of these you had to find for yourself and move in your own transportation. Despite these extreme difficulties the prisoners were administered efficiently and without detriment to themselves.

6. I desire to commend you, the officers and men of the 159th Infantry and all attached organizations, for superior performance. It has reflected great credit to all concerned.

Signed: D. A. Stroh, Major General, U.S. Army, Commanding (106th Infantry Division)[92]

92. Commendation of July 10, 1945, copies from Dr. Halle and Dr. Hammon, in EC.

Appendix A

Report on the Food Situation in Western Germany, 1945

The following report was sent to the chief of staff at SHAEF on June 15, 1945, with a brief cover letter:

Supreme Headquarters
Allied Expeditionary Force
G-5 Division
15 June 1945

Subject: Food Situation in Western Germany
To: Chief of Staff

Pursuant to your request there is attached hereto a brief summary of the food situation now existing in Western Germany. The future outlook as to the food situation contained therein is based on the best information now available.

Frank J. McSherry, G-5
Brigadier General, GSC
Deputy Assistant Chief of Staff

Food Situation in Western Germany

Summary

    1. The zone in Germany ultimately to be occupied by American, British, and French forces normally is only 60 to 70 percent self-sufficient

in respect of food. This deficit food position has been accentuated this season by military destruction, by an almost complete disruption of transport facilities, by the disorganisation of the German control and administrative system for food and agriculture, by military restrictions on the movement of food supplies, the need to feed millions of Displaced Persons, as well as by the consumption of food by millions of German refugees from Eastern Germany. These conditions, together with the interrupted flow of food from Eastern Germany and the failure to uncover any large food stocks, are resulting in ration levels in cities that are below the requirements needed for normal economic activity. This situation, if prolonged unduly, will lead to disease, unrest and a generally chaotic situation.

General Situation

2. It has been the policy of the Supreme Commander that no imported relief food would be issued in Germany except in extreme emergencies prejudicial to military operations and occupation. In view of the limited food resources in western Germany, therefore, Supreme Headquarters Allied Expeditionary Force issued a directive that allowances of rationed food for Germans would be limited to a scale based upon a maximum of 1,550 calories per day for normal consumers. Actually, rations have been well below this limit because of inadequate supplies and the need to make limited stocks last until harvest.

3. It was foreseen that German resources would have to be supplemented with imported food for United Nations Displaced Persons. Supply provision has been made accordingly. Sufficient food is available from domestic and imported supplies to meet the minimum requirements of Displaced Persons at the rate of 2,000 calories per person per day. These imported supplies have been used as sparingly as possible, however, while indigenous food has been drawn upon heavily for the feeding of Displaced Persons in camps in Germany. Food for prisoners of war has also come from German resources in large part. It was not possible to provide from Allied Army stocks for the large number of prisoners of war who fell into our hands during the last few months of the War. German civilians have, therefore, been given a lower priority than United Nations Displaced Persons and prisoners of war in the use of domestic food supplies. Substantial quantities of bread grains from German stocks were also moved to Austria and Czechoslovakia to meet critical relief needs in these countries.

Overall Deficiencies

4. The general situation described above, together with widespread general disruption resulting from operational conditions, is reflected in the low rations now received by Germans in urban centres. Representative ration allowances for normal consumers in cities of over 50,000 population vary by provinces from 700 to 1190 calories per head per day. Even these scales cannot always be met because of distribution difficulties and lack of reserves. These allowances are supplemented with unrationed items, chiefly fresh vegetables and fruit, plus such cellar stocks as remain. It is clear, however, that the low ration scales now prevailing cannot be continued if serious difficulties are to be averted. Nutritionists are generally agreed that from 1500 to 2000 calories are the minimum requirement per day for the normal consumer engaged in light work, with higher allowances for heavy workers.

5. It has now become evident, on the basis of evaluations made as accurately as conditions permit, that some imported food will have to be issued to Germans continuously from now until the domestic harvest becomes available in September. Permission was obtained from the Combined Chiefs of Staff on 7 June 1945, to issue imported wheat, in extreme emergencies, to the extent of 210,000 tons each month during June, July and August. A Wheat Control Section has been established to arrange storage, movement and milling of this wheat. It is believed that these wheat imports for civilians and the quantities of food programmed for United Nations Displaced Persons will enable the area of responsibility of this Headquarters to tide over until the coming harvest.

Deficiencies By Zones

6. It is not possible as yet to differentiate precisely as between the quantities of imported wheat for the ultimate British, American and French occupational zones pending decision regarding the boundaries between these zones. The basic consideration in making allocations between the zones are (a) the availability of domestic food supplies and (b) the population to be fed.

7. In respect to availability of indigenous food supplies, preliminary estimates for the ultimate zones to be occupied by the Western Allies indicate that stocks of major foods as of 1 June 1945 amounted to about 700,000 tons of bread grains and flour, 12,000 tons of edible fats and oils,

and 4,000 tons of cheese. The proportions of these stocks in the American-French zone are approximately 49%, 80%, 16%, 64%, and 94%, respectively. These stocks cover quantities still on farms, captured enemy stocks, and commercial civilian stocks. In view of transportation, processing and other difficulties, part of the stocks on farms cannot be counted on for urban use. Furthermore, allowances must be made for a minimum carryover for distribution to function effectively. If, for example, 50% of the 343,000 tons of bread grains in the American Zone is unavailable for urban consumption for these reasons, only 171,500 tons would remain for the 15,000,000 non-farm people during the coming three months.

8. In respect to population, a significant factor is the large-scale migrations of people from heavily-bombed areas and from actual or anticipated battle areas. Much of this migration has been towards the American-French zone and away from industrial centers such as the Ruhr. As a result, the American-French zone is now estimated to have 52% of the German civilian non-farm population of the two zones, as compared with only 46% in 1939. This changed population situation in relation to the food resources in the two zones is reflected in ration allowances that are lower for the American-French zone than for the British zone. Typical ration scales as of 1 June 1945 in cities of over 50,000 population in the British zone amount to nearly 1200 calories per person per day for three provinces and to less than 1000 calories in the other two provinces. The most serious situation in respect to food-ration allowances in the British zone is in the Ruhr industrial area, for one part of which issues of rationed foods during the first week of June amounted to only 610 calories per person per day. In the American-French zone typical ration scales on a provincial basis for cities of over 50,000 population provided 1,000 calories or less per day, with the range extending down to 700 calories per person per day in Hessen-Nassau.

Maximizing Self-Sufficiency

9. One of the major efforts of this Headquarters has been the re-establishment of a German administrative system for food and agriculture. In most areas, satisfactory progress has been made. German officials of these organizations and the Military Government Detachments exercising supervisory control over them have worked hard to put into effect a uniform and coordinated program of food collection, distribution, rationing and prices. These efforts are being supplemented with facilities which under present circumstances can be provided only by the Army. Assistance

in transporting food and agricultural supplies is a case in point. Arrangements are being instituted for the resumption of production by German industries of essential items needed in producing and processing food. Among these items are fertilizers, pesticides, repair parts for machinery, fuel, binder twine and food containers.

10. German farmers have been working early and late to get every available acre of land seeded before the end of the planting season. Military transport has been used to distribute domestic stocks of seed in order to put them where needed as quickly as possible. It is estimated that approximately 3% only of the land normally in cultivation is idle this season, and crop prospects so far are promising. Farm workers have been given top priority in the release of prisoners of war. This, together with the recruitment of unemployed urban workers for farm labour, is expected to meet harvest needs.

Outlook

11. Germany as a whole is normally 85% self-sufficient in respect of food and, on the basis of restricting consumption to minimum requirements, all of its food needs could be met from its own production. This, however, would require the normal movement of food—principally potatoes, bread grains and sugar—from the surplus areas of eastern Germany to the deficit areas of western Germany. So far, there has been no arrangement with the Russians to permit this movement to occur. Unless food is forthcoming from the Russian zone, overseas imports will again have to be resorted to during the 1945–46 consumption season to avoid disease and unrest.

12. In looking to the coming winter and the remainder of the 1945–46 consumption year, ration levels will be dependent upon the outcome of the current crop and upon the amount of food shipments from eastern Germany or other sources. If rations are restricted on the assumption of no food receipts from the outside, it is probable that ration allowances this winter would have to be too low to permit normal economic activity or even maintain health. Production adjustments involving an increase in food crops, notably bread grains and potatoes, and a reduction in livestock numbers can be made in 1946, but this will not result in any substantial increase in self-sufficiency until the 1946–47 consumption year. A production program designed to effect such adjustments is in preparation.

Conclusions

13. The present food situation in Western Germany is critical. It is estimated, however, that the 630,000 tons of imported wheat will meet the minimum food needs of German civilians prior to the next harvest.

14. Unless arrangements are made for the movement of adequate food from surplus areas in the Russian occupational zone to the deficit areas of western Germany, overseas imports will again be necessary during the 1945–46 consumption season.

15. Food-production and utilization programs are being planned on an integrated basis for the occupational territory of the western Allies. It is highly desirable that arrangements be effected with the Russians so that Germany as a whole may be treated as a unit in respect to matters relating to food production and utilization. This could entirely obviate the need for food imports from overseas.

Source: OMGUS, Adjutant General Files, U.S. Group CC, in Box 22, RG 260, WNRC.

Appendix B

Volumes of the Maschke Commission

The following is a complete list of the twenty-two volumes of the Wissenschaftlichen Kommission für deutsche Kriegsgefangenengeschichte [Scientific Commission for the History of German POWs].

Böhme, Kurt W. *Die deutschen Kriegsgefangenen in Jugoslawien, 1941–1949* [German Prisoners of War in Yugoslavia, 1941–1949]. Mit einer Einführung von Erich Maschke zur gesamten Schriftenreihe [With an Introduction to the entire series by Erich Maschke]. Vol. I, Pt. 1. Munich, 1962.

Böhme, Kurt W. *Die deutschen Kriegsgefangenen in Jugoslawien, 1949–1953* [German Prisoners of War in Yugoslavia, 1949–1953]. Vol. I, Pt. 2. Munich, 1964.

Cartellieri, Dieter. *Die deutschen Kriegsgefangenen in der Sowjetunion—Die Lagergesellschaft: Eine Untersuchung der zwischenmenschlichen Beziehungen in den Kriegsgefangenenlagern* [German Prisoners of War in the Soviet Union—Life in the Camps: An Investigation into Social Relations in POW Camps]. Vol. II. Munich, 1967.

Fleischhacker, Hedwig. *Die deutschen Kriegsgefangenen in der Sowjetunion: Der Faktor Hunger* [German Prisoners of War in the Soviet Union: The Issue of Hunger]. Mit einer Einführung von Erich Maschke [With an Introduction by Erich Maschke]. Vol. III. Munich, 1965.

Ratza, Werner. *Die deutschen Kriegsgefangenen in der Sowjetunion: Der Faktor Arbeit* [German Prisoners of War in the Soviet Union: The Issue of Work]. Mit einer Einführung von Erich Maschke. Vol. IV. Munich, 1973.

Bährens, Kurt. *Deutsche in Straflagern und Gefängnissen der Sowjetunion* [Germans in Penal Colonies and Prisons in the Soviet Union]. Vol. V, Pts. 1–3. Munich, 1965.

Schwarz, Wolfgang. *Die deutschen Kriegsgefangenen in der Sowjetunion: Aus dem kulturellen Leben* [German Prisoners of War in the Soviet Union: Their Cultural Life]. Mit einer Einführung von Erich Maschke. Vol. VI. Munich, 1969.

Böhme, Kurt W. *Die deutschen Kriegsgefangenen in sowjetischer Hand: Eine Bilanz* [German Prisoners of War in Soviet Captivity: A Summary]. Mit einer Beilage von Johann Anton [With an Addendum by Johann Anton]. Vol. VII. Munich, 1966.

Robel, Gert. *Die deutschen Kriegsgefangenen in der Sowjetunion: Antifa* [German Prisoners of War in the Soviet Union: Anti-Fascists]. Vol. VIII. Munich, 1974.

Böss, Otto. *Die deutschen Kriegsgefangenen in Polen und der Tschechoslowakei* [German Prisoners of War in Poland and Czechoslovakia]. Vol. IX. Munich, 1974.

Jung, Hermann, *Die deutschen Kriegsgefangenen in amerikanischer Hand: USA* [German Prisoners of War in American Captivity: USA]. Vol. X, Pt. 1. Munich, 1972.

Böhme, Kurt W. *Die deutschen Kriegsgefangenen in amerikanischer Hand: Europa* [German Prisoners of War in American Captivity: Europe]. Vol. X, Pt. 2. Munich, 1973.

Wolff, Helmut. *Die deutschen Kriegsgefangenen in britischer Hand: Ein Überblick* [German Prisoners of War in British Captivity: A Survey]. Vol. XI, Pt. 1. Munich, 1974.

Faulk, Henry: *Die deutschen Kriegsgefangenen in Grossbritannien: Re-education* [German Prisoners of War in Great Britain: Reeducation]. Vol. XI, Pt. 2. Munich, 1970.

Jung, Hermann. *Die deutschen Kriegsgefangenen in Gewahrsam Belgiens, der Niederlande, und Luxemburgs* [German Prisoners of War in Belgian, Dutch, and Luxembourgian Captivity]. Vol. XII. Munich, 1971.

Böhme, Kurt W. *Die deutschen Kriegsgefangenen in französischer Hand* [German Prisoners of War in French Captivity]. Mit einem Beitrag von Horst Wagenblass [With an Essay by Horst Wagenblass]. Vol. XIII. Munich, 1971.

Böhme, Kurt W. *Geist und Kultur der deutschen Kriegsgefangenen im Westen* [Spiritual and Cultural Activities of German Prisoners of War in the West]. Vol. XIV. Munich, 1968.

Maschke, Erich, with Kurt W. Böhme, Diether Cartellieri, Werner Ratza, Hergard Robel, Emil Schieche, and Helmut Wolff. *Die deutschen Kriegsgefangenen des Zweiten Weltkrieges: Eine Zusammenfassung* [German Prisoners of War During World War II: A Summary]. Vol. XV. Munich, 1974.

Reck, Michael [pseud.]. *Tagebuch aus sowjetischer Kriegsgefangenschaft, 1945 –*

1949 [A Diary on Soviet Captivity, 1945–1949], edited by Kurt W. Böhme. Beiheft [Supplementary Volume] 1. Munich, 1967.

Böhme, Kurt W., and Helmut Wolff, eds. *Aufzeichnungen über die Kriegsgefangenschaft im Westen* [Personal Notes on the POW Experience in the West]. Beiheft 2. Munich, 1973.

Selected Bibliography

Primary Sources

Benz, Wolfgang, and Angelika Schardt, eds. *Kriegsgefangenschaft: Berichte über das Leben in Gefangenenlagern der Alliierten von Otto Engelbert, Kurt Glaser, Hans Jonitz, und Heinz Pust*. Munich, 1991.

Buisson. *Historique du service des prisonniers de guerre de l'Axe, 1943–1948*. Paris, 1948.

Butler, Rohan, and M. E. Pelly, assisted by H. J. Yasamee, eds. *Documents of British Policy Overseas*. Ser. I, Vol. I: *The Conference at Potsdam, July–August, 1945*. London, 1984.

Chandler, Alfred D., Jr., Stephen E. Ambrose, *et al.*, eds. *The Papers of Dwight David Eisenhower: The War Years*. 5 vols. Baltimore, 1970.

Chandler, Alfred., Jr., and Louis Galambos, eds. *The Papers of Dwight David Eisenhower: Occupation, 1945*. Vol. VI. Baltimore, 1978.

Cohen, Bernard M., and Maurice Z. Cooper. *A Follow-Up Study of World War II Prisoners of War*. Washington, D.C., 1953.

Coles, Harry L., and Albert K. Weinberg, eds. *Civil Affairs: Soldiers Become Governors*. Washington, D.C., 1964.

Conférence Internationale de la Croix-Rouge, ed. *Rapport du comité international de la Croix-Rouge sur son activité pendant la seconde guerre mondiale 1er septembre 1939–30 juin 1947*. Geneva, 1948.

Cowgill, Anthony, Christopher Booker, and Thomas Brimelow, eds. *The Repatriations from Austria in 1945: The Report of an Inquiry*. 2 vols. London, 1990.

Deutsches Büro für Friedensfragen, ed. *Das Schicksal der deutschen Kriegsgefangenen des Zweiten Weltkrieges in französischer Gewahrsam*. Stuttgart, 1949.

———, ed. *Das Schicksal der deutschen Kriegsgefangenen des Zweiten Weltkrieges in amerikanischer Gewahrsam*. Stuttgart, 1949.

———, ed. *Das Schicksal der deutschen Kriegsgefangenen des Zweiten Weltkrieges in der Sowjetunion*. Stuttgart, 1949.

Deutsches Rotes Kreuz–Suchdienst, ed. *Zur Geschichte der Kriegsgefangenen im Westen*. Bonn, 1962.

Eisenhower, Dwight D. *Crusade in Europe*. Garden City, N.Y., 1948.

Eisenhower, John S. D., ed. *Letters to Mamie*. Garden City, N.Y., 1978.

Kindleberger, Charles P. *The German Economy, 1945–1947: Charles P. Kindleberger's Letters from the Field*. Westport, Conn., 1989. With a historical introduction by Günter Bischof.

Mann, Fritz. *Frühling am Rhein, Anno 1945: Das Drama der deutschen Kriegsgefangenen im Lager Remagen-Sinzig*. Frankfurt am Main, 1965.

Medical Department, U.S. Army. *Preventive Medicine in World War II*. Washington, D.C., 1969. Vol. IX of Medical Department, *Special Fields*. 42 vols.

Murphy, Robert. *Diplomat Among Warriors*. Garden City, N.Y., 1964.

Smith, Jean Edward, ed. *The Papers of General Lucius D. Clay: Germany, 1945–1949*. 2 vols. Bloomington, 1974.

Summersby, Kay. *Eisenhower Was My Boss*. New York, 1948.

Truscott, Lucian K. *Command Missions*. New York, 1954.

Secondary Sources

Books

Abelshauser, Werner. *Wirtschaft in Westdeutschland, 1945–1948: Rekonstruktion und Wachstumsbedingungen in der amerikanischen und britischen Zone*. Stuttgart, 1975.

Albrich, Thomas. *Exodus durch Österreich: Die jüdischen Flüchtlinge, 1945–1949*. Innsbrucker Forschungen zur Zeitgeschichte, I. Innsbruck, 1987.

Ambrose, Stephen E. *The Supreme Commander: The War Years of General Dwight D. Eisenhower*. Garden City, N.Y., 1970.

———. *Eisenhower: Soldier, General of the Army, President-Elect, 1890–1952*. Vol. I of 2 vols. New York, 1983.

———. *Eisenhower: The President*. Vol. II of 2 vols. New York, 1984.

Bacque, James. *Other Losses: An Investigation into the Mass Deaths of German Prisoners of War at the Hands of the French and Americans After World War II*. Toronto, 1989. German ed., Berlin, 1989. American ed., Los Angeles, 1991.

Bailey, Ronald H. *Prisoners of War*. Alexandria, Va., 1981.

Barker, Thomas M. *Social Revolutionaries and Secret Agents: The Carinthian Slovene Partisans and Britain's Special Operations Executive*. New York, 1990.

Best, Gary Dean. *Herbert Hoover: The Postpresidential Years, 1933–1964*. Stanford, 1983.

Bethell, Nicholas. *The Last Secret: The Delivery to Stalin of Over Two Million Russians by Britain and the United States*. New York, 1974.

Bridgman, Jon. *The End of the Holocaust: The Liberation of the Camps*. Portland, 1990.

Broszat, Martin, Klaus-Dietmar Henke, and Hans Woller, eds. *Von Stalingrad zur Währungsreform: Zur Sozialgeschichte des Umbruchs in Deutschland.* Munich, 1989.

Carell, Paul, and Günter Böddeker. *Die Gefangenen: Leben und Überleben deutscher Soldaten hinter Stacheldraht.* Berlin, 1980.

Cunningham, John F., ed. *Controversies in Clinical Nutrition.* Philadelphia, 1980.

Dinnerstein, Leonard. *America and the Survivors of the Holocaust.* New York, 1982.

Dower, John W. *War Without Mercy: Race and Power in the Pacific War.* New York, 1986.

Dunaway, David K., and Willa K. Baum, eds. *Oral History: An Interdisciplinary Anthology.* N.p. (American Association for State and Local History in cooperation with the Oral History Association), 1984.

Farquharson, John E. *The Western Allies and the Politics of Food: Agrarian Management in Postwar Germany.* Leamington Spa, Eng., 1985.

Foschepoth, Josef, ed. *Kalter Krieg und Deutsche Frage: Deutschland im Widerstreit der Mächte, 1945–1952.* Göttingen, 1985.

Foy, David A. *For You the War Is Over: American Prisoners of War in Nazi Germany.* New York, 1984.

Fox, Stephen. *The Unknown Internment: An Oral History of the Relocation of Italian Americans During World War II.* Twayne Oral History Series, IV. Boston, 1990.

Fussell, Paul. *Wartime: Understanding and Behavior in the Second World War.* New York, 1989.

Gansberg, Judith M. *Stalag USA: The Remarkable Story of POWs in America.* New York, 1977.

Hirschfeld, Gerhard, ed. *Genocide: Jews and Soviet Prisoners of War in Nazi Germany.* London, 1986.

Horne, Alistair. *Macmillan, 1894–1956.* London, 1986. Vol. I of Horne, *Macmillan.* 2 vols.

Keegan, John. *The Second World War.* New York, 1989.

Krammer, Arnold P. *Nazi Prisoners of War in America.* New York, 1979.

Krieger, Wolfgang. *General Lucius D. Clay und die amerikanische Deutschlandpolitik, 1945–1949.* Stuttgart, 1987.

Lochner, Louis P. *Herbert Hoover and Germany.* New York, 1960.

Lyon, Peter. *Eisenhower: Portrait of the Hero.* Boston, 1974.

Maier, Charles S. *The Unmasterable Past: History, Holocaust, and German National Identity.* Cambridge, Mass., 1988.

Marrus, Michael. *The Unwanted: European Refugees in the Twentieth Century.* New York, 1985.

Maschke, Erich, ed. *Zur Geschichte der deutschen Kriegsgefangenen des Zweiten Weltkrieges.* 22 vols. Munich, 1962–1974. For a complete listing, see Appendix B.

Melanson, Richard, and David Myers, eds. *Reevaluating Eisenhower: American Foreign Policy in the 1950s.* Urbana, 1987.

Mühlfenzl, Rudolf, ed. *Geflohen und vertrieben: Augenzeugen berichten.* Königstein, 1981.

Niethammer, Lutz. *Die Mitläuferfabrik: Die Entnazifizierung am Beispiel Bayerns.* 2d rev. ed.; Berlin, 1982.

Peterson, Edward N. *The American Occupation of Germany: Retreat to Victory.* Detroit, 1977.

———. *The Many Faces of Defeat: The German People's Experience in 1945.* New York, 1990.

Piccigallo, Philip R. *The Japanese on Trial: Allied War Crimes Operations in the Far East, 1945–1951.* Austin, 1979.

Schwan, Heribert, and Rolf Steininger. *Als der Krieg zu Ende ging.* Frankfurt am Main, 1981.

Smith, Arthur L. *Heimkehr aus dem Zweiten Weltkrieg: Die Entlassung der deutschen Kriegsgefangenen.* Stuttgart, 1985. .

Smith, Jean E. *Lucius Clay: An American Life.* New York, 1990.

Sorge, Martin. *The Other Price of Hitler's War: German Military and Civilian Losses Resulting from World War II.* New York, 1986.

Steinhoff, Johannes, Peter Pechel, and Dennis Showalter, eds. *Deutsche im Zweiten Weltkrieg: Zeitzeugen sprechen.* Munich, 1989.

Steininger, Rolf. *Deutsche Geschichte, 1945–1961: Darstellung und Dokumente in Zwei Bänden.* Frankfurt am Main, 1983.

Streit, Christian. *Keine Kameraden: Die deutsche Wehrmacht und sowjetische Kriegsgefangene, 1941–1945.* Stuttgart, 1978.

Sullivan, Matthew Barry. *Thresholds of Peace: Four Hundred Thousand German Prisoners and the People of Britain, 1944–1948.* London, 1979.

Tent, James F. *Mission on the Rhine: Reeducation and Denazification in American-Occupied Germany.* Chicago, 1982.

Terkel, Studs. *"The Good War": An Oral History of World War II.* New York, 1984.

Tolstoy, Nikolai. *The Minister and the Massacres.* London, 1986.

Trittel, Günter J. *Hunger und Politik: Die Ernährungskrise in der Bizone, 1945–1949.* Frankfurt am Main, 1990.

Wyman, Mark. *DP: Europe's Displaced Persons, 1945–1951.* Philadelphia, 1989.

Yahil, Leni. *The Holocaust: The Fate of European Jewry.* New York, 1990.

Ziemke, Earl F. *The U.S. Army in the Occupation of Germany, 1944–1946.* Washington, D.C., 1975.

Articles

Ambrose, Stephen E. "Ike and the Disappearing Atrocities." *New York Times Book Review,* February 24, 1991, pp. 1, 35–37.

Frohn, Axel. "Das Schicksal deutscher Kriegsgefangener in amerikanischen Lagern nach dem Zweiten Weltkrieg: Eine Auseinandersetzung mit den Thesen von James Bacque." *Historisches Jahrbuch*, CXI (1991), 466–92.

Holt, Daniel D. "An Unlikely Partnership and Service: Dwight D. Eisenhower, Mark Clark, and the Philippines." *Kansas History*, XIII (Autumn, 1990), 149–65.

Knight, Robert. "Harold Macmillan and the Cossacks: Was There a Klagenfurt Conspiracy?" *Intelligence and National Security*, I (1986), 234–54.

Mason, James B., and Charles H. Beasley. "Medical Arrangements for Prisoners of War En Masse." *Military Surgeon*, CVII (1950), 341–43.

Nolan, Cathal J. "Americans in the Gulag: Detention of U.S. Citizens by Russia and the Onset of the Cold War, 1944–1949." *Journal of Contemporary History*, XXV (1990), 523–45.

Smith, Arthur L., "Der geplante Tod?" In *Deutschland zwischen Krieg und Frieden: Beiträge zur Politik und Kultur im 20. Jahrhundert,* edited by Karl Dietrich Bracher, Manfred Funke, and Hans-Peter Schwarz. Bonn, 1990.

Tent, James F. "Simple Gifts: The American Friends Service Committee and the Establishment of Neighborhood Centers in Occupied Germany." *Kirchliche Zeitgeschichte*, II (Spring, 1989), 64–82.

Unpublished Material

"Accounts of a Forgotten Army." *Timewatch* (BBC), 1990.

Bischof, Günter. "Between Responsibility and Rehabilitation: Austria in International Politics, 1940–1950." Ph.D. dissertation, Harvard University, 1989.

Burianek, Otto. "The Politics of Rectification: The U.S. Army and Displaced Persons in Munich, 1945–1951." Ph.D. dissertation in progress, Emory University.

Eisterer, Klaus. "Französische Besatzungspolitik in Tirol und Vorarlberg: Aspekte der sozialen, politischen, und ökonomischen Entwicklung, 1945/46." Doctoral dissertation, University of Innsbruck, 1990.

"Rewriting History." *Fifth Estate* (CBC), 1991.

Contributors

STEPHEN E. AMBROSE is Boyd Professor of History and director of the Eisenhower Center at the University of New Orleans. Ambrose was an editor of the *Eisenhower Papers* and is the author of *Supreme Commander* and five more books on Eisenhower, including his highly praised two-volume Eisenhower biography. He has recently completed a three-volume study of Richard Nixon. His popular textbook on post-war United States foreign policy, *Rise to Globalism,* has just appeared in its eighth revised edition. Ambrose is at work on two books on the 1944 Normandy invasion and will edit with Günter Bischof *Voices of D-Day,* a selection of the best oral histories from the Eisenhower Center's D-day collection.

THOMAS M. BARKER is professor of history at the State University of New York at Albany. An authority on central European military history and nobility, Barker is proficient in ten languages. He is author of *The Slovenes of Carinthia* (2d ed., 1984) and *The Military Intellectual and Battle: Raimondo Montecucolli and the Thirty Years' War* (1976). His books *Double-Eagle and Crescent: Vienna's Second Siege and Its Historical Setting* (1968) and *Social Revolutionaries and Secret Agents: The Carinthian Slovene Partisans and Britain's Special Operations Executive* (1990) have both been translated into German.

GÜNTER BISCHOF is assistant professor of history and associate director of the Eisenhower Center. Coeditor of *Die Bevormundete Nation: Österreich und die Alliierten, 1945–1949* (with Josef Leidenfrost) and *The Marshall Plan and Germany* (with Charles S. Maier), as well as the new journal *Contemporary Austrian Studies* (with Anton Pelinka), Bischof is finishing a book provisionally entitled *The Leverage of the Impotent: Austria in the Cold War, 1945–1955.* Bischof is a native of Austria.

ALBERT E. COWDREY is chief of the Special History Branch, the Medical History Branch, the General History Branch, and the Conventional War Studies Branch, U.S. Army Center of Military History. Author of three general history books, Cowdrey also authored *The Medics' War* (1987) and *War and Healing: Stanhope Bayne-Jones and the Maturing of American Medicine* (1992); he is coauthor of *United States Army in World War II: Medical Services in the European Theater of Operations* (with Graham A. Cosmas).

RÜDIGER OVERMANS, specialist in German military and economic history of World War II, is a historian for the Militärgeschichtliches Forschungsamt in Freiburg, Germany, the official German military history office. He is preparing the final volume, *Germany in 1945,* of the acclaimed ten-volume German history of World War II. Overmans is a native of Germany.

ROLF STEININGER, professor of history and director of the Institute for Contemporary History at the University of Innsbruck, has been one of the most prolific historians on post–World War II Germany. Author of a dozen books, including a popular two-volume history of postwar Germany and a massive collection of documents on the Rhine-Ruhr Question of 1945–1946, Steininger also has had his widely acclaimed book on the Stalin Notes recently translated into English as *The German Question: The Stalin Note of 1952 and the Problem of Reunification* (1990). Steininger is a native of Germany.

JAMES F. TENT, professor of history at the University of Alabama–Birmingham, is a specialist on the postwar German occupation. Author of a book on the American reeducation program in Germany, *Mission on the Rhine,* Tent recently has written a book on the Free University of Berlin that has been translated into German. He is at work on a book about American relief programs during the German occupation.

BRIAN LORING VILLA, professor of history at the University of Ottawa, is a specialist on World War II American military and diplomatic history; he has taught at West Point (1967–1970). His highly acclaimed *Unauthorized Action: Mountbatten and the Dieppe Raid* (1989) won the John W. Dafoe Foundation and the Keith Matthews book prizes, as well as the American Historical Association's Birdsall Prize. He is at work on a book dealing with amateur historians.

Index

Abzug, Robert H., 57

ACVA. *See* American Council of Voluntary Agencies (ACVA)

Adenauer, Konrad, 37, 167, 174

Agarossi, Elena, 63–64

Agriculture in Germany, 11–12, 104

Aldington, Lord, 183, 185–87, 192, 194, 197, 198, 198 *n*30

Alexander, Sir Harold, 61–62, 64, 185, 190, 193, 194, 195

Ambrose, Stephen E., 8, 25, 84, 209–10, 232

American Council of Voluntary Agencies (ACVA), 107–108

American Friends Service Committee, 70, 107

American prisoners of war, 19, 19 *n*, 20, 221

Anderson, Clinton P., 109–10

Arnim, Jürgen von, 30

Attlee, Clement, 68

Austria: displaced persons in, 2, 209–10; German surrenders in, 61–62, 64, 209; repatriations from, 185–86, 189–95; postwar conditions in, 209–11

Bacque, James: allegations by against Eisenhower, xiii, 1–2, 8, 20, 29, 53, 75–76, 79, 95, 196, 200, 205; editions of *Other Losses*, xvi-xvii; conspiracy theory of, 1–2, 55, 56, 200, 207; on number of German POW deaths, 1, 20, 22–23, 78, 79–80, 84, 85, 89–90, 95, 176; on Patton, 4, 4 *n*8; omissions in, 4–5 *n*10, 23, 62, 72, 84, 204, 231 *n*87; on the British, 6 *n*12, 55, 56, 64–65, 67, 69; on transportation networks, 7 *n*16, 95–96; flaws in *Other Losses*, 21–25, 59, 66 *n*32, 76, 77, 85, 89–90, 199–201, 204–206, 211–27; on food rationing, 12 *n*31; on food shortages, 21–22, 71–73, 95–96, 112, 178, 211 *n*34; and POW deaths as "Other Losses," 22–23, 200–201; on Eisenhower's "hatred" of Germans, 23, 25, 29; allegations by against Eisenhower's staff, 56–57; on unconditional surrender policy, 58, 67; on disarmed enemy forces (DEFs), 59–61; on "myth" of Russian gulags, 65–66; on civilian agencies in Germany, 70–71, 108, 179; on release of prisoners, 76–77; on recommended dietary allowances (RDA) for humans, 97; on the Maschke Commission, 174, 175, 203, 203 *n*10; and historical evidence, 199–234; use of oral-history evidence by, 211–27; and comparisons of American POW/DEF camps to German concentration camps, 229–33

Belgium, 68, 98–99

Benz, Wolfgang, 173–74

Bethell, Nicholas, 189, 189 *n*14

Béthouart, General, 6 *n*13

Bischof, Josef, 8–9

Böddeker, Günter, 177, 228
Böhme, Kurt, 18, 20 n56, 79, 91, 92, 164, 203, 219, 221, 222, 231
Booker, Christopher, 189
Braine, Sir Bernard, 197, 188 n10, 197 n28
Brandt, Willy, 172–75, 203
Braun, Dieter, 216–17
Brech, Martin, 224, 224–25 n72
Brimelow, Lord Thomas, 189
British: and German POWs/DEFs, 5–6, 9, 17, 56, 63, 65, 67, 68, 69, 70, 100; and category of "surrendered enemy person-nel" (SEPs), 9, 178; reaction of to con-centration camps, 16–17; Bacque's views on, 55, 56, 64–65, 69; on Eisenhower's staff, 55–56; and labor reparations policy, 68, 69, 70; reluctance of to dis-close severity of occupation policy, 75
British prisoners of war, 19
Buisson report, 149–51, 164
Bülow, Claus von, 198

Cameron, Neil, 222
C.A.R.E. See Cooperative of American Re-mittances to Europe (C.A.R.E.)
Carell, Paul, 177, 228
Carinthia, 188, 190, 192, 193, 210
Casablanca conference, 57, 58, 66
Catholic Relief Services, 107
CCS. See Combined (Anglo-American) Chiefs of Staff (CCS)
Cheetham, Sir Nicolas, 197 n28
Churchill, Winston, 33, 58, 62, 68, 72, 74, 103, 184, 193, 195, 206 n15
Clark, Mark, 206–11, 207 nn18–19, 219 n56, 225
Clausewitz, Carl von, 196
Clay, Lucius D., 17–18, 25, 36, 72, 105–108
CNC. See Combined Nutritional Committee (CNC)
Collins, Joan, 198
Combined (Anglo-American) Chiefs of Staff (CCS), 57, 60–62, 64, 70, 72
Combined Civilian Affairs Committee (CCAC), 64, 100

Combined Nutritional Committee (CNC), 107
Committee of Relief Agencies Licensed to Operate in Germany, 108
Concentration camps, 2–4, 16–17, 33, 57, 67, 229, 230, 232
Cooperative of American Remittances to Europe (C.A.R.E.), 107
Cowgill, Anthony, 189, 195, 195 n23, 197

Davies, Michael, 187
Denazification policy, 12–13, 34–36, 38
"Disarmed enemy forces" (DEFs), 5, 9–10, 58–64, 147 n, 178
Displaced persons (DPs), 2–5, 8, 10, 208–209, 217
Doenitz, Karl, 66
Dower, John, 231–32
DPs. See Displaced persons (DPs)
Draper, Gerald, 197 n28
Dulles, John Foster, 37
Dutch civilians, 96–97

EAC. See European Advisory Commission (EAC)
East Germany, 37, 38
Eden, Anthony, 67
Eichmann, Adolf, 67, 229
Eisenhower, David, 29
Eisenhower, Dwight D.: Bacque's allega-tions against, xiii, 1–2, 20, 29, 53, 54, 75–76, 79, 95, 196, 200, 205; on dis-placed persons, 4 n8; and food shortages, 6, 6 n13, 21–22, 71–73, 102, 109; on surrender of Axis troops in Tunisia, 8, 30; reaction to concentration camps, 16, 33; and blanket release of disarmed Ger-man forces, 17; expressed hatred toward Germans of, 23, 25, 25 n65, 30–33, 38, 233; German ancestry of, 25, 29–30; family of, 29–30; on plans for postwar occupation of Germany, 30–31; Crusade in Europe as work of, 31; and nonfrater-nization policy, 33–34; and denazifica-tion policy, 34–36; and Patton, 34–35; and German recovery, 36–38; as army

chief of staff, 36; as supreme Allied commander in Europe, 36–37; 1959 visit to Germany of, 37–38; as president, 37; limitations on authority of, 53–55, 57, 67; leadership style of, 54; on politics, 56–57 n7; and imposition of disarmed enemy forces (DEF) status, 59–61; and labor reparations policy, 68–70; and concern about disclosing severity of occupation policy, 75; on release of prisoners, 76–77; and troop morale, 205–206; and Clark, 207 n20; on lack of shelter, 209
Eisenhower, Ida Stover, 29
Eisenhower, John, 25
Eisenhower, Mamie, 25, 31, 33
Eisenhower, Milton, 30
European Advisory Commission (EAC), 57–60, 62, 69, 76

Fehling, Helmut M., xvi
Fisher, Ernest, 25, 194, 202 n7
Food rations, 9, 12, 12 n, 17, 22, 56, 98–102, 106, 109, 111, 208, 238
Food shortages, 6, 6 n, 9, 10–12, 17–18, 21–22, 61, 71–73, 95–112, 96 n2, 178, 209–11, 231, 235–40
Foster, John, 214–15
France and German POWs, 65, 68–70, 144, 145, 149–52, 164–66, 169
Franke-Prasse, Rolf, 219
French prisoners of war, 63
Fussell, Paul, 212–13

Garson, H. L., 55
Gavin, Sir William, 103–104
Geneva Convention: and German POWs sent to United States, 8; and disarmed enemy forces (DEFs), 59–60, 178; Soviet Union's refusal to sign, 62–63, 133, 153; Germany's signing of, 130
German prisoners of war: deaths of, based on Bacque's allegations, 1, 22–23, 78, 79–80, 84, 85, 89–90, 95, 163–69, 176; number of, 2, 5, 5 n11, 9, 141, 143–55, 163, 170–71, 215, 217; British treatment of, 5–6, 6 n12, 9, 17, 56, 63, 65, 67–70, 100; captured in Tunisia, 8–9; transferred to United States, 8–9, 216; and food shortages, 10, 100–102, 231; American vindictiveness against, 13, 16, 57, 232–33; camps of, 13, 137, 146–55, 164–65, 170–71, 176, 218–34; deaths of, 13, 19–20, 53, 78–92, 92 n, 148–49, 151, 154, 155, 170–71, 176–77, 217; in Soviet custody, 19, 19 n52, 65–66, 68, 69, 70, 144, 145, 152–55, 168, 170–72, 175; deaths as "Other Losses," 22–23, 79–80, 84, 200–201; Allied policies on, 57–76; in French custody, 65, 144, 145, 149–52, 164–66, 169; and denazification policy, 67–68; and labor reparations policy, 68–70; administrative sources on, 127–39; clarifications on terminology concerning, 127–29; wartime sources on, 129–31; postwar registrations and statistics on, 131–36; reports and documentation on, 136–39; in United States custody, 144, 145, 146–49; postwar West German statistics on, 156–63; archival collections and historiography on, 201–205; oral-history evidence from, 215–27
German Red Cross, 9–10, 91, 132, 133, 150
Germany: displaced persons in, 2–4, 10–11; food shortages in, 6, 10–11, 17–18, 21–22, 61, 71–73, 95–107, 235–40; transportation network in, 7–8, desperate conditions in, 10, 74–75; agriculture in, 11–12, 104; houses destroyed in, 11; denazification and demilitarization of, 12–13, 34–36, 38; division into three zones for Allied occupation of, 30–31; Morgenthau Plan for, 32–33; recovery of, 36; reunification of, 37, 38; Flensburg government of, 66; government of, 66; Swiss role in, 66; civilian agencies in, 70–71, 107–108, 178–79; wartime losses of, 139–42, 160–62, 167. *See also* East Germany; West Germany
Goebbels, Josef, 63
Gordon, Nicholas, 225

Grasett, A. E., 72, 73, 104–105
Greiner, Hermann, 222–23
Griffith, Wendell H., 100–101
Grisell, Ted, 226 n75

Halle, Shea, 224, 226
Hammon, Albert, 224–25
Harrison, Earl Grant, 4 n8
Harrison Report, 3, 208
Helms, Jesse, 188
Herr, Anton, 219
Hilldring, John, 106
Himmler, Heinrich, 190
Hitler, Adolf, 30, 31–32, 128 n2, 194, 207, 232
Hočevar, France, 192
Hologschwantner, Hans, 223
Hoover, Herbert, 108–11
Hopkins, Harry, 62
Horne, Alistair, 186
Hughes, Everett, 96
Hull, Cordell, 62

Inter-Governmental Committee on Refugees, 4 n84
International Committee of the Red Cross. See Red Cross
Irving, David, 230 n84
Italy and German DEFs, 62, 63–64, 69

Japan and American and British POWs, 19, 19 nn54–55, 92 n, 221 n63
JCS 1067, pp. 6, 17, 33–34, 36, 61, 70–72
Jesser, Harald, 218–19
Jews, 2–4, 16, 199, 208–209, 230, 232. See also Concentration camps
Jolliffe, John, 197, 198 n29

Keegan, John, 189
Keightley, Sir Charles, 185, 190, 192
Kennedy, John F., 201
Kenner, W., 55
Kindleberger, Charles P., 10 n25
Kirk, Alexander, 191
"Klagenfurt Conspiracy," 185–89, 191
Knight, Robert, 184, 191, 191 n, 195
Kräftner, Sepp, 223

Labor reparations policy, 68–70
Lauben, Philip S., 22, 84, 214
Littlejohn, Robert, 75
Low, A. R. W. "Toby." See Aldington, Lord

McAllister, Jack, 226–27
McCloy, John J., 105–106
McCone, John, 38
McCreery, Richard, 185, 192
Maclean, Fitzroy, 192
Macmillan, Harold, 185–86, 188 n10, 192, 201
Maier, Charles S., 230
Marshall, George C., 8, 16, 21, 33, 34, 54–55, 70, 111, 205
Maschke, Erich, 175, 202, 203
Maschke Commission: statistics on POWs, 5 n, 19 n52, 143–46, 154, 163–64; description of German POWs, 13, 53, 228, 231; reliability of, 139, 156, 221 n62, 231; statistics on POW fatalities, 148, 217; volumes of, 171–74, 180, 202–204, 241–43; and Willy Brandt, 172–73; workings of, 175–77; Bacque's views on, 174, 175, 203; and categories of DEF and SEP, 178; and food shortages, 178
Mennonites, 107
MIAs. See Missing in action (MIAs)
Miller, A. B., 97
Missing in action (MIAs), 91, 141
Missing persons, 132–34, 157–60, 166–67
Mitchell, Brian R., 96
Model, Walter, 9
Molotov, 62, 153
Montgomery, Bernard, 57, 67, 69, 189
Morgan, Sir William D., 64
Morgenthau, Henry, 32–33, 70
Morgenthau Plan, 32–33, 36
Moss, William, 213, 233
Murphy, Robert, 229

NATO. See North Atlantic Treaty Organization (NATO)

Nazis, trials of, 67–68. *See also* Denazification
Nicolson, Nigel, 188, 193–94
Nonfraternization policy, 33–34
North Atlantic Treaty Organization (NATO), 37
Norway, 68

Oral-history evidence, 211–29
Other Losses (Bacque). *See* Bacque, James
"Other Losses" category, 22–23, 79–80, 84, 200

Patton, George S., 4, 16, 34–35
Pincher, Chapman, 195 *n*23
Pleven Plan, 37
Pogue, Forrest, 55
Potsdam conference, 12, 58, 68, 72, 75
Potsdam Declaration, 36
POWs. *See* American prisoners of war; British prisoners of war; French prisoners of war; German prisoners of war; Soviet prisoners of war
Prisoner of War Transient Enclosures, 13, 170, 221
Prisoners of war. *See* American prisoners of war; British prisoners of war; German prisoners of war; Soviet prisoners of war
Prisoner of war camps. *See* German prisoners of war; *Rheinwiesenlager* ("Rhine meadow camps")

Quakers. *See* American Friends Service Committee

Recommended dietary allowances (RDAs), 97, 97–98 *n*6
Red Cross, 9–10, 70, 91, 97, 130, 132, 133, 150, 152, 165, 178–80
Repatriations, from Austria, 185–86, 189–95
Rheinwiesenlager ("Rhine meadow camps"): conditions in, 13, 137, 148–49, 164–65, 170–71, 217–34; map of, 14–15; diplomatic and political context of, 52–77; Bad Kreuznach-Bretzenheim, 148, 176, 222; Büderich, 148, 176, 222;

Heidesheim, 148, 176, 222; Remagen-Sinzig, 148, 152, 176, 217, 222–23, 225–26; Rheinberg, 148, 176, 220, 221, 222; Wickrathberg, 148, 176, 220, 222, 226–27; mortality of prisoners in, 155, 168–70, 176, 222, 228; Dietersheim, 164; Andernach, 224–25; implied or attempted comparisons of to Nazi concentration camps, 229–33. *See also* German prisoners of war
Rommel, Erwin, 215
Roosevelt, Franklin, 30–31, 32, 67, 96, 108, 184
Rosenman, Sam, 96
Russia. *See* Soviet Union

Schmidt, Helmut, 175
Schneider, Michael, 221 *n*62
Schranzhofer, Karl, 223
Schwan, Heribert, 177
SHAEF. *See* Supreme Headquarters, Allied Expeditionary Force (SHAEF)
Smith, Arthur, 84, 139
Smith, Bradley, 63–64
Soviet prisoners of war, 18–19, 63, 92 *n*, 170
Soviet Union: and food shortages, 12; and German POWs, 19, 19 *n*52, 65–66, 68, 69, 70, 144, 145, 152–55, 168, 170, 171–72, 175; on reunification of Germany, 37; and status of Berlin, 38; on European Advisory Commission, 57; demands for German labor by, 62, 65–66, 68; refusal of to sign Geneva Convention, 62–63, 65, 133, 153
Stalin, Joseph, 62, 72, 184, 185, 230
Stettinius, Edward, 63
Stone, Norman, 195 *n*23
Strang, Sir William, 74
Stur, Otto, 224
Supreme Headquarters, Allied Expeditionary Force (SHAEF): and population upheaval in Central Europe, 2, 10; and food shortages, 6, 9, 71, 97, 98, 102, 103, 105, 210; and transportation, 7; and German POWs sent to United States, 8; and blanket release of disarmed German

forces, 17; Marshall's attention to, 54;
British in, 55–56; and labor reparations
policy, 68
Surrender policy, 58–59, 62–64, 66, 67
"Surrendered enemy personnel" (SEPs), 9,
178
Swiss role in Germany, 66

Teheran conference, 58, 62, 65
Terkel, Studs, 212
Theodoracopoulos, "Taki," 198
Thomas, Hugh, 197, 197 n28
Thurmond, Strom, 188
Tito, Josip, 185, 190, 210
Tolstoy-Miloslavsky, Nikolai Dimitrievich:
personal background of, 183–84; homo-
phobia of, 184 n3; on the "Klagenfurt
Conspiracy," 185–89; libel action
against, 187, 203; supporters of, 188,
188 n10, 193, 195, 197–98; flaws in
work of, 189, 196–97; Knight's debate
with, 191; as advisor for BBC's "British
Betrayal," 195–96 n24
—works: *The Secret Betrayal*, 184; *Stalin's
Secret War*, 184, 184 n3; *The Victims of
Yalta*, 184; *Half Mad Minister*, 185 n5;
The Minister and the Massacres, 185,
185 n5; *The Coming of the King*,
188 n11; *The Quest for Merlin*, 188 n11
Transportation problems, 7–8, 7 nn, 95–
96, 110, 217
Trials of German war criminals, 67–68

Truman, Harry, 36, 107, 108–10, 110 n29,
209
Truscott, Lucian, 35–36
Tryon-Wilson, Teddy, 189

Unitarians, 107
United Nations Relief and Rehabilitation
Administration (UNRRA), 98, 211
UNRRA. *See* United Nations Relief and
Rehabilitation Administration (UNRRA)
USSR. *See* Soviet Union

Volkssturm, 23, 84, 200
Voltaire, 52

Watts, Nigel, 186, 187–88, 198
Waugh, Auberon, 197
Weinberg, Gerhard, 175 n7, 203
Weiss, George, 222
West Germany, 37, 38, 111, 134, 135–36,
171, 174–75, 202, 203
Wilson, Woodrow, 32
Wimmer, Josef, 223
World War II casualties, 2, 139–42, 160–
62, 167

Yalta conference, 2–3, 58, 67, 68
Yalta Repatriation Agreement, 189, 190,
192
YMCA, 178–79
Yugoslavia, 185, 189–90